MW00604792

ROBERT BURNS

A Long Way Home

From Sweden to Cedarhome, a trail of tears and triumphs

First published by Kindle Direct Publishing 2019

Copyright © 2019 by Robert Burns

All rights reserved. No part of this publication may be reproduced, stored or transmitted in any form or by any means, electronic, mechanical, photocopying, recording, scanning, or otherwise without written permission from the publisher. It is illegal to copy this book, post it to a website, or distribute it by any other means without permission.

First edition

ISBN: 978-0-578-53336-0

This book was professionally typeset on Reedsy.
Find out more at reedsy.com

In memory of my mother, Annabelle Carlene (Freberg) Burns, every bit a Swede

"A people that take no pride in noble achievements of remote ancestors will never achieve anything worthy to be remembered with pride by remote descendants."

— Thomas Babington Macaulay,
19th century British historian

Contents

Maps, Chart and Photos

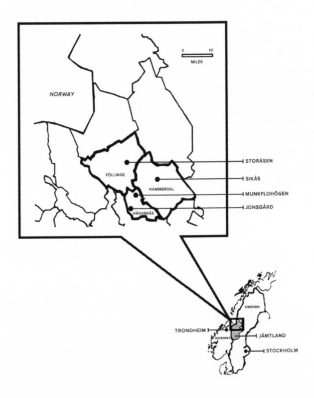

John and Anna Hagglund grew up just east of the Norwegian border and were married in Hammerdal parish in 1852. (All maps created and illustrated by Robert Burns and Libby Burns)

1. Jonsgård, Häggenås parish, Jämtland, Sweden
2. Trondheim, Norway
3. Newcastle, England
4. Liverpool, England
5. Londonderry, Northern Ireland

John and Anna and their five children journeyed from their farm in west-central Sweden in June 1867 to the Norwegian port of Trondheim. From the east coast of England, probably at Newcastle, they traveled to Liverpool and crossed the Atlantic to Quebec aboard the SS Peruvian, via Londonderry.

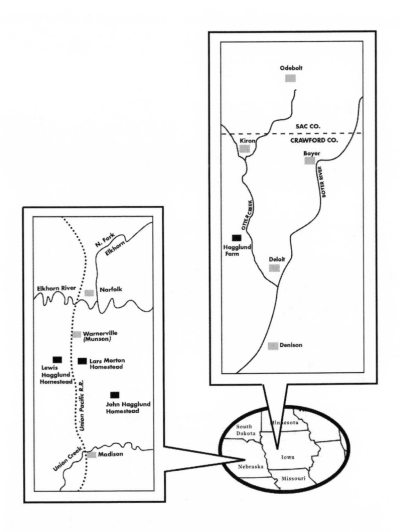

The Hagglund farm in Crawford County, Iowa was just west of Otter Creek, about two miles south of what became the town of Kiron. When they moved to Madison County, Nebraska in 1880 they were several miles northeast of the town of Madison and southeast of the homesteads of their son, Lewis, and their son-in-law Lars Morton and daughter Christine.

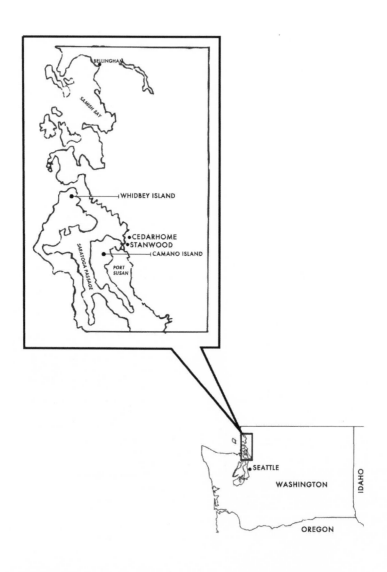

John and Anna made their final home at Cedarhome, a village on the highlands above Stanwood, in Snohomish County, Washington.

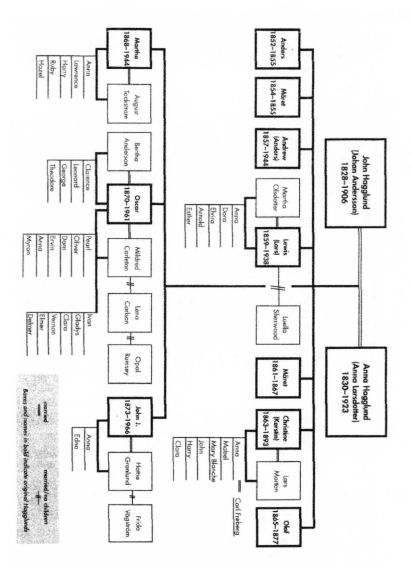

*Individuals framed in boldface are the 12 original Hagglunds — John and
Anna, plus 10 children*

John and Anna Hagglund during the Nebraska homesteading years, circa 1880s. Photo courtesy of Suzanne Hawley.

Rear, left to right: John J. Hagglund, Martha (Olsdotter) Hagglund (niece of Anna Hagglund), Lewis Hagglund, Ella (Olsdotter) Nims (sister of Martha Olsdotter Hagglund), Earl Nims, August Tackstrom, Martha (Hagglund) Tackstrom, Oscar Hagglund and Andrew Hagglund. Front, left to right: Hattie Hagglund (wife of John J. Hagglund), John Hagglund, Anna Hagglund and Bertha Hagglund, wife of Oscar. Circa 1900.

Author's Note

For most of my life I was hopelessly incurious about my Swedish ancestors. They seemed dream-like, too distant to matter.

When I think now of what awakened me to the idea of learning and telling their story, I think of a Swede named Berta Svensson and a letter she wrote to her Uncle Emil more than half a century ago. Berta's words were polite but pained: "I have never seen you or heard from you." She knew her uncle only from an old photo her mother kept after he emigrated to America from their native Sweden in 1893, ten years before Berta was born. Suddenly, in the evening of her life, she felt a surge of curiosity about the man in the picture frame.

"As we grow older, we think of our relatives," she wrote. "When we are young, we don't."

In time, that simple truth grabbed me, too.

Like Berta, I was growing older. When I began my research in 2014, I was nearly the same age Berta was when she wrote to the uncle she had never met. Like her, I found my thoughts gravitating to a subject I had spent a lifetime largely ignoring: my roots. I began to think about the paths that preceded mine, about the people who walked them, and about how my life's journey is an extension of theirs.

I realized that like a poorly preserved painting, the detail and color of my Swedish ancestors' lives had faded. Some features had disappeared.

Like Berta, I felt a stirring, a need to learn about these faint figures of the past and in so doing, rescue their history for generations of descendants still too young to care. I had come to realize that the distance I once thought made my ancestors' lives irrelevant to mine was in fact the very thing that made them important.

I had pitifully little understanding of where to begin. Raised in a town so thoroughly Scandinavian that the Swedish language was taught in high school, I had every opportunity to learn about my heritage. It was there for the asking. Regrettably, I never asked.

Like Berta, my perspective changed with age.

I came upon Berta's letter in 2014, three years after my mother, Annabelle (Freberg) Burns, died and shortly before the passing of my father, Robert Burns. Their deaths, and whispers from the past like those in Berta's letter, launched me unexpectedly on a genealogical exploration that ultimately resulted in this book. What sustained me in this pursuit was the thought that in learning about my ancestors I might learn about myself. And I did. I learned that the challenges that have tested me are small compared to the obstacles my ancestors overcame. They bore scars of 19th century living — disease, hardship, isolation, early deaths and more – human hallmarks of a period in rural America that is widely forgotten.

By coincidence, Berta had touched my life twice previously, although I never met her. As a college freshman in 1974 I wrote to her for no reason other than wanting to use the Swedish language skills I had been learning that year at the University of Washington. She was a random relative I had never heard of before. Her address was affixed to an old envelope my mother found. Berta wrote back twice. I wrote a second letter, but for reasons I don't recall — most likely related to my youthful indifference — our correspondence ended. How I regret that now.

Eleven years later, when I and my wife Liz moved from New York to Brussels, Belgium, our proximity to Sweden gave rise to an impulse to reconnect. I sent Berta another letter, this time in English. It found its way to a younger relative who, after informing me that Berta had died in 1977, invited me and my family to visit, which we did in 1985. We met relatives old and young and were shown the former homes of Berta and others, including the man she called Uncle Emil.

Emil was my grandfather, Carl Emil Freberg. Like Berta, I hardly knew him. Unlike Berta, I could not blame distance. He lived just a few miles from the home where I was raised. I was eight when he died at age 90; In my mind's eye, I see a dour expression beneath a shock of white hair, but I can't recall his voice. He plays a key part in my family history, but this book is not mainly about him. It is about the Swedish immigrant family he married into, headed by John and Anna Hagglund, ordinary people who traveled extraordinary paths through stretches of American history that are oddly foreign to many of us in the 21st century.

The Hagglunds seem to have recorded few details of their lives, so even the easiest parts of their story were sometimes hard to find. Surely they wrote and received many letters; this was an era in which nearly everyone who could write did so, and at length. And yet, no letters to or from the original Hagglunds survived, as far as I could tell.

Even their photos were mysteries – most with no names, no dates.

With the patient help of many people — relatives, amateur genealogists, record keepers of every sort and even a practitioner of water witching — I followed the family's journey from its beginning in rural Sweden to its end at Cedarhome, a quiet village in Washington state where they – and Carl Emil Freberg — lived their final years.

I traveled to all four states in which the Hagglunds lived – Minnesota, Iowa, Nebraska and Washington — and walked some of the ground they had trod. I searched and studied in libraries as modest as the public library in Norfolk, Nebraska and as majestic as the Library of Congress on Capitol Hill. I visited church basements, graveyards, old homesteads, museums, government archives, private homes, courthouses and newspaper offices, including one with stacks of newspapers so old the yellowed pages disintegrated in my fingers like ash from an ancient tomb.

From these sources I collected and weaved together ancestral threads that eventually formed a tapestry of history that even Berta might have admired.

At times on my journey I could sense the fall of the Hagglunds' footsteps, almost hear their accented voices. It was as if faces freeze-framed in old photos — like the one of Carl Emil Freberg that his niece had admired back home in Sweden — had momentarily come to life.

My account is not the last word. Pieces of the story remain undiscovered. For example, what prompted John and Anna to become Baptists in defiance of the Church of Sweden? Why, upon emigrating, did they pick Minnesota as their initial destination? Did they ever regret leaving their homeland? How did they deal with language and other social barriers in their adopted country? Answers to these and other intimate questions are hidden in the sands of time.

It is possible that clues to the Hagglunds' thoughts, fears, and hopes are contained in letters, diaries or other papers that escaped my search. Having failed to find those, my goal was to sketch at least the outlines of their journey and set it in the context of their times. I hope my modest success will be seen as having shored up the foundation of Hagglund history, and that it will enable — perhaps inspire – another descendant to find and tell those parts that eluded me.

I aimed to get every fact correct, but inevitably I will have failed. Any errors are mine alone. Even some things that appear accurate now may look different later. New information will emerge to alter an aspect of the story line or contradict some of my conclusions. That is as it must be.

One note about my intent: I had no desire to grow the biggest family tree. By design, I limited my focus to just one branch, the one that begins with John and Anna Hagglund. I followed this branch of the family tree only through John and Anna's offspring, and with one exception I followed it no further. The exception is the family of their daughter Christine. I tracked her family because it leads to my own. Christine was my great grandmother; her eldest daughter, Anna, was Carl Emil Freberg's bride, and my mother was the Frebergs' youngest child.

Wandering the paths of Hagglund history, tracing the contours of their lives and discovering the tears and triumphs of their time has been a revelation. It has shown me that their striving helped form the bedrock on which future generations, including mine, were built. I admire and thank them for that.

The Hagglunds were a stoic, optimistic lot. This family trait showed itself time and again during my research. As one of John and Anna's grandsons put it, "high hopes were part of the family nature." I sensed this in a casual note that another descendant, Hazel Booth, wrote to my parents in September 1996.

In neat handwriting at age 90, Hazel mentioned the passing of her cousin Elmer Hagglund. She had seen him just the other day; he looked pale and thin. "When I asked him how he was, he said 'so-so.'"

Three days later he was dead.

"Life is full of changes all the time," Hazel concluded. "We just accept them and keep on going."

Robert Burns
April 2019
Reston, Virginia

I

The First Goodbye

1

The Decision to Leave

Summer's arrival is normally cause for celebration in Sweden, but 1867 was not normal. It was the coldest year of the century – so persistently cold that frosts in May and June crippled crops across the country's midsection and north, marking the second of three straight years of failed harvests. Historians have called this Sweden's period of deprivation rather than full-on famine, yet food was so scarce that the deprived were reduced to eating tree bark.

In the countryside, the gloom spared few.

Among the exceptions were an ordinary farmer named Johan Andersson and his wife, Anna Larsdotter. At the start of that damp and discouraging summer, they had reason to celebrate. They were saying goodbye to Sweden and hello to hope.

Johan and Anna were ready to start over, to leave behind their homeland and the confining, unfulfilling life it had given them. Years of toil in the rocky soil of Jämtland county had taken a toll on body and soul. Midlife was approaching, and the outside world beckoned. They were among 39 Jämtlanders who left for the United States in 1867, and as conditions worsened the numbers grew. Over the next two years, 597 would follow – still a trickle compared to the million-plus from across Sweden who would catch "America fever" in the coming three decades.[1]

Having cleared their plans with authorities, Johan and Anna in late June made their way west. They entered Norway and crossed its narrow waist through forests of spruce and pine to the ancient port city of Trondheim, about 150 miles from home. There, in a sheltered harbor on the southern shore of a towering fjord, they embarked on a journey that surely was as exhausting and bewildering as it was exhilarating.

Johan was 39, Anna 37. Five children were in tow, harnessed to their parents' hopes for a brighter future in a distant land from which they would never return.

The family was headed to America on the leading edge of a mid-century wave of emigration by Swedes willing to trade the familiar at home for the unseen abroad, to abandon the poverty they had inherited for a prosperity they might find on their own. Johan and Anna's destination was Red Wing, Minnesota, a pioneer settlement and recent Dakota Sioux village on the west bank of the Mississippi River.

Everything in their lives was about to change – even their names. They would become the Hagglunds – John A. Hagglund and Anna Hagglund. (The name selection appears to have followed the common Swedish practice of combining terms from nature, in this case "hägg," which is a type of tree known in English as bird cherry or hackberry, with "lund," which means grove, as in a grove of hackberry trees. So, the name was Hägglund, but in English the vowel "a" was substituted for the Swedish "ä".)

The name change was a matter of choice. The reason for it is a matter of speculation. It may have reflected Johan and Anna's feeling that in every sense they were starting anew.

In 19th century Sweden, parents named their children by

4

patronymic custom, meaning a child's surname was derived from his or her father's given name. Thus, Johan and Anna's eldest son, Anders, was known as Anders Johansson – Johan's son. In America, he would take the name Andrew J. Hagglund. His brother Lars Johansson would become Lewis G. Hagglund. Kirsten Johansdotter – daughter of Johan – would be Christine (sometimes spelled Christina) Hagglund. The baby of the family, 1-year-old Olof Johansson, became Oliver Hagglund.

Märet Johansdotter, age 6, was to take the name Martha, but fate had other plans for her.

Neither Johan nor Anna, and certainly not any of their children, could have foreseen how far the next decades would take them or where the odyssey would end. Nor might they have imagined that the twists and turns would be of interest generations later. To them, in the moment, the struggles may not have seemed exceptional or even worth retelling. But to a 21st century descendant looking back to imagine it all, their triumphs were special and their story worth preserving.

Johan and Anna left no known record of their lives in Sweden or their reasons for leaving. Even so, it's not hard to imagine why they wanted out. The disastrous state of farming in the 1860s was likely one important reason.[2] As Baptists, regarded by the state as heretics, their pursuit of religious freedom was another. They may also have been influenced by the buzz created by former countrymen whose letters from America raved about life in a seemingly boundless land of plenty. In the end, it probably was an accumulation of things that convinced Johan and Anna the time was right and the opportunity worth the risk.

Maybe it was as simple as the old saying: Some people are movers, and some are stayers.

* * *

Dream Big

Fifteen years before Johan and Anna took that first step, they exchanged marriage vows in a parish called Hammerdal in the remote upper reaches of Jämtland county, a sparsely populated expanse of mountains, woodland lakes, small farms and hard winters. Situated in the Norrland region of central Sweden, Jämtland is at roughly the same latitude as Anchorage, Alaska, and is about the size of Vermont and New Hampshire combined. For nearly 500 years, until the mid-17th century, it was a province of Norway.

Anna had grown up in Hammerdal parish; Johan was a newcomer. Most of what I could learn about their young adult years, including the intersecting of their life paths, came from church records in Hammerdal and the adjacent parishes of Föllinge and Häggenås.

In Sweden's system of local government at the time, the key to both religious and civil administration was the parish. It can be thought of as a local district comprised of multiple clusters of homes and farm compounds. A parish was both a congregation and a territorial subdivision of the Church of Sweden, the institutional enforcer of Lutheranism, which was made the state-sanctioned religion by King Gustav Vasa in the mid-16th century and remained so until the year 2000.

Starting in the 17th century, parish clergy were required to keep records of local births, baptisms, marriages and deaths, as well as a yearly accounting of individuals moving in and out of the parish. They even rated a person's character and recorded his or her level of literacy and yearly progress in religious instruction. The style, thoroughness and frequency of this recordkeeping varied greatly by parish, as did the quality of penmanship, which ranged from elegant to awkward and occasionally resembled chicken scratch.

A person moving out of a parish – or out of the country – was required to obtain an exit certificate ("flyttningsattest" in Swedish) from his or her parish minister. It contained the person's name, birth date and birth place, and usually several other details like occupation and marital status. It was to be presented to the minister in the destination parish. Remarkably, many of these and other preserved local records have been digitized.

Hammerdal parish marriage records identify Johan as a farmhand ("drängen," in Swedish, sometimes abbreviated "Dr.") and Anna as a farmer's daughter ("bondedottren"). He was 24. She was 22. Both were of the peasant class, meaning they were born poor, stuck in a generations-long cycle of hardship.

In tradition-bound, pre-industrial Sweden, peasants had little chance of redirecting their life's destination. They might dream big but go nowhere. The best a young man could hope for, ordinarily, was to inherit a sliver of his father's small patch of arable land – and even that could be beyond reach if, as in Johan's case, he was not the eldest son. A young woman had even fewer options. She was expected to marry and bear children. Perhaps this made the vision of success in more liberal America a big dream worthy chasing.

2

Anna Meets Johan

A nna was born March 24, 1830 on a Hammerdal farm called Prästgården (priest farm, or parsonage), operated in support of the parish minister and his family. This did not mean Anna's parents had a special place in the church; the farm was just another place of peasant employment. The family was there for about two years; they moved short distances numerous times before settling in a Hammerdal village called Sikåskälen shortly before Anna set out on her own.

Anna's father was Lars Henriksson. Thus, she grew up as Anna Larsdotter – daughter of Lars – a surname she would drop only after reaching America, where she adjusted her maiden name to the less foreign-sounding Larson but normally called herself Anna Hagglund, following the American custom of taking her husband's surname. (Had she and Johan stayed in Sweden, she would have remained Anna Larsdotter for the rest of her life.)

Lars Henriksson, born in 1800, was originally from Gästrikland, an area in the southern part of Gävleborg county, east and south of Jämtland.

During portions of Anna's youth, Lars was a crofter ("torpare" in

Swedish), or tenant farmer. This meant he rented for his family a small plot of land, with cottage, under a contract that required him to work a set number of days – perhaps 150 – on the landowner's estate in lieu of cash rent. Anna's mother, Märet Olofsdotter, also was obliged to work for the estate owner, in addition to caring for her children. Märet was born in 1793 in Föllinge, a parish next door to Hammerdal.

These were sturdy Swedes. Anna's mother lived to be 96 and her father 91 – roughly double the average life expectancy for Swedish men and women of that era. Both died at Sikåskälen.

Anna had three siblings. The oldest, Hans, was born in May 1825 and died the same year; Catharina came next in September 1826, and a younger brother, Olof, was born in September 1832. Years later, Olof and several members of his family would follow Anna to America and play a significant role in the Hagglund story.

Catharina stayed put on her parents' farm at Sikåskälen and in 1851 married a neighbor, Jonas Olofsson, who moved onto her family's farm. They had two daughters, Lisbeth and Märet.

Anna's mother actually had three daughters. One was born and baptized on December 28, 1828 but died the same day or possibly was stillborn. Her name was Anna. As was customary in that era, the family gave the same name to the next-born girl, and two years later that would be the future wife of Johan Andersson.[3]

Johan was from the same region of Sweden as his bride – the west-central area bordering Norway, although details of his childhood are sketchy. His birth record is the only one in the family that eluded me. Numerous parish records agree on the date, March 12, 1828, but not the place. Most cite the ancient province of Dalarna. But at least two say he was born farther north in Jämtland.

Johan's parents, Anders Anderson and Kerstin (sometimes spelled Cherstin or Kjerstin) Matsdotter, both were born and raised in the village of Färnäs in Dalarna's Mora parish and were married there on July 25, 1813. Like most peasant-class Swedes of that era, they stayed where they were put. Färnäs is situated along a narrow band of moderately fertile soil in a geologic depression known as the Siljan Basin, sometimes called the Siljan Ring because it forms a nearly perfect circle. Färnäs is at the north end of Lake Siljan and stands a stone's throw east of the larger town of Mora, which also is the name of the parish.

Anders and Kirsten had their first four children in Färnäs, starting with a boy named Anders in July 1814. He was followed by Mats in October 1816, Kerstin in September 1820, and Anna in October 1825. For unknown reasons, they moved in 1828 to Jämtland county, about 170 miles to the north. In a country of tightly bound kinship networks a move of such distance was unusual and would suggest a disruptive episode in the family. Whatever the trouble was, it would not be the last.

In parish records, a handwritten notation of the family's departure from Mora parish says simply, "1828 to Jämtland." It does not mention the month or specify the parish in Jämtland.

It's unclear whether the family moved before or after Johan's birth in March, but logic suggests they waited out the winter before making the trek. So, while he probably was born in Dalarna, Johan grew up in Jämtland, although he apparently returned briefly to Dalarna at age 10 before going back to Jämtland. One wonders whether this mobility in childhood influenced his tendencies as an adult.

I don't know where Johan's family first settled in Jämtland, but by 1833 they were living in Föllinge parish in a farm village called Storåsen, a remote area of aspens, silver birches and evergreens about five miles west of Gåxsjön lake. There the last of Johan's siblings were born – Jonas in April 1833, Olof in May 1835 and Erik in June 1838. Thus, Johan was the fifth of eight children – two girls and six boys.

Records held by the Swedish National Archives say that during the Follinge years, Johan's father was a "nybyggare," which can be translated as settler or frontiersman and suggests that he settled the family on previously uninhabited land. Other official records refer to him as a "dalkarlen," meaning he was from the old province of Dalarna, whose people were known for self-reliance and individualism and valued for their skills in timber cutting and construction. The people of Dalarna also were known for handicrafts; the province is home to the Dala horse, the brightly painted wooden horse that forest workers originally carved as toys for their children and that later became a widely known symbol of Sweden.

The portion of Dalarna province where John's parents grew up was known then as Kopparberg but was renamed Dalarna county in 1997. (Perhaps the best way to explain this rather confusing distinction between a province and a county is that provinces are older and narrower land divisions that today denote cultural and historical differences but serve no administrative function. The county of Jämtland, for example, includes the territory of two provinces: Jämtland and Härjedalen.) Kopparberg (today's Dalarna county) was an agrarian area shaped by centuries-old traditions and limited by its isolation from centers of commerce.

In his detailed study of 19th century emigration from a single parish in Dalarna – Rättvik, adjacent to the Andersson family's Mora parish – historian Robert C. Ostergren wrote that the meager amounts of arable land in and around Rättvik were not enough to sustain the local economy. Many families had less than one acre of tillable land to sustain a household often crowded with multiple generations. This suggests a possible explanation for Johan's father's decision to move the family north.

What little I know about Johan's early years comes from local church records, plus fragmentary recollections shared by unspecified descendants in a short narrative compiled for a 1983 Hagglund family reunion in Everett, Washington. To my knowledge, this is the only family record of its kind, supplemented with a videotape of the reunion. The written account offers telling insights and details, and, while it is incomplete and at times inaccurate, it helped inform my research. When citing it in the pages ahead I will call it simply the Everett account.

My own research revealed that at age 10, Johan learned the first of many hard lessons about the fragility of life. His father died March 16, 1838 in Fölinge parish. He was 52. The official death record does not specify a cause, but the Everett account says he was killed by a falling tree while working in the woods.

"Very shortly after that accident, he (Johan) and his mother moved to a new home where, about a year later, she died, broken-hearted over the loss of her husband," it says. That summation, while lacking dates, locations and other details, largely aligns with the limited information I found in parish records, which show that Johan's mother died 15 months after her husband, in June 1839 in Färnäs, the village in Dalarna where she was born. The death record says she succumbed at age 45 to "kolik," which translates as colic, or severe intestinal distress.

Suddenly Johan and his seven siblings, including three brothers under the age of seven, were parentless. The three oldest children had reached adulthood by this time. Anders was 25, Mats was 23, and Kerstin was just short of her 19th birthday. Anna was 13. I don't know who cared for Johan and the other younger children – Jonas, Olof and Erik – after they were orphaned, or how these tragedies might have affected Johan's development. At 11 he had lost both parents in a little over a year, a circumstance that surely was jarring and perhaps scarring.

Untimely death is a recurring theme in the Hagglund story. It didn't define the family, but it tested young and old for three generations. Their resilience, demonstrated by their ability to accept loss and stick together, revealed itself as a family strength. Those who survived were exceptionally hardy; one descendant referred to the Hagglunds as "long lifers."[4]

The Everett account says that "soon after" Johan's mother died he "took his younger brother" to Hammerdal parish in Jämtland, "where he managed to make a comfortable home for himself and his brother (name unknown)." The unknown brother could only have been Erik, since it says this brother was "born after the father died." Erik was born June 29, 1838, three months after his father died.

I had little success tracking Johan and his siblings in the first few years after they lost their parents, but it's clear they moved from farm to farm within Jämtland county.

Erik is mentioned in parish records as having lived with relatives (no names mentioned) "from the age of 4." He seems to have been in the care of a man named Olof Hemmingsson in Hammerdal in the 1840s, but I could not tie those thin threads together into a coherent story or find record of Erik in subsequent years.

I could find no record of their brother Jonas during this period.

At some point in the 1840s, Johan's older brother Mats lived for a short time in Föllinge parish's poorhouse ("fattigstugan" in Swedish), possibly as a worker and possibly as a pauper, or perhaps both. Later in the 1840s, Mats moved a short distance to a farm called Sandviken, where he died on July 2, 1868. The recorded cause of death was "vattusot," which translates as "dropsy," an older term for generalized edema, usually associated with heart failure.

The eldest son, Anders, appears to have taken over their father's farm in Storåsen. He and his wife Kerstin Mårtensdotter, along with daughters Kerstin, Sara and Anna, lived there until Kerstin, the wife, died in October 1871. The following month, Anders and his daughter

Kerstin and her husband, Erik Jonsson, moved about four miles to Kaku-åsen, a farm village in Hammerdal parish.

Johan, the future John Hagglund, apparently was on his own from age 14, when he went to work on a farm in the lakeside village of Gåxsjö in Hammerdal parish. He remained there for five years, until 1847. By chance, it was the same farm where his future bride's parents, Lars Henriksson and Märet Olofsdotter, had worked as farmhand and farm maid about 30 years earlier, before they were married.

Although I could not determine exactly how Anna met Johan, parish records show their paths crossed in about 1850. That year, Anna moved from her parents' place in Sikåskälen to work as a farm maid in Sikås, a slightly larger village about four miles to the east. It was common for unmarried sons and daughters, once reaching adulthood, to leave the family farm and work elsewhere in the parish.

As it happened, Johan had moved to Sikås in 1849. He and Anna were not on the same farm in Sikås, but they were not far apart – possibly within a mile of each other.

This would seem to explain how they happened to meet. It was an encounter that might never have happened had Johan not lost both parents as a boy and wound up in Hammerdal. An eerily similar tragic circumstance a generation later – after Johan and Anna had settled in the American Midwest – would lead to a fateful encounter in Iowa in the 1890s.

* * *

Tested by Tragedy

Johan and Anna were married in Hammerdal parish on Leap Day, February 29, 1852. That summer, in late July, they moved to a farm village called Munkflohögen in Häggenås parish, about 10 miles southwest of Sikås and eight miles south of Storåsen, the village where Johan's family was living when his father died.

In Munkflohögen the newlyweds started a family. Their first child was a boy, born October 1, 1852. They called him Anders, following the Swedish custom of naming a first-born son after his paternal grandfather. Next came Märet, on September 23, 1854. She likely was named after Anna's mother.

At this early stage of their marriage, Johan and Anna were tested by tragedy – the first of many to come. On November 24, 1855, both infants, Anders and Märet, perished at the Munkflohögen farm. The circumstances are not fully explained in parish records, but a notation on the children's death record cites "brand," meaning fire, preceded by the term "inne," which could be interpreted as meaning an inside fire, or house fire. A staff researcher at the Swedish National Archives told me he interpreted the notation as "building fire." The Everett account, evidently relying on the memory of a since-deceased descendant, describes the circumstance in slightly greater detail, minus the infants' names and ages.

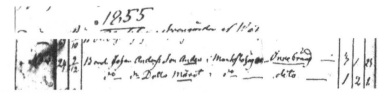

The Swedish death record for Anders and Märet says the cause was "inne brand," which could mean house fire. He was 3 years, 1 month and 23 days old. She was 1 year, 2 months and 1 day.

"A definite report states that while still very young, the two children died in a fire which destroyed their home while John and Anna were working in the field," it says.

Neither account explains the tragedy further. One is left to imagine the horror and heartbreak.

Johan and Anna did not give up. Two years later they started over. Anna had a boy on February 18, 1857. He, too, was named Anders – the one who later would be known as Andrew J. Hagglund. Then came Lars, born May 6, 1859, probably named after his maternal grandfather. Both boys would live long lives. Next came two girls – Märet, born April 26, 1861, followed by Kerstin on May 11, 1863. Unlike their brothers, they would meet unhappy ends.

In 1865, the family moved to another farm compound in Häggenås parish called Jonsgård, about five miles south of Munkflohögen and two miles east of the Hårkan River. The farm sat on a gently sloping hill overlooking a vast woodland. The Hagglunds did not stay there long, but long enough for Anna to give birth one last time. Olof was born July 14, 1865, and two years later the family was on the move again.

On June 29, 1867, less than a week after the traditional Midsummer Eve holiday marking the arrival of summer, Johan and Anna packed up their lives, dipped into a well of personal courage, and perhaps cast a final glance back at their farmhouse before setting off for Trondheim. So long as they obtained the proper paperwork from local authorities, Swedes were free to leave the county. Entering the U.S. was no problem; the U.S. government had not yet begun regulating immigration.

With no surviving record of Johan and Anna's trek to Trondheim, it's impossible to know their exact route or how long it took to reach the Norwegian port city. It almost certainly was the first time either had set foot beyond Sweden.

They appear to have given themselves a good two or three weeks to reach Trondheim; their ship did not sail until July 22. No rail line linked Jämtland and Trondheim in those days, so the family of seven likely covered the approximately 150 miles on dirt trails in an ox-drawn farm wagon and on foot. They probably crossed the border into Norway on a well-worn pilgrim's path known as St. Olavsleden (St. Olaf's Way), established in the 11th century and traversed by generations of Christians flocking to Trondheim's iconic Nidaros Cathedral.

3

Sharing Space with Rats and Disease

At the Norwegian port city of Trondheim, Johan and Anna called on Christian Henriksen, a shipping agent who handled routes to Quebec, Canada, for the Allan Line. Most Swedes who emigrated in the 19th century departed from a Swedish port – often the southern city of Gothenburg. But for Johan and Anna an easier and perhaps cheaper alternative was Trondheim, much closer to their home.

Records of the National Archive of Norway show they registered with emigration authorities on July 22, enabling them to board the *Tyne Queen*, a British cargo ship, either the same day or soon after.[5] This vessel served as part of a feeder system for larger ships steaming to America and Canada from Liverpool, England. They were registered as Johan Andersson and Kone (Wife) Anna Larsdotter, with the children recorded by their first names and ages.

This almost certainly was the first time aboard a steamship for Johan and Anna. The same is likely true for two other Jämtland families that traveled with them from Trondheim to Liverpool and from Liverpool to Quebec, also bound for Red Wing, Minnesota. They were farmer Jonas Eriksson, 37, his wife Brita Olsdotter, 39, their two children and Brita's younger sister, Kerstin; as well as farmer Morten Persson, 31, his wife Emerintia Olsdotter, 27, and their two children. If the three families didn't know each other in Sweden, they surely had time to get familiar during the voyage to America and on the final leg to Minnesota.

The rest of the *Tyne Queen* passengers were headed to places like Chicago, St. Paul, Milwaukee and La Crosse, Wisconsin.

The *Tyne Queen* was built in 1865 and launched in December of that year by the Tyne Iron Shipbuilding Co. Ltd., at Newcastle, England. At the time of John and Anna's journey, the iron-screw ship, 238 feet in length and 29.8 feet wide, was owned by the Channel Steam Ship Co., Ltd., of Liverpool.

After easing into the Norwegian Sea, the *Tyne Queen* arced around Norway's bulbous southwestern flank and entered the North Sea. It would have dropped its passengers at Newcastle on the River Tyne or a little further south at Hull.[6] From there the Hagglunds – still listed by their original Swedish names – would have gone by train across the midsection of England to Liverpool, as arranged by Henriksen, the Trondheim agent.

At Liverpool, they would have made their way to the harbor and waited to board the SS *Peruvian* for the trip across a great ocean they almost certainly had read about but never seen. The *Peruvian* was a state-of-the-art, iron-hull steamship with a clipper bow that curved gracefully upward from its forward waterline. Steam from its boiler was expelled through a single funnel, or smokestack.[7]

The British-registered schooner-style ship was built by Robert Steele & Co. at its yard in Greenock, Scotland, in 1863 and sailed its maiden voyage to North America a year later. It was part of a fleet of more than a dozen steamships of the Allan Line, founded in 1854 as the Montreal Ocean Steam Ship Company, which hauled mail between Britain and Canada under government contract.

Conditions aboard the *Peruvian* were rugged by today's standards but much improved from just a decade earlier on sailing vessels that were built to accommodate commercial cargo like fish and timber but not human passengers. The voyage was also much faster now that steam engines, not whims of the wind, powered the ship.

The *Peruvian* must have seemed gigantic. Johan and Anna might have imagined that an entire Swedish village – and then some – could fit aboard. It was 312 feet long and 39 feet wide and capable of carrying up to 2,549 tons of cargo. It was of the screw-propeller design which replaced less efficient paddle-wheel propulsion systems.

On this leg of their journey, Johan and Anna and the kids were manifested under names that were neither strictly in the Swedish patronymic tradition nor fully adapted for their new lives in America. They were Andersons. So, for example, Lars, who left Trondheim as Lars Johansson and who later would become Lewis Hagglund, was listed aboard the *Peruvian* as Lars Anderson. The daughter Kerstin was listed as Christina Anderson, and her mother was Anna Anderson.[8]

The Andersons (Hagglunds), like most immigrants, were in steerage class, the cheaper accommodations sometimes called "between-decks" because this was the area below the main deck and above the cargo hold. The more well-to-do traveled in cabin class, with easy access to fresh air. The distinction between classes referred to differences in the accommodations, but you can see it also in the way passengers were manifested. In steerage, they appeared as "laborer," "spinster" or "wife." Those in cabin class (mostly British subjects) were listed as "gentleman" or "lady."

Johan and Anna must have dug deep into their savings to pay the fare, which two years later, in 1869, was advertised at $25 per adult for steerage accommodation. That is equivalent to $400 in 2018 dollars, adjusted for inflation. The fare for children was calculated this way: $2 for each year of age for those between one and 12; no charge for those under one. The total cost for the Hagglund family, if those rates were in force when they traveled two years earlier, would have been $108, or the equivalent in 2018 of just over $1,700.

Conditions in steerage varied by vessel, but typically it was crowded, cramped and damp. Limited sanitation could make it dirty and foul smelling. Passengers shared their space with rats and disease.

The Hagglunds left no known record of their 14 days aboard the *Peruvian* (August 1-14), but American, Norwegian and Canadian records provide a sense of what it might have been like. Make no mistake, it was true equally for passengers and crew: An ocean crossing was not for the faint of heart, the impatient, the pampered or any but the most determined souls.

The *Peruvian*'s captain was W. Ballantine, a veteran of many Atlantic voyages. He was mentioned in a 1912 issue of Pacific Marine Review magazine as a mariner of "high standing in the profession." A passenger who sailed aboard the *Peruvian* six weeks after the Hagglunds, on the same Liverpool-to-Quebec route, described Ballantine as "a regular old salt, blunt, uncourteous and undignified in his manner and conversation, but a good sailor no doubt."[9]

In that era, most ships sailing to North America from Norway made Quebec City their port of call rather than New York. That was because, starting in about 1850, when Britain loosened its international trade restrictions, Norwegian sailing ships did a good business hauling Canadian timber from Quebec City to England; emigrants became the return "cargo," and a lucrative one at that. Shipping companies competing for European passengers advertised the Quebec route as shorter and cheaper than New York, where landing fees were higher.

Ship records show the *Peruvian* departed Liverpool on August 1, 1867, with 226 passengers aboard, of which 154 were in steerage, including the seven Andersons (Hagglunds).

Exiting Liverpool's River Mersey and crossing the Irish Sea on a northwest heading, the *Peruvian* sailed by the Isle of Man and pulled into the Irish port of Londonderry the same day. There it picked up 105 more passengers, bringing the total to 331.

On August 2, the vessel departed Londonderry. It likely battled hostile winds through much of the journey, judging from the ship's log for the same transit about five weeks later. That log, reproduced in a travelogue written by William E. Whyte, an Irish American, and published in 1870, showed the *Peruvian* fighting "contrary winds whole passage," yet completing the trip from Liverpool to Quebec via Londonderry in 11 days — three fewer than was required for the Hagglunds' voyage. The stability of stomachs in the Hagglund family must have been severely tested.

Their route took them approximately 2,475 miles west across the Atlantic to the entrance to the Strait of Belle Isle, a narrow waterway in eastern Canada between the northern tip of Newfoundland and the southern end of the Labrador Peninsula. From there the *Peruvian* continued west into the Gulf of St. Lawrence. As it approached the entrance to the St. Lawrence River, Captain Ballantine would have spotted on the north shore an all-white lighthouse at Pointe des Monts whose lantern helped ships steer clear of the Manicouagan Shoals.

About 30 miles downriver from Quebec City the ship would have stopped briefly for inspection at Grosse Ile, a small island with a quarantine station established in 1832 for cholera victims arriving from Britain. Cemeteries on the island contain the remains of thousands of victims of epidemics of typhus, cholera and other contagious diseases that swept through immigrant ships over the years.

As the *Peruvian* pulled into port at Quebec City on August 14, the

Hagglunds' natural excitement and sense of relief would have been overwhelmed by deep emotional pain.

Their ship had been approaching Canadian waters when tragedy again called on the Hagglunds and left with 6-year-old Märet. The only known record of this is the Everett account, which described it as follows:

"Märet became seriously ill and died just before the ship reached its destination. The cause of death is not on record, nor is the exact date of death. It seems safe to assume, however, that death must have occurred very shortly before they were to land because it is recorded that she was buried on land in Newfoundland or Nova Scotia."

I don't know where her burial was "recorded." Of the two Canadian provinces mentioned as possible burial locations, the more likely is Newfoundland, since the Peruvian's route did not take it far enough south in the Gulf of St. Lawrence to be near Nova Scotia. I checked with the staff of the main repository of vital records for the province of Newfoundland and Labrador, located in St. John's, and was told there was no record of burial of a child by this name – Maret or Martha Anderson or Hagglund or Johansdotter, her original surname.

It's possible that Maret was buried on Grosse Ile, the island in the St. Lawrence River, although I could not find her in a Canadian National Archives collection of names of nearly 5,000 immigrants who died at sea or on the St. Lawrence River or on quarantine ships at Grosse Ile between 1832 and 1922. Nor is she on the Archives' list of nearly 4,900 people buried at the Grosse Ile quarantine station between 1832 and 1937.

A Hagglund descendant, Hazel (Tackstrom) Booth, recalled at a 1983 family reunion that she had been told Märet was buried in Newfoundland and that the cost had consumed the last of the family's travel money, save for a single gold coin.

* * *

Life Aboard Ship

If any of the Hagglunds recorded observations or memories of their epic sea journey, the story seems not to have survived. One gets an idea of what it was like, however, in a letter penned by a British passenger after she, her husband and their baby made the same journey from Liverpool to Quebec aboard the *Peruvian* three years after the Hagglunds.

"I did not like the look of my sleeping place when I got in. I could not sleep at all," the mother wrote.[10] Identified as Mary Lucy H., she and her family apparently were in steerage. "It was like a small box, and some sleep above you. Dreadful hot. Could scarcely breathe."

Her 10-day journey never got easy. On the second day at sea the weather took a terrible turn. "The ship rocking very much. Sickness very bad; such a scene you never did see," she wrote. It was cold, windy and snowy. "No one could stand on deck. Down below we had to hold by a rope to keep from injuring ourselves; several were hurt. Baby and I were dashed from side to side. I was screaming, 'Oh, my baby!'"

In cabin class the experience could be much different. Just how different is made clear by a 17-year-old Scot named John Gwynn Swain in a letter to his mother back home in Edinburgh. Writing from aboard a steamship making the trans-Atlantic voyage to Quebec in June 1867 (the same summer as the Hagglunds), he described a pleasant passage, all the more enjoyable for the ocean breezes that stimulated his appetite. By his account, conditions for those between decks were nothing less than brutal. He described steerage passengers "lying like pigs vomiting in all directions, over each other and under each other, and indeed everywhere. That night the sounds I heard were awful. The steerage is right under the cabin, and consequently when lying in our bunks, and all quiet, you heard with the greatest distinctness. The retching was frightful ... and the poor babies were crying most piteously. Of course, their mothers were all too ill to attend to them."[11]

The writer of the 1870 letter, Mary Lucy, recalled arriving in Quebec, getting off the ship and walking around "Point Levi," where their luggage was examined, presumably by customs officials. This appears to refer to an area on the right bank of the St. Lawrence, across from Quebec City, that was called Pointe Levy. In more recent times it has been known as Levis. Starting in the mid-1800s, Pointe Levy's rail connections made it a major transportation center for commerce and immigration. It was the starting point for the Grand Trunk Railway that stretched west to Sarnia, Ontario, on the south shore of Lake Huron, and continued on to Port Huron and Detroit, Michigan. From there, immigrants could ride the Michigan Central Railroad to Chicago.

It seems likely the Hagglunds, as they were known now that they had reached North America, followed the same procedure as Mary Lucy, catching their train connection at Pointe Levy to head west. It's not possible to fully reconstruct this movement from official records because the U.S. government did not begin documenting immigrants entering from Canada until nearly 30 years later.[12]

Although I don't know precisely how the Hagglunds got from Quebec to Minnesota, they could not have gone the entire distance by rail alone. There were no rail lines reaching into Minnesota from points east until shortly after the Hagglunds got there. In October 1867, the McGregor Western joined rails with the Minnesota Central to complete a line linking Minneapolis to the east via Prairie du Chien, Wisconsin.

It is likely the Hagglunds connected at Chicago on a separate line reaching west to the Mississippi River at one of two Wisconsin towns – Prairie du Chien or La Crosse, the western-most railheads. From there they likely took a steamer up the Mississippi to Red Wing, about 80 miles north of La Crosse and 130 miles north of Prairie du Chien.

The Everett account says that by the time the Hagglunds boarded their train in Quebec, John and Anna's cash reserves had dwindled to just one coin.

"When the train conductor came around to collect the fares, Anna concealed the coin in her mouth and told him that they had no money left," it says. "The conductor took pity on them, talked to the other passengers, then allowed them to ride without charge."

Talk about starting from scratch.

4

No Going Back

I don't know for sure why Johan and Anna left Sweden, but the decision likely was the biggest of their lives. The feeling of home would never be the same, which is not to say they would never feel at home again. The challenge as immigrants was to form a different idea of what home meant.

Was leaving the right thing to do? Only Johan and Anna could say for sure. What is clear in hindsight is that they had the strength, spiritually and physically, to take the first fateful step beyond Sweden. Their subsequent journey was not without stumbles, but it eventually returned them to a sense of home.

In *Unto a Good Land*, Swedish novelist Vilhelm Moberg described what made his main character, Karl Oskar, certain that emigrating had been the correct decision despite his wife Kristina's longing for their homeland after settling in Minnesota.

"She must think ahead, of their children, and their children's children in time, of all the generations after them," he wrote. Johan and Anna seem to have looked at it the same way. Still, for some months or years afterward they may have retraced in their minds the path that drew them away from their former life; they may have suffered initial pangs of regret akin to those expressed by Eric Norelius, a 19th century Lutheran minister who recalled the emotions that welled inside when he cast off from his native Sweden in 1850.

"It was a day a I shall never forget," he wrote in his memoir, as translated by a colleague. "Even today, as I think of this farewell, this significant moment, my heart is ready to break." He added: "When one has been cut off from a stem where one belongs by nature and training and then grafted on another tree, one can never again have quite the same feelings and the same outlook on life ..."

The emigration movement during this period was a complex social phenomenon. Aside from the question of what motivated people like John and Anna to leave their homeland, there were competing forces at work in Swedish society. The clergy, the press and the upper classes "leagued together," in the words of historian Olof N. Nelson, in opposing the movement and ridiculing emigration as unpatriotic, if not sinful. An even more powerful force, however, was a grassroots fascination with the idea of finding a better life and greater freedom in America.

"It became a fashion," Nelson wrote in an 1899 history of Scandinavians in the United States.

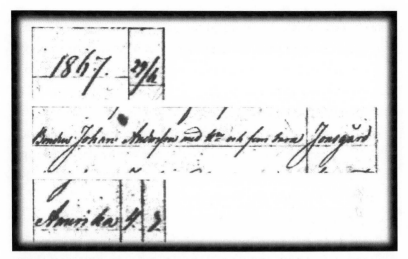

Original church records in Sweden show that "farmer Johan Andersson with wife and family" (4 males, 3 females) left their home on June 29, 1867 — destination: "Amerika"

Historians point to numerous factors that fed successive waves of emigration in the mid- and late-1800s, starting with a belief that America was an almost magical solution to the despair that gripped the Swedish countryside in the 1860s.

In his book, *Swedish Exodus*, Lars Ljungmark argued that the prospect of land ownership and jobs were the biggest factors drawing Swedes across the Atlantic amid what he called "deplorable conditions" in the homeland. He cited the 1866-68 series of crop failures but doubted this was the foremost impetus for emigration.

Did Johan and Anna leave in desperation, or were they among the relatively few in Jämtland in 1867 who saw hope on the distant horizon and were bold enough to pursue it? Were they, as the old expression goes, "building castles in Spain" – daydreaming of the unattainable? I think not. They were ready to take steps toward achieving the sense of self-worth and satisfaction that comes with owning land and a home and determining one's own destiny.

Of the 12 families and individuals who moved out of Häggenås parish that year, most went to a neighboring parish. Johan and Anna were the only ones whose destination was "Amerika," as Swedes spell it. And they seem to have started something. The following year, 1868, two more Häggenås families left for the United States, and the year after that, three more.

There was no shortage of people selling the idea of America as a beacon of hope.

In the U.S., leading promoters of immigration included state authorities, newspaper publishers, land companies, railroads, trans-Atlantic steamship lines and Swedish Americans whose letters home had great credibility. America's first land-grant railroad, the Illinois Central, dispatched agents to Sweden and Norway in the 1850s and 60s to travel throughout both countries, distribute pamphlets and place ads in local newspapers using Illinois Central materials.

Among the selling points, in addition to the prospect of home-steading, was the idea that in America you could pray and preach whenever, however and wherever you chose. At the time, Sweden's only state-sanctioned faith was Lutheranism. As leaders of the state Church of Sweden, the Lutheran clergy wielded the authority not only of the Church but also of the Swedish government. An 18th century law known as the Conventicle Act forbade any private gathering for religious services – Lutheran or otherwise – except for family prayer. Only state-regulated congregations were permitted, and only ordained clergy could preach. Offenders were fined or imprisoned; some were forced into exile.

This angered and embittered not only Swedes who split from the Lutheran church to embrace the Baptist faith but also those commit-ted Lutherans who considered the state clergy to be morally corrupt for overlooking violations of the church's behavioral standards so long as the violators called themselves Lutherans.

This gave rise to a revivalist and temperance movement fueled partly by disdain for the autocratic nature of the Church and partly by disgust with the widespread acceptance of alcohol use even among clergy. This movement prompted many nonconformists to look toward America, as described with biting anger by a Baptist minister in *A History of the Swedish-Americans of Minnesota.*

"So long as they had engaged in dancing, drinking, and an openly sinful life they were looked upon [in Sweden] as being in perfect harmony with the Lutheran faith," the minister wrote, "but as soon as they began to seek salvation for their poor souls, and did it outside of the state church, they were looked upon as dangerous and undesirable citizens."

An 1898 account paints a dark picture of this period. *History of the Swedish Baptists in Sweden and America*, by one of their most outspoken leaders, Gustavus W. Schröder, refers to "the despised Baptists, everywhere spoken against" in Sweden in the 1850s.

Others have suggested that the Baptists could be rightly accused of occasional insolence.

"Whether the cause was reasonable or not, many parishes were torn with religious strife, friends became enemies, neighbor was set against neighbor, and parent against children," George Malcolm Stephenson wrote in his 1932 book, *The Religious Aspects of Swedish Immigration: A Study of Immigrant Churches.*

In his view, the rise of a Baptist movement in Sweden, starting in the 1840s and gaining momentum a decade later, was closely tied to a Baptist attraction to the New World.

Among Baptists, emigration was seen as providential, as a part of God's plan to build up a kingdom in the New World. This belief was reflected in the Baptists' missionary zeal, and it would be seen in

Lewis Hagglund's own writings many years later.

To a degree, the state church eased its grip as the nonconformist movement grew. The Conventicle Act forbidding unsanctioned preaching was abolished in 1858, but the Baptists and other religious dissenters remained on their own path. They refused to secede from the Church of Sweden on the state's strict terms. This was not unlike circumstances in colonial America's pre-revolutionary years when the Anglican Church was predominant and Baptist dissenters were persecuted.

In his history of Swedish Baptists, Schröder quotes a Mrs. C.W. Putnam as writing in 1868:

"As we trace the progress of Baptist principles in Sweden, we must remember all the obstacles which impede their onward course. All the wealth and power and influence of the hierarchy were employed to crush out this heresy and to silence the voice of the preacher. Blows, fines and imprisonments were meted out to pastors and people. Men cast out their names as evil, and often friends and relatives disowned them."

Schroeder wrote that the persecution was most severe from about 1840 to 1880.

In Ostergren's study of Dalarna's Rättvik parish, he wrote that the prevailing atmosphere of religious intolerance partly explained why emigration was more prevalent among Baptists than in the overall Swedish population.

Ostergren speculated that these nonconformists by their nature may have been more inclined to emigrate. If true, that tendency could have been part of what guided Johan and Anna. They had joined the Baptist movement at some point in the early 1860s, if not before, and surely knew the social consequences. The Everett account says they converted "sometime after" they lost Anders and Maret in the 1855 fire.

Their conversion coincided with a period of attention-getting Baptist missionary work by two older Swedes: Anders Wiberg and Fredrik O. Nilson. Both men spent time in the United States in the early 1850s – Nilson after he had been banished from Sweden as a heretic in 1853, and Wiberg because he sought opportunities in America to minister to immigrants. Their writings drew great attention back home in Sweden.

"Next to the banishment of Nilson, the fact that Wiberg, a devout man and a scholar, had left the established church with all its allurements of comfortable living, promotion and honors, to cast his lot with the despised and persecuted Baptists, had great moral effect on the advancement of their cause in Sweden," Ernest W. Olson wrote in his *History of the Swedes of Illinois*.

In other words, these men caught the attention of a lot of ordinary Swedes, possibly including Johan and Anna, or others in Jämtland who in turn influenced them.

For Johan and Anna, their abandonment of Lutheranism changed everything.

"All of their friends turned against them; they would no longer speak to them," the Everett account said. "The loss of respect of their former friends was possibly the prime factor in the decision to migrate to the United States."

The record is clear: Johan and Anna were singled out as Baptists by the state clergy – and not in a positive way. This marked them as outliers, if not outcasts. The civil survey of Häggenås parish for 1862-1871 has a "Baptist" notation after Johan's name, and a "special" remark – "has avoided baptism" – was added for daughter Kerstin, probably in 1865, two years after her birth.[13] Some Baptists, as an act of principled protest, refused to submit their newborns to the Lutheran practice of infant baptism, sticking to the core Baptist principle that only at an age of accountability, or young adulthood, can one become a true believer and repent. In other words, they practiced believers baptism, not infant baptism. (Under Swedish law, parents were obliged to baptize their child within eight days after birth; in 1864 the limit was stretched to six weeks.)

The birth and baptism record for Kerstin included the following notation:

"The parents refused to allow the child to be baptized," adding that her father's "application" – apparently referring to his formal request for permission of the parish clergy to forego baptism – said the child would be named Kerstin. For reasons I could not determine, Johan and Anna did allow the next child, Olof, to be baptized in 1865. Perhaps they could not get official permission to forego his baptism. If so, one could imagine this being the final straw. They emigrated two years later.

No written family record has shed further light on this period of personal turmoil. The Everett account says that although Johan had been making "a good living," the backlash from the family's Baptist conversion compelled them to leave. There would be no returning, as Johan and Anna surely knew.

Only memories could take them back.

5

Minnesota for a Minute

The Hagglunds arrived at Red Wing, Minnesota, in the final days of August, completing a 1,400-mile trek from Quebec City, where they had disembarked from the Peruvian on August 14. Thus, the journey from start to finish, from Sweden to Minnesota via Norway, England, Ireland and Canada, had taken a full two months — and one child's life. A slog of that length and consequence is hard to imagine for a 21st century traveler who can fly from Sweden to Minnesota in a single day and suffer little more than jet lag.

If they arrived at Red Wing by riverboat, as seems highly likely, John and Anna might have marveled at a 340-foot-high cliff, known locally as Barn Bluff, that stands watch over the city on the upper Mississippi. When Jacques Marquette, the French missionary and explorer, wrote about his 1673 voyage of discovery along this stretch of America's grandest river, he described "bold bluffs" on either side that reminded him of "the castled shores of our own beautiful rivers in France."

Barn Bluff, just north of a centuries-old Mississippi landmark called Point-No-Point, might have reminded the Hagglunds of the more dramatic fjords they saw around Trondheim, Norway, at the start of their voyage. Almost everything else in their new surroundings, however, was unfamiliar – starting with the language.

The America that welcomed the Hagglund family of six had barely begun recovering from the Civil War, which had ended two years earlier. Ten of the 11 states that seceded from the Union had not yet been readmitted. (Tennessee was readmitted in 1866.) Minnesota may have seemed far removed from the strife, geographically and socially, but its citizens — immigrants included — did fight and die for the Union.

My account of this phase of the Hagglunds' journey is a rough approximation of events. Available documentation is thinner than for other periods, so I relied more on educated guesswork and clues and impressions from a July 2017 visit to Red Wing and Vasa, where family lore says the Hagglunds made their first home. Vasa, pronounced "VAY'-suh" by locals, is a dozen miles west of Red Wing and was so thoroughly Swedish that it had enclaves named for Swedish provinces, including Jämtland, which was south of Vasa village not far from a landmark called White Rock.

I cannot prove the Hagglunds' presence in Vasa, but I would bet heavily on it. To my knowledge, there is no surviving written record of their time in Minnesota, although in Vasa I came close to finding one. I reviewed handwritten entries in a dry goods store ledger that included names of buyers, their purchases and the prices they paid. The accounting began in December 1868, a few months after the Hagglunds had moved on to Iowa.

Vasa is both a village and a township, or locale, encompassing an area of about 36 square miles. The township is bisected by Belle Creek and bordered on the north by the Cannon River, which enters the Mississippi four miles north of Red Wing. The character of this area remained largely unchanged well into the 21st century. It is farm country, pure and simple. In summer, oceans of cornstalks flow to the horizon, interrupted only by clusters of farm buildings, narrow roads, groves of burr and white oak, and an occasional reminder of the distant past, such as a small graveyard.

I was not surprised to find that the Hagglunds left no discernible mark in Red Wing or Vasa, given that they remained only about one year and owned no property. In that short span, with the heartbreaking death of little Märet surely weighing on them, there were no new additions to the family, and, mercifully, no further loss of life. It also is unsurprising that the Hagglunds moved on quickly from Vasa; the settlement was an example of what historians of Swedish immigration call a "mother colony," a starting point for the newly arrived, some of whom then moved westward in stages – often winding up on the West Coast.

I can point to two pieces of evidence supporting my belief that Minnesota was the Hagglunds' first stop in America. The first is a passage in the 1983 Everett account that says they arrived in "an area of Minnesota where John's brother lived; we have a name, Vasa, for the town or area where they settled but can find no such name on a modern map. We do have a more definite date, August 1867." (More later about John's brother having lived in Vasa.)

It's no wonder the authors of the Everett account could not find Vasa on a map. It was tiny, and is even smaller today, although it looms large in Swedish immigrant history in 19th century Minnesota.

The second bit of evidence is the fact that the Hagglunds declared Red Wing their destination when they set sail from Trondheim. I know this from their *Tyne Queen* paperwork, which I obtained from the Norwegian National Archives. Among the scant facts recorded for each passenger was his or her destination. For Johan and Anna and their children it was written as a single word: "Redwing."

The Tyne Queen passenger list includes "Johan Andersson," age 39, "wife Anna Larsdotter," age 37, and their five children, from Jemteland (the Norwegian spelling). Ship departing July 22, 1867, destination, "Redwing."

The passenger manifest for their subsequent voyage from Liverpool to Quebec aboard the *Peruvian* lists their destination only as Quebec. It cannot be ruled out that they changed their minds about Red Wing along the way, but I found no evidence to support that scenario. I believe they stuck to the original plan. At the time, Red Wing was a common destination for Swedes, including a number who left the homeland at the same time as the Hagglunds.

"Immigrants were arriving in such numbers [in 1867] that temporary quarters were provided at Red Wing for 200," Christian A. Rasmussen wrote in *History of Goodhue County, Minnesota*.

I don't know why the Hagglunds chose Red Wing as the starting point of their American adventure. It likely was talked about in the Jämtland countryside as a promising new frontier. As early as 1850, Swedes — settlers as well as visitors — were touting Minnesota's attractions. The Swedish author Fredrika Bremer toured the state that year, traveling up the Mississippi by steamboat to St. Paul. Afterward she wrote, "What a glorious new Scandinavia might not Minnesota become!"

Minnesota was a magnet for disaffected Baptists in Sweden.

"They considered it a great privilege to be free, and they wrote back to their friends in the old country and told what they found here," a Baptist minister wrote in a 1910 collection of essays on the history of Swedish Baptists in Minnesota.[14] "Hence, others came, family after family."

I find no reason to doubt the Everett account is correct in saying the Hagglunds wound up in Vasa, but the assertion that a brother of John's lived there appears to be incorrect. It refers to the brother, without mentioning a name, a second time when speculating about why John adopted a new surname.

"It seems likely that he changed his name from Johan Anderson to John A. Hagglund because there were so many John Andersons in the town where his brother lived, and where John and his family stayed while they were in Minnesota," the Everett account says, referring to Vasa.

Indeed, there was no shortage of Andersons in Vasa; the 1865 state census counted ten households headed by Andersons, including two named John, out of 134 families in and around the village. In July 2017, I met a descendant of one of those ten. His name was Bernard Anderson, a great grandson of Bengt Anderson, who arrived in Vasa in 1855. Bernard, who was 87 when I spent part of an afternoon with him browsing in collections of old town records, told me that his farm has been in the family since Bengt bought it in 1865.[15] I was tickled to have him autograph my copy of *Vasa Illustrata*, published by the Vasa Swedish Lutheran congregation in 1905 as a "civil and churchly cultural picture" of the area.

If John Hagglund had a brother already living in Vasa in 1867, that would explain why he and Anna chose to go there. Alas, I believe that scenario is wrong.

John had five brothers – Anders and Mats were older than him; Jonas, Olof and Erik were younger. Among them, only Olof emigrated to the United States, but he left Sweden well *after*, not before, John.

By remarkable coincidence, Olof made the voyage aboard the same ship – the SS *Peruvian*.

Olof lived with John and Anna at the Munkflohögen farm in Häggenås parish from the fall of 1852 to the fall of 1853. In October 1865, at age 30, Olof married Christina Danielsdotter, a widow and 13 years his senior. The marriage record describes him as a "målaren," the Swedish word for painter. Christina and Olof had a daughter together in March 1868, Christina Olivia Olsdotter, who changed her name to Olivia Anderson after emigrating to America with her parents in 1882. By this time, the Hagglunds were living in Nebraska.

Like his older brother John, Olof became a Baptist. I don't know whether that influenced his decision to emigrate. Olof and his wife Christina are marked as Baptists in parish records in Gävleborg, a county southeast of Jämtland and bordering the Gulf of Bothnia, the northernmost arm of the Baltic Sea separating Sweden and Finland. They lived in at least two parishes – Bergsjö and Hassela – before emigrating.

Fifteen years after John and Anna and their five children left Sweden, Olof and his wife and their 14-year-old daughter Olivia retraced his brother's path aboard the *Peruvian*, departing from Londonderry on June 22, 1882 after starting out at Liverpool. They arrived in Quebec on July 2. They declared St. Paul their final destination.

The 1900 U.S. census lists Olof as a widower living with a Swedish immigrant farm family in Isanti County, Minnesota, north of St. Paul. His wife apparently had died in the years since they emigrated. Ten years later he was living in Cambridge, the seat of Isanti County, 30-plus miles north of Minneapolis. He was retired, 74 years old and living in the home of his daughter, Olivia. She was 42, unmarried and a restaurant owner.[16]

One can imagine that John and Olof would have communicated by letter during this period, but there is no known record of it, nor any indication that either visited the other.

Of John's two older brothers, Mats and Anders, I confirmed that Mats never emigrated, and that he died in Sweden. Anders remained in Sweden at least into the 1870s. If either of John's two other younger brothers, Jonas and Erik, emigrated at all, I could find no evidence of it. This leads me to conclude that the Everett account is wrong. There was no brother in Vasa. If I'm right about that, I'm left with no obvious alternative explanation for why the Hagglunds picked the Red Wing/Vasa area as their destination, other than the possibility that it was among popular choices they heard talked about in their home village in Jämtland.

As an exclusively Swedish enclave at the time, Vasa may have been a good fit for the Hagglunds, except perhaps for one thing: As Baptists, they were again in the religious minority, although not openly despised. I don't know how much it mattered to the Hagglunds, but Lutherans dominated in Vasa as they had back home in Sweden, minus the authoritarianism and cultural stigmas. In Vasa, they were led by an evangelist named Erik Norelius, a revered figure in the history of Swedish Lutherans in the American Midwest and beyond.

The Norelius name also would figure in the Hagglunds' lives in the years ahead. The connection was more than personal. It symbolized the religious rivalry – Lutherans versus Baptists – that fed undercurrents of tension in the Hagglund story.

Norelius came to America in 1850 with his older brother Anders and about 100 other Lutherans from the parishes of Bergsjö and Hassela in Hälsingland province in east-central Sweden – coincidentally the same parishes in which John Hagglunds' brother Olof lived in the 1860s and 1870s. Anders Norelius was 19 when they left in July; Erik turned 17 shortly before they arrived in October. Once settled in the

United States, both Americanized their given names – Erik became Eric and Anders became Andrew.

In a memoir originally published in Swedish in 1916, Eric wrote of the pain of leaving Sweden.

"I know that when I left my home in the Old World, I lost the feeling of having an earthly home, and I can never in this life get it back," he wrote.[17]

By the time he had made his way to Andover, Illinois, where he stayed with a Swedish Lutheran pastor named Lars P. Esbjörn, Eric was even more distressed. "While living at the Esbjörn home I had become so homesick that I was almost beside myself," he wrote.

When Eric and Andrew Norelius and their fellow Lutherans set out across the Atlantic in July 1850, their goal had been to establish a Swedish Lutheran congregation in America, but the plan fell apart in more ways than one. Some died along the way, many veered onto separate paths, and the Norelius brothers had a personal falling out. Andrew became a Baptist in 1852, much to Eric's chagrin.

Eric pitied the Lutherans who converted to the Baptist faith. He called them "prey to the spirit of error." Andrew, the brother, seemed to hint at this split in a letter to a fellow Baptist minister in May 1854 explaining his devotion to Baptist principles.

"No, I will never leave Him, I will rather suffer ridicule and persecution, even though it be from my own relatives," he wrote.

In his memoir, Eric barely mentioned Andrew, reflecting their apparent estrangement. At times in the 1860s they co-existed in Vasa as leaders of their respective congregations. Eric was Vasa Lutheran Church's first pastor in 1855, and Andrew led the Vasa Baptist Church for the first two years after it was organized in 1860.

From the get-go, the Lutherans had a leg up in Vasa. They started with 88 members; the Baptists had just 19 and never caught up. Some of the Baptists moved on to Iowa in the late 1860s – the Hagglunds and Andrew Norelius among them. It's unclear to what extent this Lutheran-Baptist rivalry drove the re-migration; I suspect that it played a part. Equally important may have been the expectation that greater economic opportunity lay to the west.

A summary of the Vasa Baptist church's history, on file at the Vasa Museum, says membership had grown to 49 by the time the Hagglunds arrived in 1867. One could imagine them joining soon after their arrival, but I was unable to find a by-name membership list. The Lutheran congregation in Vasa by 1867 was about seven times bigger than the Baptists', and the gap never narrowed.

In 1868 the Baptists built their first church, but within nine years the membership had shrunk to 36. It apparently peaked at 59 members in 1878 (compared to a high mark of more than 1,100 for the Lutherans) and dipped to 37 in 1889.

By 1896 the Baptist congregation was edging toward extinction. It had just 18 members and no pastor that year. Two years later the church building was sold to the Vasa Farmers Co-op Creamery and was moved a short distance down the street; fire destroyed the building in October 1915. I could not determine what became of the church's records.

One measure of the Lutherans' dominance in Vasa was still visible when I visited in 2017, more than a century after the Baptists disbanded. The Lutheran church is a majestic brick temple situated atop a grassy knoll. It towers over the village; its graveyard is large, well-groomed and visible from a great distance. By contrast, the tiny Baptist cemetery with about two dozen marked graves, while neatly kept, is tucked among bushes and trees, almost hidden at the other end of town, across Norelius Road — named for Eric, not Andrew — from where the church once stood.

6

Sweden in America

Vasa is an interesting story by itself. Before it had an official name, the place was known locally as Swede Prairie and then Mattson's Settlement, referring to Hans Mattson, a Swede who arrived in the United States at age 18 and accompanied a small group in search of fertile land south of St. Paul in 1853.

"We were not satisfied until we came upon the large prairie where Vasa is now located," he wrote in 1856. "On this prairie, we found the best soil and saw good oak woods in all directions."[18]

Mattson, who later enlisted in the Union Army and twice served as Minnesota's secretary of state, drew significant numbers of his countrymen to his settlement by promoting it in letters to Swedish-American newspapers, including Hemlandet, a voice of the Lutheran church with subscribers in America and Sweden. By 1856, Mattson reported, about 100 Swedes had settled in Vasa.

That same summer, the 21-year-old Eric Norelius and fellow Lutheran clergyman Nils Hokanson traveled from their homes at West Point, Indiana, to Red Wing in search of Swedes in need of ministering. On September 3, Norelius preached to an impromptu gathering at a log cabin 12 miles west of Red Wing. Norelius' biographer, Lutheran clergyman Emeroy Johnson, credits Norelius with suggesting the congregation be called the "Swedish Evangelical Lutheran Congregation in Vasa."

The name stuck, and the settlement adopted it as its own.

Vasa refers to the 16th century king of Sweden, Gustav Vasa, who organized and led a peasant revolt that began in Dalarna and eventually achieved Sweden's independence from Denmark in 1523. He later introduced the country to Lutheranism. Thus, the village of Vasa was virtually synonymous with the Lutheran Church.

"There is perhaps no other colony in America which is so purely characteristic of Sweden as Vasa," E. Marion Sigfrid Norelius, a son of Eric Norelius, wrote in 1905.[19]

The town was formally organized in 1858. Pages of handwritten notes from the first town meeting, held July 5 of that year, have been preserved – yellowed but still legible – and are available for public viewing at the Goodhue County Historical Society in Red Wing. The elegant calligraphy on the title page of the "Book of Record" is a reminder of a bygone era when penmanship mattered and artistry was a part of everyday life.

According to local lore, Vasa, though small and remote, was widely known.

"Since the first settlement, Vasa has been famed far and near," Franklin Curtiss-Wedge wrote in 1909 in his *History of Goodhue County*.

This suggests the possibility that the Hagglunds heard about Vasa while in Sweden and aimed to settle there after arriving in Red Wing.

The Swedes were proud of their little enclave, which grew rapidly in the early 1860s. The state census of 1865 recorded 695 Vasa residents and broke it down thusly: "134 families, 14 soldiers, 1 insane." That was two years before the Hagglunds arrived. Unfortunately, the census recorded no information about residents aside from their name and gender. (It did include columns to be marked if an individual was "deaf, dumb, blind, or insane" or if currently serving in the military.)

* * *

Norelius

The Norelius name comes up frequently in any review of the history of Vasa because Eric played an outsized role in the town's early days as its preeminent religious figure.

As evidence of Eric's iconic status, Vasa townspeople have lovingly organized a "Norelius Room" in a building they call the Vasa House, not far from the present Vasa Lutheran Church built in the late 1860s. On display are his 19th century silk top hat, his walnut writing desk, the wedding bedspread made by his wife Inga, and many other carefully preserved artifacts.

Erik's brother Andrew is, by comparison, a forgotten figure in Vasa; he is better remembered in Isanti County north of Minneapolis and St. Paul.[20] His story nonetheless is relevant to the Hagglunds' because their paths moved in parallel and even intersected.

Andrew is listed in the 1860 census as a Vasa resident, occupation: "Baptist clergy." He and his wife Christina had one child at the time, 1-year-old Adolph. Also living with them were Andrew's parents, Andrew and Elizabeth, who emigrated in 1853, three years after Eric and Andrew. They also became Baptists.

Andrew's two-year stint as pastor of the Vasa Baptist Church ended in 1862; two years later he joined the Union Army – Company D, Minnesota 3rd Infantry Regiment – to spend the final year of the Civil War as a chaplain. In September 1865 he returned to civilian life, serving as pastor of the Baptist church in Cambridge, Isanti County, about 75 miles north of Vasa. (He had been present as an adviser for the creation of the Cambridge church in June 1860.) He was living in Cambridge when the Hagglunds arrived in Vasa in 1867. So, while Andrew Norelius and John Hagglund would not have known each other at that point, they did a short time later.

In the spring or summer of 1868, the Hagglund and Norelius families headed for Iowa – probably not together, although they ended up at the same place: a tiny Swedish settlement in Crawford County. The timing of the Norelius move was remembered differently by some of his associates, but he and the Hagglund family seem to have been part of a purposeful but loosely organized Swedish Baptist re-migration that followed a westward pattern from Illinois and Minnesota to west-central Iowa in the late 1860s. Some continued on to eastern Nebraska.

The Hagglunds may never have intended to stay in Vasa for the long haul. If that was the case, what prompted them to choose west-central Iowa as their next stop? My guess is that the choice was linked to events involving Andrew Norelius and a handful of his fellow Baptist leaders.

The Everett account has little to say on this score.

"We have no information concerning what John did in Minnesota during the time they stayed in that state," it says, adding, "They found very few reasons to stay."

One reason not to stay, perhaps, was the sting of winter. In his *History of Red Wing, Minnesota*, Christian A. Rasmussen recounted the story of a postman and his stagecoach driver delivering mail on an especially cold day in the winter of 1867, the year the Hagglunds arrived. The two men sat on the front of the coach, he wrote, "silently huddled in their buffalo coats endeavoring to obtain whatever protection they could" from a biting wind. The stage entered Red

Wing and pulled up to a hotel. A man came out to greet them with a lantern.

"The postman jumped down but there was no response from the driver, even when they called to him. They finally removed him from the seat and found he had frozen to death in the bitter cold and the horses had brought the stage in without guidance."

I don't know what sort of accommodations the Hagglunds had that winter in Vasa. One could imagine they found room and board on a farm in exchange for their labor. Perhaps the arrangement allowed them to save enough money to pursue more promising prospects in the far reaches of Iowa, where their Baptist faith might be more mainstream.

The Everett account offers additional details about the move to Iowa.

"The Hagglunds, along with a group of 'friends and neighbors,' left Minnesota in the fall of 1868 and traveled by wagon train to the area now called 'Kiron' in Crawford County, Iowa," it says.

As best I could determine, they left in the summer, not fall. More intriguing is the reference to the Hagglunds having traveled with a group. No names are mentioned in the Everett account or any other family record, but the reference to "friends and neighbors" suggests that others in the Vasa area moved with them.

One of their fellow travelers might have been a Vasa family headed by David Ludwig Johnson, a Swedish immigrant with a non-Swedish sounding first name. He was a Baptist and one year older than John. He had an adventurous youth, having emigrated from Sweden in the 1840s by hiring on as a ship's cabin boy and then stealing away during its stop in London and repeating the process on a voyage to New York. He sailed to San Francisco to join the 1849 California gold rush, returned to Sweden, got married and returned to America, winding up in Minnesota in about 1860.

The 1865 Minnesota state census counts David and his wife and six children as Vasa residents, and five years later they were living in Crawford County, Iowa, in the same township where the Hagglunds had resettled. An 1875 Iowa plat map shows the Johnsons were near-neighbors, living less than two miles east of the Hagglund farm. Judging from census data, the Johnsons likely arrived in Iowa in 1868, or, at the latest, 1869. (Their youngest child, born in Iowa, was not yet two when the 1870 census was taken in July, meaning they could have arrived in Iowa as early as August 1868. The rest of their children were born in Minnesota.)

The chief instigators of this Baptist re-migration to Crawford County may have been two Swedes known as the Star brothers, Carl and Peter. They had Americanized their surname – switching from Stjärnström to Star – and converted to the Baptist faith in September 1853 at Galesburg, Illinois. They later moved to a place in north-central Iowa known as Swede Bend, which was not a town but a cluster of settlements along a wide bend in the Des Moines River near present-day Stratford.

At Swede Bend, the Star brothers got to know Andrew Norelius, who was the first pastor of the Swedish Baptist church there from the summer of 1856 to early 1857, before he moved to Vasa. The Star brothers stayed put while Norelius became a traveling preacher, spreading the word in various towns in Iowa, Illinois and Minnesota, including Vasa.[21] After he was discharged from the Union army in September 1865 and returned to preaching in Cambridge, Minnesota, Andrew also served there as county treasurer, postmaster and a justice of the peace.

What prompted the next set of movements is unclear, but Norelius and the Hagglunds had reached a turning point, steering both families' history in the same new direction.

As recounted years later by Andrew's son George,[22] the Norelius family moved from Minnesota back to Swede Bend in May 1868 with three other families, traveling by covered wagon. In George's recollection, a short time later Andrew received a letter from a friend telling him about attractive land available farther west, along Otter Creek in Crawford County. George said his father was "so impressed with the letter that he made plans immediately to leave for this new community."

The letter writer was Carl Star, Andrew's old friend from their days together in Swede Bend in the 1850s. Star had moved from Swede Bend to the Otter Creek area in 1867.

In late June 1868, Andrew set out to join Star on Otter Creek, leaving his family temporarily in Swede Bend, according to his son's account. It was during this visit that Andrew decided Star had been right about this promising, unsettled prairie; he bought an 80-acre parcel near Otter Creek at what later became the village of Kiron, a few miles north of where the Hagglunds settled that same summer.

A nearly identical timeline was offered by O.M. Nelson in his book, *Swedish Settlements in Iowa*. He wrote that Andrew arrived in the Kiron area in June 1868. The timing is significant because it coincides with the Hagglunds' move.

It seems likely that John and Anna hitched their wagons, figuratively speaking, if not literally, to one of several groups of Swedes who trekked the approximately 250-300 miles from southeastern Minnesota to Crawford County, by way of Swede Bend, in the summer of 1868. This group migration, incidentally, was the approach recommended by the railroad companies eager to draw settlers farther west. One suggested that "a few families of tried and true friends" move together. "Then, if occasion requires, they can be of mutual assistance to each other, their wives and children are society for each other, and there is very little danger of suffering from either loneliness or homesickness."

Whatever the exact sequence, it's clear the Hagglunds were part of a westward migration of devout Baptists who would help create a Swedish colony on a new frontier.

II

The Iowa Years

7

On Otter Creek

The Hagglunds settled on 40 acres of virgin soil barely a stone's throw from Otter Creek, a broad-shouldered stream that cuts a path along western Iowa's slope toward the Missouri River. Their foothold was modest – a speck on a vast grassland that unfolded in gentle waves, like a rolling sea in shades of green and gold.

"As fertile and desirable as any in America," boasted a pitchman for the railroad that sold the Hagglunds their patch of prairie.[23]

To John and Anna and their four children it couldn't have looked much like home, this remote stretch of empty space on the narrow edge of civilization, more than 4,000 miles from Sweden. But they made it home, nonetheless, for a dozen years of hard farming and hard times.

They persevered, but it got no easier as the years passed.

In 1880, having added three children and sadly lost another, John and Anna would leave Iowa and move 120 miles west across the Missouri River into Nebraska. There they would claim a homestead four times the size of their original Iowa farm and make another try at starting over. Before the turn of the century, however, personal tragedy would strike yet again, setting off a string of events that eventually brought the family to the shores of Washington state's Puget Sound.

Once John and Anna left the Midwest they never returned, and for more than a century the details of their story – the struggles in Sweden, the journey to Minnesota, the hardships in Iowa and Nebraska, and the pathway to the Pacific slope – lay largely unexplored.

In a generational twist, my daughter, Elizabeth Ann Burns, who grew up in Virginia and had never set foot in Iowa or known of the ancestral connection, moved there for a job in 2014 and got married there in 2015, completing a circle that started with the Hagglunds' arrival nearly a century and a half earlier.

* * *

A Pioneering Time

In the summer of 1867, as the Hagglunds began their journey from Sweden, several newly transplanted Swedish families — mostly Baptists — arrived in Iowa's Otter Creek area from Swede Bend, 80 miles to the east. In search of unclaimed land on which to start a new Swedish community, some of them initially had traveled by horse and wagon all the way to the Missouri "bottoms," or floodplain, along the river that forms most of Iowa's western border. Disappointed by the lay of the land, they turned back.

On the return trip, by one account, they stopped at the Crawford County outpost of Denison, where they met an agent of the Providence Western Land Company. He persuaded them to check out an unsettled area several miles north along Otter Creek. The newcomers liked what they saw and bought land for $3 an acre. A year later they were joined by more Swedes, including the Hagglunds, who had pulled up stakes in Minnesota.

Together they began building new lives.

It was a pioneering time, a period that changed the face and future of the United States. The Civil War was over – the fighting, at least. The economy was growing. Industrialization was advancing quickly, powered in part by European immigrant labor in factories and mines. Railroads and telegraph lines were stretching westward, enabling and energizing migration and transforming a nation.

The federal government was in a hurry to settle its newly pacified western lands – many of them "acquired" from Indian tribes. The Homestead Act of 1862 was widely advertised as a chance for the adventurous and the ambitious to claim free land. Railroad companies and land agents assured settlers they had little to fear from native tribes; the Indians had been relocated west of Iowa in the 1850s.

The stage was set not just for internal migration but also for a rush of non-English speaking European arrivals. The emergence of steamship travel in the 1860s made Atlantic crossings faster, more affordable and less arduous, and immigrants were generally welcomed on the Western frontier. Swedes were warmly embraced.

In his assessment of what made Scandinavians good neighbors, the Rev. William M. Haigh of Illinois wrote in 1897 that they were industrious, thrifty, "trained to simple habits," and not afraid of work.[24]

Swedes were "much sought after here," one prominent Iowa land agent[25] wrote in 1867, and as a local account put it later, "Swedish families came in successive waves from Minnesota to congregate in Otter Creek and Stockholm townships until the region was almost entirely Swedish."

A local historian, William H. Hart, wrote admiringly of the Swedes and their choice of settlements in his 1914 account of the history of Sac County, the next county north of Crawford and home to many Swedish immigrants who initially settled near Otter Creek.

"No people from the continent of Europe are quicker to learn the language and adopt American customs than the Swedish people," Hart wrote. He lovingly described the Iowa prairie as "a garden of sunshine and delights" – a farmer's nirvana, a newcomer's dream.

To many Swedes, America was a beacon of hope during a dim period in their homeland, where no amount of thriftiness or hard work would deliver prosperity. Coming mostly from rural areas, many were drawn to the American frontier, rather than to cities, by the dream of farm ownership. John A. Erickson was one such pioneer. He came to the Otter Creek area one year before the Hagglunds. Back home in southern Sweden he had been "convinced he could never realize his ambition, which was to become the owner of landed property in the land of his birth," Frederick W. Meyers wrote in 1911 in a comprehensive history of Crawford County.

The westward advance to Iowa and beyond by American-born settlers and immigrants alike was more than a trend. To many it reflected the "manifest destiny" of white Americans to claim for themselves the whole of the North American continent. It was an imperialistic destiny based on belief in white American superiority, which "Providence has given us for the development of the great experiment of liberty," New York newspaper editor John O'Sullivan famously proclaimed in 1845.

It is unlikely the Hagglunds felt this nationalistic fervor. The destiny they sought was highly personal, manifested by the risks they were willing to take to cross the Atlantic and begin anew. They simply wanted a better future for their children.

Iowa was where it would begin.

* * *

Riches of Soil

Iowa is uniquely situated on the American landscape — not far from the geographic center, framed by two of the great rivers that drain the continent: the Mississippi on the east and the Missouri on the west. Historian Dorothy Schwieder has called Iowa "the Middle Land." I think of it as a Mesopotamia – the Greek word for a land between two rivers, like the ancient and fertile region between the Euphrates and Tigris that roughly corresponds to modern Iraq. Iowa, to its everlasting advantage, is blessed with riches of soil, not oil.

Iowa's pattern of settlement began mostly along the Mississippi before shifting westward and drifting as far as the upper Des Moines River toward the center of the state. These early settlers initially avoided the open prairie farther west, thinking that because this area was largely treeless the soil would be ill-suited for growing crops. This pattern began to change when the Civil War ended in 1865 and "railroad fever" gripped the nation; settlers pushed farther west, and the possibilities seemed endless.

West-central Iowa truly was a frontier when John and Anna arrived on Otter Creek in the summer of 1868. Around them lay vast stretches of wilderness devoid of humanity. Dwellings here and there among softly rounded hills were so crude they often had no windows, which one traveler said made little difference since "I could usually discern through cracks in the walls or roof if it was night or daybreak."[26]

Denison, about a dozen miles south of the Hagglunds' place, was the nearest organized town.

The railroad had not quite reached the Otter Creek area. There was no electricity, no plumbing, no post office, no telegraph service, no churches, and few people. There were no roads in the usual sense of the word. People traveled dirt paths by foot or on ox-drawn farm wagons, as the Hagglunds had back home in Sweden.

There were few named towns in this part of Crawford County. Settlements were known by natural landmarks. There was Mason's Grove and Burnt Wood, as well as Three Bee Tree Grove and Half-Mile Grove. These referred to narrow stands of timber – black walnut, bur oak, hickory, linden, elm, hackberry and others – hugging the Boyer River (pronounced BOO'-yer) and its tributaries, including creeks called Buffalo, Paradise and Otter. Trees attracted settlers because they offered ready fuel for homes and logs to erect houses, barns and fences. (Some trees also attracted honey bees, whose stores of sweetness were in great demand, which explains why a grove of bee trees was considered a major landmark.)

Mostly, the Swedes faced open prairie crowned by a flowing mane of grasses. These thick-rooted natural grasslands were the dominant land feature in Iowa in the mid-1800s, covering about three-quarters of the surface of the state before disappearing as plowshares exposed the virgin soil and crop farming took root.

I was struck by a description of the native prairies attributed to Basil Hall, a British naval officer who traveled the region in 1828. He is said to have observed, "The charm of a prairie consists in its extension – its green, flowery carpet, its undulating surface, and the skirt of forest whereby it is surrounded." Hall admired the American term, "Looking-Glass Prairie;" the prairie's color and character so reminded him of the sea, he said, that "I almost forgot where I was."[27]

Where a visitor like Hall saw charm, the settlers saw challenges. The prairie could be lonely and forbidding. It was beautiful in its own way, but it could be a source of punishing blows from Mother Nature, the likes of which the Hagglunds had never seen.

A local historian painted an almost poetic word picture of the frightful power of a prairie fire.

"It was a common, almost yearly, sight when the vast, limitless sea of amber-tinted grass was burning continuously for 20 miles, fanned and pressed speedily forward by a high wind," William H. Hart wrote in his history of Sac County, whose southwestern corner abuts northeastern Crawford County.

"It appears like a vast army mowing down solid columns of an enemy."

A near neighbor of the Hagglunds, Carl N. Waldemar, recalled many years later that his father would set backfires to protect their home from an approaching prairie fire.

"When the fire came with a hard wind it looked like a lake of fire," he wrote.[28] "It jumped over the tops of the tall grass in a hurry."

An 1876 travel guide described these fires as "fearfully exciting" – "the most awful yet grandest scene of prairie life" and a "rewarding" feature of cross-country train travel. Though published to promote the new transcontinental rails, this guidebook noted that prairie fires were sometimes started by sparks from locomotives.[29]

* * *

Denison — the town, the legend

Crawford County was a backwater in the mid-1850s when an enterprising preacher-turned-businessman, New York native Jesse W. Denison, hit upon an idea for striking it rich in what some called the New West. In the execution of his plan he incidentally jump-started the Swedish settlement along Otter Creek.

Denison acquired thousands of acres of government land by buying up property warrants held by war veterans, including men who fought in the Revolutionary War. Known as bounty-land warrants, this entitlement was offered by the federal government as both an incentive and a reward for military service.

Specifics varied by state, but under Iowa law, a qualifying veteran could use his warrant to claim up to 160 acres of unoccupied public land. Most of these veterans lived in Northeastern states and preferred to sell their warrants rather than use them to establish an Iowa residence. The genius of Denison's plan was his bundling of these warrants and using them to acquire one large, mostly contiguous area. This gave him considerable sway among local officials and businessmen.

Denison and his investment partners bought bounty-land warrants by the dozens from veterans willing to sell them for pennies on the dollar. Denison personally hauled these documents to the General Land Office branch in Council Bluffs, Iowa, and filed claims for thousands of acres in targeted parts of Crawford County, including the area that would become the town that bears his name.[30]

Incidentally, the most famous bounty-land claimant in Crawford County was the man who would become the 16th president of the United States, Abraham Lincoln. As a veteran of a 1832 skirmish with Sac Indians that came to be called the Black Hawk war, he used his warrant to claim a 120-acre parcel in 1860 in Goodrich township, about six miles northwest of what would become the town of Denison and a few miles southwest of where the Hagglunds later settled. Lincoln used a surrogate to file his claim and pay his real estate taxes; he never lived on his parcel.[31]

Denison sensed a chance for quick profit – "making a handsome thing," as he once put it –but he also played the long game. He launched his project in 1855; he and partners in Rhode Island formed the Providence Western Land Company to raise capital for the purchase of about 20,000 acres of bounty land in Crawford County. He calculated, correctly, that a railroad connection to Council Bluffs would soon be constructed through this area, creating a corridor for new settlements and ensuring the success of his investment.

In early 1956 Denison wrote to his land company partners: "You will never make money faster than by buying up land warrants at less than $1 an acre, as you now can." Over the next several years they paid the old soldiers – and in some cases, the widows of war dead – as little as 60 cents an acre, then sold the land for many times that price. For example, in 1859 Denison used the bounty warrant he purchased from the widow of Private Joshua Young, killed in the War of 1812 as a member of the Maine Militia, to claim 120 acres, including a parcel a couple of miles northwest of what would later be the Hagglund farm.

An 1868 advertisement by Denison's land company painted an alluring – and entirely accurate – picture of fertile prairie in all directions.

"The soil is a dark loam, with a due mixture of sand and clay, being adapted to the raising of stock or grain," it proclaimed.

As evidence of his knack for self promotion, the town that Denison established at the center of his empire, at a fork in the Boyer River, was named after him. At his energetic urging, it became the county seat but never achieved the greatness he envisioned. To his credit, he remained a town leader; he established a Baptist church whose parsonage many years later was the venue for the wedding of a granddaughter of the Hagglunds.

Denison became a local legend. In an 1875 report, the *Chicago Inter-Ocean* newspaper said the founder of the little Iowa town was "a Moses in those days."[32]

Jesse Denison is remembered in Crawford County as a benevolent visionary, but he was not universally admired in his day. In a letter to the local newspaper in April 1870, the school board president called him a "shyster," claiming he had fleeced buyers of what he misrepresented as "tip top lands."

It would not be a stretch to say Denison's shrewd tactics and salesmanship sowed the seeds for Crawford County's first Swedish community, which grew out of the prairie a dozen miles miles north of Denison. The small party of Swedes who had explored, then turned away from, the Missouri River flats in the summer of 1867 were said to have followed Jesse Denison's personal steer toward Otter Creek. They initially voted to name their settlement after the stream, but it came to be called Kiron for reasons still in debate.

In an August 1868 letter to his partners in the Providence Western Land Company, Denison wrote that he had sold land along Otter Creek to more than 20 Swedes "who have just arrived." He mentioned no names. Although the Hagglunds were among the newly arrived, they were not among these 20-plus buyers; John and Anna bought their land a few months later from a railroad.

Denison foresaw a ripple effect from dealing with these immigrants.

"Selling to those Swedes will have a good tendency, as it will open the door for others who otherwise would not have thought of Crawford County," he wrote.

He was right. The Otter Creek/Kiron area was known for many years as reliably Swedish — so much so that as late as 1903 the town had a Swedish-language newspaper, the *Kiron Svenskan*, to serve what remained of the non-English speaking immigrants.[33]

Non-Swedes in the area commonly referred to it simply as "the Swede settlement."

"It is a region of well-kept homes and highly cultivated fields and bespeaks on every hand the careful methods, the prudence and the unremitting toil of the old world," Meyers wrote in his account of Crawford County's early years. "One can tell that he is in the Swedish settlement by the distinctive look of the homes and of the farms."

That distinctive appearance – alas, any visible reminder of Kiron's Swedish origins – was gone by the early 21st century. Kiron took on the look of a town struggling for survival. During a 2018 visit I learned the only gas station in town had just closed, putting another damper on hope. Old-timers noted the steady loss of familiar Swedish surnames as younger generations left for jobs in Des Moines and beyond.

Before it became Kiron, some called the settlement "Swedeboy," but the name didn't stick. Perhaps it sounded as demeaning to the Swedes then as it does to me today. An 1868 guidebook mentioned Swedeboy, "four miles above Deloit," as one of several promising new settlements featuring "a steady and industrious class of citizens who are already arranging for a meeting and a school-house."

Among them were the Hagglunds.

8

The Baptists

Bonds between the Otter Creek Swedes were forged by more than hardship and hard work. They also had religion to draw them closer – except when it drove them apart.

The Baptists among them, including John and Anna Hagglund, wasted no time organizing themselves.

They gathered in the makeshift home of Carl P. Frodig on August 16, 1868, declared their faith in God and formed a congregation. Frodig, incidentally, was more than a meeting host. He preached, performed baptisms, officiated at marriages, acted as an unofficial doctor, built coffins, delivered funeral sermons and buried the dead.

Forming a congregation was a matter of some urgency. As the Rev. S. Bruce Fleming wrote in a 75th anniversary account, these newly arrived Swedes were accustomed to services on Sundays. "The immigrants found themselves in a community without a church, without a preacher. To these who had fled from religious regimentation this presented a vital problem," he wrote in his 1943 account.

The settlement's Swedish Baptist Church was the first in Crawford County and is still active today as the First Baptist Church of Kiron, minus an explicit Swedish affiliation. To their credit, the church members have preserved their history by retaining a substantial, though far from complete, collection of original records.

Among church documents that Pastor Bruce Kaihoi permitted me to review in 2015 was a booklet whose Swedish title translates as "History of the First Swedish Baptist Assembly in Kiron, Iowa," covering the period from its founding to its 25th anniversary in 1893. Thirty-five years later, material from this document was incorporated into a broader English-language history of the church through 1928.

The 1893 report, entirely in Swedish, named the congregation's first members – dirt-poor immigrants whose "hearts were filled with gratitude and joy to God." These 17 Swedes who gathered on August 16 to organize their congregation included "J. Hägglund" and "Mrs. Hägglund." (They used the proper Swedish spelling.) All "gave testimony of their Christian faith and experience, adopted the Baptist Confession of Faith ..., and accordingly formed themselves into a Swedish Baptist Church."[34]

Rev. Fleming, the church's pastor from 1942 to 1944, wrote in his 75th anniversary account that this first gathering was a momentous event for the immigrant Swedes.

"These families had fled persecution and were now making their homes in Freedom," he wrote.

C. J. Johnson, one of the first settlers, recalled years later that his fellow Swedes had become fed up with the state church of Sweden and its intolerance of dissenters.

"After being persecuted for many years, many of the inhabitants who had heard of this country with religious liberty decided to leave their own land and set sail for the other side of the sea, and thus we find the reason for the large number of Baptists who first settled in Otter Creek valley," Johnson wrote in a 1915 remembrance.

The Kiron congregation, unlike a larger American Baptist assembly in Denison, was purely Swedish. Members met Sundays in neighbors' homes because they had no chapel. In 1869 they began holding services in a newly built school house known as the "Star school," named for Carl Star, a leading Baptist, one of the settlement's founders and later a justice of the peace, on whose property it was built. This likely was where the Hagglund children had their first formal schooling.

Church membership grew modestly. In the first two months after the founding in 1868, a total of 13 new members were added, and by year's end membership stood at 31. A year later it reached 52. When the Hagglunds left in 1880 the total stood at about 150.

This was a devout community. Louis J. Ahlstrom, who came to Kiron from Rockford, Illinois, in 1881 and served nearly five years as the church's pastor, later recalled leading revivals in which "the whole settlement would trek several miles to the Boyer river for baptismal service with (dozens of) candidates, singing, *'On Jordan's stormy banks I stand, and cast a wistful eye, unto that happy Canaan's land, where my possessions lie.'*" Ahlstrom's account of eighty years of Swedish Baptist history in Iowa was published in 1933.

Andrew Norelius, the preacher who had ministered to Baptists in Vasa, Minnesota in the 1860s and who moved to the Otter Creek area the same summer as the Hagglunds, took over as pastor in March 1870, with the congregation's membership at 81. Soon, trouble invaded. As recalled in Fleming's 75th anniversary account, "a few families moved in with the intention of disturbing the peace of the church. This they were somewhat successful in doing, for several members left the church and joined the trouble-making faction." It seems that more than "several" departed, although the tide swung back and forth. Membership stood at 87 when Norelius left the pulpit in December 1873, but dissension grew over the winter and by spring only 36 members were left.

Fleming referred to this as a period of "internal troubles" and "discouragements," and a 1918 history of the church described "contentions" that became so severe that the church was "nearly disorganized," which I take to mean nearly disbanded. I found no indication of where the Hagglunds stood on the issues that divided the congregation, but they apparently were among the core group that remained loyal.

The initial set of troubles apparently was overcome, as membership by 1876 had jumped to 160, marking what Fleming called "a most happy state-of-affairs."

That year, perhaps encouraged by the congregation's sudden revival, they decided to build a chapel in Stockholm township on two acres in the southwest corner of the northwest quarter of Section 17, about three miles northeast of the old Hagglund farm and about a mile south of the original Kiron settlement. The building was moved in 1899 when the town shifted a mile west to accommodate the railroad's arrival.

The Swedish cemetery is situated about a half mile west of the original church location.

More than a century later, the First Baptist Church of Kiron stood at 107 Clover Street. When I visited in 2015 and again two years later, a footlocker in the basement was filled with ledger books and other original records – some from the early years but most from the 20th century. I found among them a single-page gallery of photos of men and women described as the church's founding members. One is identified as John Hagglund. The collection contains an undated photo of the original wood-frame church with members standing outside among saplings apparently planted when the church was built.

The church records reveal snippets of life in the early years, including the care with which hard-earned pennies were tracked by church officers. For example, they meticulously accounted for donations used to build and maintain the first chapel.

In a hand-written note in Swedish above his signature, Carl Frodig, the first pastor, described the "subscription" – the plan for raising construction funds. His note is an account of a meeting held by church members on June 13, 1876. Members discussed their estimate of construction costs, although no figure is mentioned in the summary. (Carl Star, an original member, wrote in 1928 that the chapel was built for $1,800 and that a parsonage was added the following year for $277.)

At that June 1876 meeting, the parishioners decided each would donate $5 for every 40 acres of land owned (husband and wife together), and that the landless among them should pay $5. Women, if employed, would give $3. It was agreed that in no case should a church member be made poor by his contribution.

They also voted to allow members to contribute materials or labor in lieu of 50 percent of their cash contribution.[35]

A separate ledger of church funds, written with impeccable penmanship in Swedish, was titled "The Swedish Baptist Church Congregation in Kiron, Crawford County, Iowa, 1876." It indicated John Hagglund had contributed 16 days of painting; his labor was valued at $2.50 a day, which meant his payment in kind ("gåfva genom arbete" in Swedish) totaled $40. Among others on the list, jack-of-all-trades Frodig was credited with 15½ hours of work at $2.50 per day, or $38.75.

An 1876 ledger in Swedish Baptist Church archives in Kiron shows that in June, John Hagglund was credited with a $40 in-kind contribution for painting.

The Hagglunds apparently remained active in the church until they left for Nebraska. An entry in an 1879 ledger credits John with an in-kind contribution of $6.54 for four days of painting.

At about this time, the church encountered problems even more severe than the 1870-73 setback under Andrew Norelius. The renewed unrest apparently touched Norelius, as well, even though he no longer was the pastor. The Ahlstrom account says that in 1879, "doctrinal differences" arose between Norelius and the church, and he "withdrew." Another account, which I obtained from archival holdings of the Isanti County Historical Society in Minnesota, says the 1879 rift "led to his exclusion,"[36] meaning Norelius was expelled. Norelius died in Iowa in April 1927 and is buried in Kiron Cemetery.

The Ahlstrom account says the late 1870s turmoil stemmed from disagreement over incorporation of the church, a move meant to provide legal protections for church property. This may have upset those Swedes for whom the memory of religious authoritarianism in the homeland was still fresh. Church leaders decided to go ahead with incorporation, "and that brought on the storm," Ahlstrom wrote.

Church struggles persisted in various forms.

"As time moved on, there seemed to be no solution to the problem," the Fleming account said without explaining the problem, beyond citing a "misunderstanding" among members. A sizable segment of the congregation broke away to form their own Church of God, later called the Evangelical Free Church, and Baptist membership shrank to 36. By this time the Hagglunds had left Iowa.

9

Landowners at Last

I collected nothing close to a complete record of the Hagglunds' 12 years in Iowa, but by reviewing county land and tax records, state and federal census documents, church records, newspapers and local histories I got a fuller picture of this period than was possible for the writer of the Everett account in 1983.

The Everett account emphasizes the Hagglunds' devotion to the Baptist faith but says very little about their Iowa farm and makes no mention of Otter Creek. It says they traveled by wagon train from Minnesota to Crawford County, where John bought a small parcel of land in 1869 under the Pre-emption Act. That was an 1841 law allowing people to buy up to 160 acres of public land for as little as $1.25 an acre – pre-empting a public bidding process.

My research, however, revealed a different path to landownership for the Hagglunds. I also found that financial complications a decade later would more or less force John and Anna off their land, apparently hastening their decision to try their hand at homesteading in Nebraska.

On my first visit to Crawford County in May 2015 I reviewed county land records handwritten on heavy lined paper bound in large hard-cover ledgers. These bundles of local history stand on shelves in carefully organized vaults in the county courthouse, a stately marble building erected in 1904 on Denison's Broadway. On a return visit three years later, I searched tax records in similarly sturdy ledgers that showed no sign of having been disturbed in this century or last; dust had settled atop these books like a light coating of sand. Some stood untouched for decades after the pioneer chapter of Crawford County history had closed.

These land and tax records revealed the Hagglunds made two land purchases – one more successful than the other.

On November 16, 1868, shortly after they arrived in Crawford County, the Hagglunds signed a contract to buy 40 acres from the Cedar Rapids & Missouri River Rail Road Company. The parcel was the northwest quarter of the northwest quarter of Section 25. (A quarter of a section is 160 acres, and thus a quarter of a quarter is 40 acres.) This tract of land stands about two miles south of present-day Kiron. At the time, there was no Kiron nor any town at all nearby.

The railroad in 1860 had been granted more than 950,000 acres of public land to build lines connecting Cedar Rapids in east-central Iowa and Council Bluffs on the state's western border at the Missouri River – thus the railroad's name. Across the river from Council Bluffs is Omaha, Nebraska, which would become headquarters of the Union Pacific and the eastern terminus of its portion of the first transcontinental railroad, completed in May 1869.

The land grant to the Cedar Rapids & Missouri River came with attractive bonuses, as was common at the time. In addition to the land on which the tracks would be built, the railroad was given outright ownership of land that in some cases extended 15 miles from each side of the proposed line. The goal, to the perceived benefit of the state as well as the railroad, was to sell as much of this adjacent land as possible to settlers, thus creating and expanding communities whose farms and businesses would provide additional traffic for the railroad.

"The commencement of work on the road will give a strong impulse to business and [immigration], and the increase in population and wealth will be even more rapid than it has been in the past few years," the Cedar Rapids & Missouri River company's chief engineer, W.W. Walker, wrote in a report to his boss in June 1860.[37]

Walker predicted that revenue from the company's sale of acreage along the rail line would cover the entire cost of building it, even if buyers paid as little as $4 an acre on average. This land, he wrote, was endowed with "unsurpassed fertility," echoing the company's public sales pitches.

Eleven years later Walker would sign off on the final paperwork for the Hagglunds' first land purchase.

I did not locate the Hagglunds' purchase contract, but it likely was what they called a "short time plan," one of three types of land deals offered by the rail company. The pricing and sale terms are explained in detail in an obscure booklet, "Iowa: The Home for Immigrants," published in 1870 by the state's newly established Board of Immigration to begin a campaign promoting the state to potential settlers.

The railroad offered a ten percent discount to buyers who paid full price in cash up front. A second option was the short time plan in which the buyer paid one-quarter of the full price in cash up front and the balance in annual payments over three years, with a six percent yearly interest charge payable in advance each year. This seems to have been the option chosen by the cash-poor Hagglunds.

The third option was called a "long time" plan. It required an upfront payment of two years' interest on the purchase price, at 10 percent per year, but nothing more for two years. In the third year the buyer paid one-quarter of the principal, with the remainder paid in installments over three additional years.

On November 18, 1871, three years after the contract was signed, the Iowa Rail Road Land Company signed over to the Hagglunds a warranty deed granting ownership of their 40-acre parcel.[38] (The seller's name had changed because in 1869 the Iowa Rail Road Land Company was formed to handle sales of the railroad's excess land.)

The warranty deed on file at the county courthouse says ownership of the 40 acres was transferred "in consideration of the sum of $220." That figure tracks closely with an example of terms published by the Iowa Rail Road Land Company in 1871 to illustrate how easy it could be to buy their land on a "short time" plan. In the example, in which a buyer contracted for 40 acres at $5 an acre, he would make four separate payments over three years starting with a cash payment up front of $50 plus $9 interest on the balance. A year later he would make a principal payment of $50 plus $6 interest, followed a year later by another $50 and $3 interest. At the end of the three years he would pay a final $50.

In that illustrative case, the total would be $218. Since the Hagglunds paid $220, the terms of their deal may have been almost the same as in the example.

Although the Hagglunds appear to have paid $5 an acre, its value for property tax purposes initially was $3 an acre. By 1871 the assessed value had risen to $5 an acre.

The deed the Hagglunds received in November 1871 says these were "the same premises contracted to be sold to John Hagglund by the Cedar Rapids & Missouri River Rail Road Company" on November 16, 1868 "in pursuance and fulfillment of which said contract, this conveyance is made and executed."

It must have been a proud moment for John and Anna, land owners finally, although it seems they had little money to spare for sod-busting and equipping the farm, not to mention digging a well, building fences and erecting a house and outbuildings. Still, this

40-acre parcel was practically an empire, albeit a primitive one, compared to any farm the Hagglunds could have aspired to own in Sweden. It was home, or at least the makings of home.

The Hagglunds' warranty deed was notarized on November 29, 1871 and filed with the county recorder on January 27, 1872. With impressive precision, a notation in the margin of Warranty Deed No. 132 says it was filed at 2 p.m. on that date. It was signed by the Iowa Rail Road Land Company's vice president, W. W. Walker, the former chief engineer of the Cedar Rapids & Missouri River railroad.

The 40 acres thus became the property of John Hagglund, "to have and to hold" by him and "his heirs and assigns forever." There were two small caveats.

First, the company reserved the right to declare a 100-foot-wide right of way for any future rail line it might choose to build on any portion of the Hagglunds' property. No line was ever built there, but other railroad influences came into play later.

Second, the company reserved the right to mine and remove "by such means as they might deem proper" all coal, minerals and oil from the land without being held liable for damage to the land. In the event mining operations were undertaken, the company would pay the Hagglunds $25 an acre for any land it used to extract the products.

No mine was dug.

It's hard to imagine that the Hagglunds, or any of the other newly arrived Swedes with limited knowledge of English, could have fully understood the terms of their purchase, given the legal lingo – "... said Grantor doth hereby covenant with the said Grantee that it is lawfully seized of said premises ..."

If there were a competent lawyer for hire in Denison, the county seat, the Hagglunds would have been hard pressed to afford his services. (In his "Guide to the Rocky Mountains," published the same year the Hagglunds arrived in Crawford County, T.G. Turner, a lawyer in Indiana, wrote that Denison had two attorneys and one doctor – "all highly ornamental but not extremely useful.")

And yet, it somehow worked out. The Hagglunds held and farmed those 40 acres for ten years while weathering many storms — financial, personal and natural.

By coincidence or design, the Hagglunds' nearest neighbor was a Swede from the parish in Jämtland where John grew up. He was known as Olof Wick (sometimes spelled Weik or Vik). His name in Sweden had been Olof Jonsson and he was raised on a lakeside farm compound known as Laxviken in Follinge parish. John Hagglund had spent most of his youth in Föllinge, about eight miles south of Laxviken.

Olof and John were the same age. Could they have been childhood friends? Olof's wife, Elisabeth Pehrsdotter, also was from Föllinge and was the same age as Anna. (Anna's mother also grew up in Föllinge.)

Olof and his wife and their four children emigrated in June 1870, three years after John and Anna. The Hagglund and Wick farms in the Otter Creek area were catty-corner from each other, connected at a road crossing where the southeast corner of Section 23 meets the northwest corner of Section 25. In 1881, the year after the Hagglunds moved to Nebraska, Olof and his family moved to Clark County, Washington, and in 1903 they moved to a Swedish immigrant settlement called Albin on the Wyoming-Nebraska border.[39]

The Hagglunds undoubtedly felt connections with many Swedes in the Otter Creek settlement, but none were as closely linked to Jämtland as Olof and Elisabeth Wick. By the time I started exploring the area in 2015, the old Wick place was long gone.

On a sultry May afternoon that would soon deliver its promised thunderstorm, I found the old Hagglund farm along a narrow dirt-and-gravel road that marks the northern boundary of Section 25.

Approaching the farm from the east, the road carried me over a gentle crest and then descended toward Otter Creek, whose deeply gouged banks suggested a history of flooding. I crossed the creek on a wood-plank bridge which later that year was replaced by a steel-girder span.

The Hagglund place appeared to have changed little over the years other than the disappearance of the original house and farm buildings. In their place was a grass field, a small grove of apple trees and a modest house built near the spot where the Hagglund place had stood. With a little imagination one could see family members working the fields, loading the corn crib, feeding the oxen and hauling buckets of well water to the house.

The rest of the former Hagglund homestead is still farmed – and it retains a connection to Otter Creek's earliest settlers. As of 2018, it was owned by the William Q. Norelius Trust. William's father, Everett A. Norelius, owned it before him. Everett was a son of George Norelius, who would figure in the Hagglund story early in the 20th century. Everett's grandfather was Andrew Norelius, the Baptist minister who had previously preached in Red Wing and Vasa, Minnesota. Everett was a graduate of Grinnell College and a prominent local lawyer starting in the 1930s; the Norelius Community Library in Denison is named for him.

In 2017, I met with a local man, Robert "Bobby" Wulf, who told me that in the mid-1980s, Everett Norelius sold to him the six-plus acre parcel on which the old Hagglund home stood. Wulf described it as a two-story wood-frame house, which he said burned down in the late 1980s shortly after he had thoroughly remodeled it. He said the fire consumed his records, including photos.

In my pursuit of a photo of the house, in 2018 I mentioned the fire to a Kiron insurance agent, John M. Larson. To my surprise, he said he had responded to the blaze as a volunteer firefighter.

He unhesitatingly recalled that it was a severely windy day; in his recollection the wind had knocked together electrical wires near where they entered the house, sparking a fire that burned it to the ground. He said he had been inside the house as a youth because he was friends with children of the Argotsinger family that lived there in the 1950s and 60s.

Dean Argotsinger was one of those children. I found him on his family's farm near Deloit in May 2018. He told me that his father, upon returning from World War II service in the Navy, had married a local woman and moved onto the Norelius property in a crop-sharing arrangement. Dean said he lived there from birth in 1952 to age 14 when his family moved to their current farm several miles to the south. Speaking with me inside his machine shed, Dean recalled the old Hagglund home as being two stories and square-shaped with a chimney protruding from the center of a steeply pitched roof. The house faced south, overlooking the farm fields. It had a partial basement, he recalled, that was lined with rough-cut timbers and contained a coal-burning stove, a coal bin and a root cellar.

Alas, I never did find a photo. The mental picture will have to do.

It probably took the Hagglunds some years to develop their land into a fully functioning farm. To do that they had to borrow money, as did most farm families.

Shortly after taking title to the property, John and Anna in July 1872 mortgaged the farm for $276.50, presumably to buy the equipment and other resources required to run it. The mortgage holder was a Denison man named W.A. McHenry, who partnered with his brother in several local businesses, including banking and insurance; they also were land agents for the Iowa Railroad Land Company, which means they might have arranged the land sale to the Hagglunds in 1868.

This mortgage was not the kind we think of in the 21st century, and not just because the dollar amount seems small. It was to be paid off in 17 months, with 10 percent interest, in just two payments – $138 due on April 1, 1873 and $138.50 seven months later. Considering how new they were to American farming, and the undeveloped state of their land, this debt had to have been a steep hill for the Hagglunds. The records make no suggestion that they were delinquent, but a hand-written note in the county's mortgage records says the loan was "paid off in full and discharged" on March 13, 1875, more than a year beyond the final payment deadline.

That same day – March 13, 1875 – paperwork for a new mortgage was filed with the county Recorder's Office.[40] This one was for a similar amount but came to a very different result. The new mortgage, for $280, was structured as nine separate promissory notes in amounts ranging from $5 to $50. The notes were to be paid off at varying intervals over five years, starting with a $20 payment due in March 1876.

Importantly, this mortgage's terms allowed for the possibility of a third party making the payments. (The Hagglunds were required to pay "or cause to be paid" the amounts due each year.) That may have been a standard provision rather than something the Hagglunds requested, but it would prove useful in 1878, a pivotal year for the Hagglunds as Crawford County landowners – and not in an entirely good way. This was the year they sold the farm with the bulk of their mortgage yet to be paid. It also was the year that a separate Hagglund land deal seems to have begun to crumble, pushing John and Anna to an unhappy turning point just two years before they decided to seek better fortune on the Nebraska side of the Missouri River.

10

Competing for Settlers

The Hagglunds' early years in Crawford County coincided with tumultuous change sweeping a country not yet 100 years old, driven by two powerful and rapidly accelerating forces: railroads and immigration.

Immigrants were fuel for America's economic engine, and the rural "western" states' thirst for more was fed by the railroad companies, which at the time of the Hagglunds' arrival were on the verge of completing the first transcontinental line. The railroads also were barreling toward financial disaster, which would shock the young nation's economy just as the Hagglunds were getting settled.

An industrializing, ambitious America was approaching what Mark Twain later dubbed the Gilded Age, a glittery period marked by unfettered capitalism, corrupt politicians and misplaced hopes — corporate America's formative years, in other words. Nowhere on the financial and social landscape was this more evident or more consequential than in the railroad business, which counted on the federal government to subsidize rail construction costs and on immigrants to lay track and to form new settlements in western states and territories.

The railroads overbuilt and over-promised in a period of cutthroat competition; they created false hope in many communities, but they also enabled immigrant families, including the Hagglunds, to pursue their American dream.

States competed for immigrants without concern for federal limitations because there were none; not until 1875 was regulation of immigration deemed a federal responsibility.

Swedes in America did their part to promote immigration. Some returned to Sweden for visits sponsored by railroad land agents or state immigration agencies.

Iowa's Board of Immigration, whose mission was to outmaneuver neighboring states like Minnesota in the competition for new settlers, tried to appeal to immigrants' yearning for farm ownership. In its 1870 report on settlement of government lands, the board said the United States had five and a half million land owners, of whom four million were farmers.

"In no other country in the world have so large a proportion of the citizens an absolute interest in the soil, and indeed, history furnishes no parallel," it said. In Iowa, it added, there was still room for "all who will only exercise ordinary industry."

The welcome mat was out, and the industrious came to Iowa in droves. From a population of 574 in 1865, the year the Civil War ended, Crawford Country by the time the Hagglunds appeared three years later had topped 1,600. By 1875 it had nearly quadrupled to 6,038 – of which one-fifth were immigrants – and there were 361 souls in the Otter Creek area, where it became possible to count residents when it officially became a "township" in 1872. The town of Kiron was established a year later in the neighboring township of Stockholm.

A township – sometimes called a congressional township – is not a town. It is a district drawn and marked by government land surveyors under an ingenious grid system dating to 1785. Known as the cadastral system, it was first proposed by Thomas Jefferson as the "rectangular survey system." A township typically is comprised of 36 one-square-mile parcels called "sections" of 640 acres each. A section often was sold in quarters of 160 acres each and further subdivided by halves (80 acres) and quarters (40 acres). A township sometimes contained multiple towns.[41]

Tracking townships in Crawford County can be confusing because boundaries changed during the Hagglunds' time. Their farm initially was within the borders of Milford township, but in 1875 the lines were redrawn to create additional townships, and the Hagglund land then fell within Otter Creek township.

By 1880 – the year the Hagglunds pulled up stakes and left Iowa – Crawford County's population had topped 12,400, including 676 in Otter Creek township.

Today's Crawford County, more than a century later, is not much bigger – about 17,000 people. It is still farm country, although the farms are mostly owned by corporations, not families. A sense of timelessness stretches across the furrowed fields, the gravel roads and the clumps of trees that hug creek beds and encircle farmhouses. It's not hard to imagine the screeching of wagon wheels and pounding of horse hooves from the time the Hagglunds worked this fertile earth.

* * *

"Dug-out" Days

I don't know how the Hagglunds envisioned their future when they arrived in the upper reaches of Crawford County, about 80 miles west of the Des Moines River and 50 miles east of the Missouri. Did they think this would be the final stop on their immigrant journey, and that western Iowa would be their permanent home? Or did they see it as a stepping stone to a future farther west?

Their first hope, most likely, was to own farmland and to be among fellow Swedes as they raised their children. Having made the move with like-minded Swedish Baptists from Minnesota and north-central Iowa, they could count on companionship, if little else.

Unfortunately, I have no letters or other correspondence that John or Anna may have exchanged with relatives in Sweden after arriving in the United States. I don't know whether doubt or regret ever crept into their new lives, which were tested in ways they are unlikely to have anticipated when they left Sweden. For example, they could not have expected that their first home on the Iowa prairie would be a dirt-lined cave.

Fittingly, the Hagglunds settled next door to Stockholm township, although the name arrived after them. The name choice reflects the immigrant flavor of this part of Crawford County; there were families of Johnsons, Carlsons and Larsons, as well as Winquists, Nelsons, Andersons and Ericksons. These families were part of what amounted to a Swedish colony extending north from the Otter Creek and Stockholm townships into the lower reaches of two adjoining counties – Ida and Sac. Short distances to the south, east and west were settlements of Irish and Germans. The Germans were Crawford County's dominant ethnic group. They established their own colony just west of Kiron and called it Schleswig for the Schleswig-Holstein area of Germany from which many of them had come.

The Swedes' farms were mostly within a few miles of Otter Creek, which flows in a southerly direction just east of the original Hagglund property and spills into the Boyer River about five miles downstream at Deloit, a town that grew up after Mormons settled a nearby area called Mason's Grove in the early 1850s. The Boyer, which follows a southwesterly path to the Missouri, was shallow and hardly navigable. This meant Kiron-area farmers had no easy means of getting their grain or livestock to market – not that they had much to sell in their first years.

Denison had the closest rail station until 1877 when the Maple River Railroad Company built a line that arced north of Kiron, from Carroll County on the east to Monona County on the west, passing through the town of Odebolt about 10 miles north of Kiron. Having a rail station at Odebolt "made a new life in the farming community around Kiron," early settler C. J. Johnson wrote in his 1915 remembrance, because it provided a more manageable way to get farm products to market.[42]

Johnson said the Swedes' first harvest was in 1869, which happened to be a particularly good year throughout Crawford County. "Farmers are feeling good – in fact, everyone – over the present bright prospects," after a local harvest that was expected to "astonish the state," the *Denison Review* newspaper reported in July 1869. The Swedes grew mostly wheat, having been advised by American farmers to the south that corn was a poor prospect.

Johnson recalled that David Ludwig Johnson, the Swede who likely had been a Vasa, Minnesota, neighbor of the Hagglunds, used what was called a "dropper" to cut his and his neighbors' grain — an advancement from the hand-held scythe.

"This was a wonderful machine to see as there had never been a harvesting machine in the settlement before," C. J. Johnson wrote. He did not mention how they got their harvested grain to market, but I presume that farm wagons hauled it over rutted trails to Denison until new rail lines shortened the distances.

The first train tracks to enter Crawford County were built by the Cedar Rapids & Missouri River Rail Road Company, led by John I. Blair, a New Jersey businessman described by one writer as a "human dynamo let loose in railway-mad Iowa."[43] Having started at Cedar Rapids in eastern Iowa, the line reached Denison in 1866. This fulfilled Jesse Denison's hopes and was ballyhooed as the leading edge of a transportation revolution that would soon benefit all in west-central Iowa.

"The fecund prairie awaits the plow, from whose furrows shall spring plenty," said a booklet published in 1868 to trumpet the expected arrival of more rail connections. "The pleasant groves invite settlers to joyous homes, and altogether give promise of the coveted advantages of a highly civilized condition."

For the present, however, conditions for the dirt-poor Swedes — including the Hagglunds — were notably primitive. They made do with "dugout" homes, sometimes called "soddies." These were dark, sometimes damp one-room living spaces, often 12 feet wide and 14 feet long, half or more dug by hand into a hillside. The front part was built up with strips of sod, with a door in the middle. A sheet-iron pipe attached to the cook stove was pushed up through the earthen "roof."

"In 1868 and 1869 the incoming settlers made the dirt fly for C. Carlson, J. Hendrickson, N.P. Erickson, J. Hagglund," and several other Swedish immigrants, C.J. Johnson recalled in his account of Kiron's early years. Indeed, the 1870 census shows Carl Carlson and Nils P. Erickson were close neighbors of the Hagglunds.

Johnson remembered John Hagglund as well as the "dugout" days.

"During the summer of 1869 there were a number of dugout houses built which were owned and occupied by the following families as near as the writer can remember," Johnson is quoted as recalling in a later account about Swedish Baptists in Iowa, "namely: Charles Carlson, J. Hendrickson, Carl Peter Frodig, Nils Peter Erickson, John A. Hagglund," and 13 others he recalled by name.

"It was certainly not very inviting to come from Sweden to this barren country and move into a small dugout house with only one room," Johnson wrote, "but it does not harm one to pass through different experiences in his life and learn something new from self-denial."

One of those "different experiences" was recalled years later by Peter Star, one of the settlement's original pioneers and brother of Carl Star. Peter said he was lying down in his dugout to rest after dinner when he noticed a silent, uninvited visitor.

"The head of a rattlesnake was slowly protruding from between the sods and then drew back," he said. "I then took a leather tong from my tool shelf above my head, held it right under the hole in the wall where the snake had disappeared. When he again stuck his head out far enough, I pinched him tightly and pulled him out and held him until he was dead. He had many rattles on his tail."[44]

C.J. Johnson got the itch to check out the Otter Creek area when he heard Andrew Norelius describe its farming possibilities. "To plow up the land you just had to hitch the team to the plow and go right along," he recalled Norelius telling him. In fact, breaking the prairie sod was not easy work. It required several yokes of oxen and an especially heavy plow. Many new arrivals hired sod-breaking help.

Johnson knew the area as well as anyone. He was "enumerator" for Stockholm township in the 1880 federal census, meaning he counted all the noses, door to door. He considered himself a historian.

"I intend to show to the younger generation what hard times their forefathers have had to open up a country which now looks almost like a paradise compared with that of forty-eight years ago, [1867] when the Otter Creek valley, as well as Missouri valley, was nothing but a wilderness where the grass in the summers grew up as high as a man's head and deer were roaming over the prairie and rattlesnakes had their habitations as well as other wild animals," he wrote.

Indeed, the wildlife was diverse, even exotic: elk, mink, badger, fox, grey wolf, wild turkey, Canada geese, pelicans, sandhill cranes, prairie chickens, beaver, muskrat and otter.

11

A Growing Brood

Perhaps as a sign of confidence in their future, John and Anna began expanding the family shortly after arriving in Iowa. The four who came with them from Minnesota ranged in age from three to 11, Andrew being the oldest and Oliver the youngest. The first Iowa addition was Martha, born three days before Christmas, on December 22, 1868. If I'm correct in my estimate that the family made the journey from Vasa that summer, then Anna would have traveled while pregnant.

Next came Oscar, born April 13, 1870.

When Anna greeted her final arrival, John J., on September 1, 1873, she was 43 years old.

Each of the three was born at home on Otter Creek.

The state did not require the recording of births until 1880, and many went unrecorded until the 1920s, according to the Iowa State Historical Society. Years later the state began retroactively documenting births from the earlier era in what it called a "delayed birth certificate" program.

Martha's birth was not recorded, even retroactively, as far I can tell, but the births of her two younger brothers are included in the delayed birth certificate records. In both cases, Andrew (born in Sweden) submitted a witness statement — a sworn, written affidavit. In September 1942, at the age of 85, he confirmed the date of birth for Oscar Frans Hagglund.

"I am thirteen years older than my brother and was at home at the time of his birth," Andrew wrote.

In January 1943, he submitted a similar sworn statement for John J. Hagglund.

"I am the older brother and I was at the house when the child was born," he wrote.

Shortly after their arrival in Iowa, probably before they could speak much English, the Hagglunds appeared in their first federal government census. It spelled their name "Hegland," probably reflecting the family's pronunciation of the first vowel in their adopted surname, which is not an "a" but rather an "ä," a Swedish vowel not used in English. To the American ear it sounds like a soft "e." Thus "Heg-land."

The 1870 census, taken in July, lists eight family members, as John was not yet born. Anna was 40 years old and "keeping house." Forty-two-year-old John was described simply as "farmer." Two of the children were "at school" – Andrew, age 13, and 11-year-old Lewis. The four others were "at home." Christine was seven, Oliver was two days short of his fifth birthday, Martha was going on two, and Oscar was three months. Interestingly, Christine is listed as "Katie" – another attempt at Americanization, perhaps by the census-taker. It did not stick.

I cannot be sure how much schooling the Hagglund children received.

The census did not begin recording information about education levels until 1940. In that year, Andrew indicated he did not go beyond the 5th grade, although I learned through additional research that as an adult, he took high school-level courses by mail. Oscar and John J. got no further than 5th grade, according to the census, whereas Martha indicated she quit after the 8th grade.

The 1870 census counted the Hagglunds as residents of Milford township, which at the time encompassed the lower portions of what became the separate townships of Otter Creek and Stockholm. The nearest post office was called Boyer River, situated near Deloit, about five miles south of the Hagglund farm. Until the Kiron post office was established in 1872, mail was delivered to the Swedish colony once a week by horseback.

The Hagglund farm on the northwest 40 was modest even by local standards. In 1870, only two years after their arrival from Minnesota, the family had 20 of their 40 acres in cultivation, mostly growing wheat. This suggests to me that John had hired what were called "breaking brigades" — teams with several yoke of oxen pulling broad plows capable of breaking the prairie's leathery sod into long strips. Alternatively, the Hagglunds and other Otter Creek farm families may have shared their own sod-busting labor, going from farm to farm breaking virgin prairie. A farmer plowing alone could ordinarily break only a few acres a year.

The Hagglunds' crop that year yielded 700 bushels of spring wheat, 100 bushels of Indian corn and five bushels of Irish potatoes. They also produced 15 pounds of butter that year, probably for their own use.

The estimated total value of what the census called "all farm production, including betterments and additions to stock," on the Hagglund farm for the 12 months ended June 1, 1870 was $177. That was the lowest total among the 63 farms in Milford township. Most recorded at least twice the Hagglund total; many were in the $2,000 range, although the most prosperous farms had much more acreage than the Hagglunds.

Raising grain in Crawford County, be it wheat or corn, was not a short path to riches. In 1874 a local farmer calculated that grains yielded a county-wide average of $12.75 per acre, only $1.25 more per acre than the combined costs of seed, planting, harvesting, threshing, moving to market and interest on the land. "Rather an uphill business," he concluded.

The value of the Hagglunds' farm equipment – estimated in the census at $30 – suggests how poor they were, although John probably bought more once he got the first mortgage in 1872. According to an 1870 Iowa Board of Immigration publication, the "necessary outfit" for working a 40-acre farm included a plow and other implements costing between $50 and $90, plus a team of oxen or horses and a wagon and yoke at a total cost of between $250 and $450.

The Hagglunds in 1870 had no oxen, mules, sheep or hogs. Their livestock was valued at $200 – one horse, two milk cows and three "other cattle."

The estimated cash value of their farm was $400. That is nearly twice what they paid for the land and twice the land's assessed value, but it is less than every other farm in the township, most of which were larger in size. Many were valued at over $3,000.[45]

* * *

Panic and Plague

This was the start of a difficult stretch for the Hagglunds – as farmers and as a family. They endured personal tragedy, a national economic calamity, a local diphtheria epidemic, and angry outbursts by Mother Nature, including a deadly tornado.

The Everett account says the Hagglunds farmed their acreage "not too successfully."

They did not struggle alone. In his 1911 history of Crawford County, Frederick W. Meyer wrote that the decade of the 1870s was tough for most farmers. That was an understatement. Corn prices were disappointingly low. The *Sac Sun* newspaper, in adjacent Sac County, reported on December 6, 1872 that some families were burning corn to heat their homes because it was cheaper than wood. "They can't sell corn for even 15 cents (a bushel) in cash now, and that is less than it costs to raise it," it said.

On a national level, the American financial system nearly came unglued in what became known as the Panic of 1873. The disaster was rooted in land speculation and failed railroad investments. A New York bank known as Jay Cooke & Co., which earned riches by marketing government bonds that financed the Civil War effort, later invested in railroads, chiefly the Northern Pacific that would link Duluth and Seattle. When that project faltered, Jay Cooke & Co. went belly up in September 1873, triggering a run on banks. The panic led to more bank failures. The stock market crashed, and on the 20th of September the New York Stock Exchange closed — the first panic-driven closure in its history.

"The blackest day in the financial history of Wall Street was passed today," a *Chicago Times* reporter wrote under the headline, "Pandemonium in New York."[46]

Credit markets froze. Farm prices tumbled, factories closed, and unemployment soared. The pain spread widely; many former Civil War soldiers lost jobs and became transients, giving rise to "tramp" and "bum" as common American terms for the homeless and wandering poor.

National recovery did not begin until 1878.

Not only were farm market conditions bad during the 1870s but Crawford County suffered other calamities – severe winters, devastating hailstorms, disastrous prairie fires and damaging winds. Also, "grasshopper plagues" descended on Crawford County and wide stretches of the Great Plains each year from 1873 to 1876, destroying cropland.

"The air is thick with them as they come down like showers of snow," one settler said of the insect invasion.

In his 1914 book, *History and Stories of Nebraska*, historian Addison Erwin Sheldon wrote that damage in his state peaked with "the great grasshopper raid" of July 1874. "All the corn was eaten in a single day," he wrote. "Where green fields stood at sunrise nothing remained at night but stumps of stalks swarming with hungry hoppers struggling for the last bite."

Word of the spectacle spread. One evening that July, an immigrant wagon passed through Denison bearing a sign whose message was quoted two days later on the front page of the local newspaper: "D—N THE GRASSHOPPERS!" Fascination with these destructive buggers was reflected in the newspaper coverage, which was constant. The Denison Review quoted an anonymous "northwestern Iowa doctor" as saying of the grasshoppers, "They are a very hardy insect. It takes quite a freeze to kill them. Immerse one in water for three hours and he will come to have a better masticative and digestive faculty than ever."

The weather posed challenges unlike any the Hagglunds had seen in central Sweden. According to Carl Waldemar's account of life along Otter Creek, a tornado struck on Easter Sunday, 1878. From his description of the twister's easterly path it likely touched down near the Hagglunds' place in Section 25 and again a mile or two to the east. One schoolhouse and six farm dwellings – some almost within a stone's throw of the Hagglund place – were struck, including that of Olof Larson. Waldemar mentioned that the house of another near neighbor, John Larson, "was whirled up in the air" with several people inside, including John Larson and his wife, other family members, and a neighbor, Anna Wick, a daughter of Olof and Elizabeth Wick, the Swedes who were near neighbors of the Hagglunds.

"They made the first air trip in this vicinity," Waldemar wrote.

Some were injured.

John Larson was killed.

* * *

Enchantments in "Fairy-land"

Life for Iowa's pioneers was hard in ways barely imaginable today. They made do with little.

"As a rule, their earthly possessions consisted merely of strong arms, good health, ambition to succeed and faith in God," C.J. Johnson wrote in his remembrance.

The conveniences and opportunities that we enjoy – indeed, take for granted – in the 21st century had not even been imagined by the Hagglunds in the 1870s. It's often said those were simpler times, but I'm not sure they were. Slower, yes. But not always simpler. The electric age had not reached the Hagglunds; they did without the simplicity of lighting their home with the flip of a switch, heating a room with the turn of a dial, filling a wash basin with the turn of a spigot, expelling their household waste with the flush of a toilet, or communicating long distances with the immediacy of a phone call or email. The automobile had not yet arrived; the Hagglunds' feet (and ox-drawn wagons) were their wheels. Train travel was common, but air travel was a distant dream.

Life in those days could be inconvenient in more profound ways. Disease killed with an impunity we would not recognize today.

Simply staying alive was not simple.

Communicable diseases like scarlet fever were a frightful enemy of the newcomers.

The threat of disease, and the fear it inspired in the years before true medical professionals arrived on the prairie, gave rise to innumerable "miracle cures" for ailments of every description. The newspapers were filled with ads for cheap, surefire remedies. "Radway's Ready Relief" was pitched in newspapers in 1874 – "cures the worst pains in from one to twenty minutes." A bottle sold for 50 cents, with no mention of ingredients. A Denison ad for the Philadelphia-based Thorpean Institute promised, "The worst cases of cancer cured in a short time."

While swindlers lurked, these prairie pioneers survived by their wits.

Even by 1874, six years after the Hagglunds had arrived, the old timers were marveling at their progress.

"There is but a small number of our population who know of the sufferings, deprivations and hardships of the early settlers of the Boyer Valley," an old timer wrote in the Denison Review newspaper on February 11, 1874. "Now, the new settlers can find a market for any commodity and can buy at a neighboring store any necessary [sic] he needs. It was not so a few years ago; then the nearest market was Council Bluffs [about 60 miles by rail southwest of Denison], and the means of transportation were ox-teams." The writer, who signed only his initials – G.C.L. – may have been George C. Lawson of nearby Dowville, an early settlement originally called Crawford and now known as Dow City.

While these hardy people surely felt pride in their accomplishments, they might have scoffed at the rosy picture of prairie life painted by the railroad companies.

An 1871 advertisement by the Iowa Rail Road Land Company

offered this sunny outlook:

"The climate is healthful and bracing," it said. "The air is pure and dry, and there is much less liability to fevers and malarious diseases than in most new countries." (At the time, the term "country" was commonly used to mean a region or a settled area; before Nebraska had a name, for example, fur traders called it either the "Missouri country" or the "Platte country." Today we might refer to Washington state's Yakima Valley as hop-growing country.) The ad described winters as "without much snow, with little or no rain or mud."

Providence Western Land Company, the outfit that more-or-less created Denison and nearby settlements in the 1860s, ran newspaper ads in the 1870s that made it sound like prospective settlers could hardly afford NOT to buy its land.

"Offers for sale on terms so easy that any live man may not be without a home!" it exclaimed.[47]

The state Board of Immigration was even more flowery in its description of this sparsely populated prairie.

"Day after day, for weeks, the sun is veiled in a hazy splendor, while the forests are tinged with the most gorgeous hues, imparting to all nature something of the enchantments of fairly-land," it said in 1869.

The pioneers themselves may have been given to a little exaggeration now and then, or so it would seem from tales told by Carl Waldemar, who was five when his Swedish immigrant family arrived on Otter Creek in 1867 and put down stakes about a quarter mile north of the Hagglund place on the opposite bank of Otter Creek, making them one of the Hagglunds' nearest neighbors.

In an account that Waldemar wrote for the local newspaper many years later, he recalled that as a boy he bagged a lot of ducks, quail and other wild game.

"Once I killed eight large ducks with one shot in our pond," he claimed. "It was not unusual to kill two or three with one shot. I also did a lot of trapping in my young days. Many times, I was out hunting when it was 25 degrees below zero and a blizzard, so I could not see my hand if I stretched it out in front of my eyes."

He also claimed, "When I was five to eight years old I killed many snakes that were twice as long as I was myself. I cut their heads off to be sure of it."

The Hagglund children surely had their own adventures in the wide-open spaces of Crawford County, but aside from mentions of their schooling, I found little written record of how they spent their days along Otter Creek. Waldemar wrote in his "Pioneer Memories" that Andrew Hagglund was the Baptist Church's superintendent of Sunday school for several years, presumably in the mid- and late 1870s when he would have been in his late teens and early 20s.

"It was all conducted in English except the morning sermon," Waldemar wrote, because church leaders believed the children would have a harder time learning English at public school if Sunday school was conducted in Swedish.

It seems safe to assume that the Hagglund children engaged in some of the same fun and games as those described by Waldemar, who also wrote about his fishing techniques, adapted for the seasons, on local ponds and in Otter Creek.

"I used to catch the fish with hook in the summer," he wrote. "In the winter before the ice was too thick, I pounded on it with an ax and stunned the fish. Then I cut a hole and pulled the fish out with my hands. Lots of fish in the creek, all we could eat."

12

'A Terrible Scourge'

The birth of John J. Hagglund in September 1873 concluded 21 years of childbearing for Anna. But the cycle of family tragedy that began in Sweden with the deaths of John and Anna's first two children in 1855, followed by their loss of Märet 12 years later, had not ended.

Heartbreak hit again on October 12, 1877. On that date the Hagglunds lost 12-year-old Oliver.

Iowa did not begin the practice of registering births and deaths until July 1, 1880, so there is no known official record of the cause of Oliver's death. It seems likely but not 100 percent certain, based on my review of cemetery records, that he died of diphtheria. He may have been a victim of one in a series of epidemics that caused alarm locally and struck communities coast to coast in the second half of the 19th century. The devastation is not widely remembered today. Thanks to vaccine, diphtheria in the United States is largely a disease of the past.

In his account of life in the Kiron area, C.J. Johnson recalled the late-1870s epidemic in grim detail. He said it killed nearly 40 local children, most aged five to 14.

"There seemed to be no remedy at hand to check the disease, and it spread from house to house as long as there was anyone left to take it," Johnson recalled 40 years later. "During that time there were no undertakers, nor did we use to buy coffins, and the writer [Johnson himself] had all that he could do that winter making coffins of black walnut lumber, of which we had an abundance."

Kiron Cemetery records closely match Johnson's recollection.[48] Although the records are in some cases incomplete, I counted at least 37 children buried there who died of diphtheria between December 1876 and December 1877. The worst periods were December 1876 to January 1877 and the month of May 1877.

Four years after the epidemic, an Iowa doctor, Ward Woodbridge, said this of diphtheria: "It is a terrible scourge, snatching away the youth, beauty and promise of our land."

Diphtheria is a highly contagious bacterial infection. Children are especially vulnerable. As evidence of its cruelty, the disease was once known as the "Strangling Angel of Children."

The first symptoms are a sore throat, fever, loss of appetite, croup-like coughing and difficult breathing, followed by formation of a thick, fibrous membrane on the nasal tissues and throat. The throat can swell grotesquely, leading to suffocation. In some cases, death is caused by damage to the heart, kidneys or other organs from a toxin secreted by the bacteria.

The organism that causes diphtheria was not identified by scientists until 1884. Treatment with antitoxin began in the 1890s and a vaccine was developed in the 1920s, but effective immunization did not begin in the United States until the 1940s.

Lacking any family record, doctor's report or official death certificate, I could not establish with certainty that diphtheria was Oliver's killer. The only direct evidence is the Kiron Cemetery registry's chronology of burials, which includes Oliver in a long string of child deaths attributed to diphtheria, without further explanation.

The cemetery ledger lists 27 other local children who died ahead of Oliver in 1877, starting Januarty 7. Each was taken by diphtheria. Three Berggren children – 4-year-old Anna, 1-year-old John and 6-year-old Emma – died on the same day, May 13. Their 2-year-old sister Lydia died 14 days later. The Berggrens were Swedish immigrants living a mile or two north of Kiron in the Sac County township of Wheeler.

Following Oliver on the list are three Baker children who died within a two-week period in late November and early December, ages nine, seven and three. It's hard to say just how many children this epidemic killed; it apparently began in late 1876, if not earlier. Iowa did not establish a state board of health until 1880, and record-keeping in remote areas like Crawford County was haphazard.

The *Sac Sun*, a newspaper in nearby Sac City, reported on December 29, 1876 that diphtheria had struck hard. "Near Kiron, Crawford County, last week 18 children were buried – one family losing all their children, five in number, two of them dying on the same day."

A *Kiron News* obituary of Catherine Olson, another of the Swedish pioneers, said diphtheria killed two of her children in February 1877 "during the time when the diphtheria wave went over the settlement and when very few homes was not visited by this plague taking some members from each circle of the early settlers."

All these years later, it's hard to grasp the scope of the scourge, the depth of the grieving.

The disease was so horrifying that local officials at times deliberately under-reported it.

"The greatest difficulty which the state board of health has to meet is the disposition of local authorities to cover up and misrepresent the disease," a Denison newspaper reported in November 1888. "In many places they have an idea that it would hurt the town to have it known that diphtheria was prevalent, and so they call the disease membranous croup, or something else that doesn't sound so frightful."

Oliver was buried in Kiron Cemetery – known in those days simply as the Swede cemetery – on October 14, two days after he died. His grave is unmarked, a haunting sight that can make searching for ancestors seem like chasing ghosts.

The cemetery is a small oasis on a wide expanse of farmland. It is a peaceful patch, a final gathering place for neighbors from a quieter time – easily overlooked but for a cluster of burly, wind-worn trees standing watch over the graves.

I located Oliver's grave in 2015 with the help of a local man, John Larson, an insurance dealer who happened also to be keeper of the cemetery records. The records, which date to 1868, include hand-drawn grid maps identifying each grave, with a number for each that corresponds to names on an accompanying list. Oliver's is grave No. 2 in a group of nine in the south half of Burial Lot 53. I found no evidence he ever had a headstone.

It saddened me to think that little Oliver remained there on the open prairie, abandoned, it seemed, and forever alone after his family had moved west.

As it turns out, he was not entirely alone. He was joined, in a manner of speaking, by friends of his extended family. I discovered this long after my visit.

Once my Hagglund research had progressed to the point where I had traced the full arc of their lives, and the lives of their immediate descendants, I was able to understand the significance of the names of others buried in Oliver's portion of Lot 53. They were one and in some cases two generations younger than Oliver. So, while he would not have known them, the family connection is real, and it means Oliver was not alone.

Among those buried beside Oliver is Elwood Gustaf Anderson. A sister of his was a longtime friend of Anna (Morton) Freberg, who was the eldest daughter of Oliver's older sister, Christine. In other words, Anna Freberg would have been Oliver's niece had he lived another five years to see her come into the world.

The first to join Oliver in the small burial plot, in November 1921, was Adeline Anderson, an infant daughter of Elwood and his wife, Edith. Adeline lived "only a few hours," according to a local news account. In July 1923, their next-born, Jane Edith Anderson, likewise lived less than a full day and was put to rest next to her sister. Elwood was buried beside them in 1953, followed by Edith in 1968.

I might not have given a second thought to the Andersons when I initially saw the names, but for the fact that Edith was listed in the cemetery records as having purchased a $25 "care contract" in 1919 to keep the plot trimmed. At that time, none of her relatives were buried there, which made me wonder why someone outside the Hagglund family would pay to maintain the plot. This stuck in my head.

I initially had no idea who Edith might be, but during a later phase of my research I found that Anna Freberg had made friends in this area in about 1900 with a woman named Anna Mathilda Anderson, who turned out to be Edith's sister-in-law. (I will refer to Edith in more detail, and to Anna Freberg's friendship with Anna Mathilda Anderson, in a later chapter.) So, while taking a fresh look at the Kiron cemetery records much later I recalled the "Anna-Anna" connection, and it was not difficult to figure out the Andersons' indirect link to Oliver.

Little Oliver rests beneath a grass blanket near the base of an evergreen tree. He was not forgotten by his family, of course, but the absence of a headstone made him invisible to the rest of us. Finding him, if that's the right phrase, was one of the greatest thrills of my quest to reconstruct the history of the Hagglund family. Although I know him only through paper records, I felt his presence there in a way that is hard to put into words.

The hand-written entries in the cemetery ledger include Oliver's parents' names and place of origin: "Jämtland, Sweden."

In a column labeled "occupation," the entry for Oliver says simply, "farmer boy."

Yes, he was just a boy. He lived 12 years, two months and 29 days.

13

Kiron, Then and Now

T he Hagglunds would have considered Otter Creek their home, since the town of Kiron did not exist until five years after they arrived, and they never lived in the town limits. Oliver Hagglund's place of death in 1877, for example, was recorded as Otter Creek. Until 1873 the community had no official name. That year, the folks of Stockholm township successfully petitioned Washington for their own post office, which meant they had to come up with a name. They chose "Kiron," which the locals pronounce 'KI'-run.'

Where they got the name is a matter of dispute. Some say it was an accidental misspelling of "Kidron," a brook near Jerusalem cited in the Bible. Carl Waldemar, one of the Hagglunds' nearest neighbors on Otter Creek, credits his father, Waldemar Peterson, with suggesting the biblical reference. "Through a mistake, the "d" was left out," he said, "so they let it go at that."[49]

In an account published in the *Odebolt Chronicle* newspaper in 1938, however, George Norelius offered his own, quite different, explanation. He said some favored "Swedesburg," but "for some unknown reason it was suggested by Lars Olson and Andrew

106

Norelius, (George's father) that the town be called 'Kiron' after a settlement in Manchuria." (There is a city called Kirin in the Manchuria region of eastern China, and Baptist missionaries were working in that area in the mid-1800s, but that's the closest I come to a rationale for associating the town with Manchuria.)

Whatever the case, little Kiron still stands, although it relocated about one mile to the west in 1899, just enough to shift it from the boundaries of Stockholm township to just inside Otter Creek township. The move was triggered by a financial dispute between local landowners and a railroad that wanted to build a line westward through Kiron, branching off from the Chicago and Northwestern main line at what was then the village of Boyer, about five miles east of Kiron.

The railroad company and the landowners in Kiron couldn't agree how much the company should pay for the right-of-way, so the company looked elsewhere. It found a more accommodating seller in Nels Peter Swanson, who agreed to take $500 for his 100 acres in Section 12, which the railroad used to build a station and start a new town from scratch about a mile west of Kiron.

The response in Kiron was a classic illustration of the belief in the make-or-break power of rail connections. Fearing economic irrelevance, many in the bypassed town chose to swallow their pride. Shortly after the new Kiron was laid out in August 1899 on gently sloping land that just months earlier had been a corn field, people and businesses in "old" Kiron packed up and moved to the new one.

The *Denison Bulletin* newspaper called the move an example of progress "in the push and hustle of the last days of this century." In its November 20, 1899 edition, the paper wrote, "Half a hundred workmen are pounding nails day and night to get the buildings in shape for occupancy before the cold weather sets in."

Even the original Swedish Baptist Church was moved – and not easily. A student of Kiron history, Glenn Gustafson, told me in 2017 that a local man, Waldo Winquist, had recalled for him the trouble it took to haul the building to its new location. Whereas it likely would be transported by hydraulic trailer today, the solution in 1899 was to improvise a set of large harnesses, attach them to teams of horses borrowed from several farmers, and pull the church in as straight a line as possible across fields and dirt roads. Fences in the way were removed. Or so the story goes.

The original Kiron simply vanished. When I looked for traces in 2018, I found none.

A 1908 state atlas shows the rail line passing just north of "Old Kiron" and running directly into "Kiron." The line – built by the Boyer Valley Railway Company, which was bought out by the Chicago and Northwestern in June 1900 – ran from Boyer to Kiron, continued in a southwesterly direction through Schleswig, then turned sharply south through Monona County to the town of Mondamin near the Missouri River – a total distance of 61 miles. The line was abandoned in the 1950s, relegating Kiron to a future of economic stagnation.

By 2018, I could discern just three visible reminders of Kiron's years as a rail stop. One was a mural of a locomotive painted on the side of a maintenance shed. Another was a street name on the south end of town – Railroad Street – paralleling the former track, not far from grain silos that had been built trackside. The third was an abandoned and dilapidated little two-story building that had served as a rail "section house," providing shelter for men who maintained the Chicago and Northwestern track during the years it ran through Kiron.

The best source of history for a little town like Kiron is its newspapers. Unfortunately, no copies of the town's earliest papers, including the Sentinel, seem to have survived. The same seems true for nearby Boyer, whose paper, the *Record*, failed to live up to its name, leaving no record of that town's earliest years.

The original Kiron consisted of 10 residences, two general stores, one blacksmith shop, one wagon shop, one lumber yard, a doctor's office, a post office, one church building with parsonage (the Baptist church) and one schoolhouse.

The new town that started in 1899, however, had important advantages, including newspaper boosterism.

A local paper had this to say about new Kiron in 1902:

"At present and in fact since its removal to its new site, Kiron has enjoyed a steady growth, the taxes are low, the school and church advantages most excellent, and the people are of a high class with an exceptionally small number of objectionable characters."[50]

"Objectionable characters" probably was a reference to slackers and petty criminals but may also have included those who simply liked to frequent the local saloons. Drinking, though common, had been frowned upon by many townsfolk – including the Hagglunds – since Kiron's earliest days. At the turn of the century, a temperance movement was gaining steam nationwide; its leaders in Iowa called the church-led crusade a "war against the cohorts of King Alcohol." Kiron was part of the battlefield, as reflected in church records that I reviewed, including handwritten summaries of weekly meetings of the Baptist Young People's Union (a local group that trained future church leaders). One such summary described the main topic at a meeting in Kiron on February 17, 1903:

"As it was a temperance meeting, it was discussed which was the best way to fight against the chief agency of the devil on earth – legalized drunkard making," the meeting notes said.

The national campaign against alcohol peaked with passage of Prohibition in 1919, officially the 18th amendment to the Constitution. Over time, the movement lost steam, and while the Amendment was repealed in 1933, some states remained dry.

Times changed, even in Kiron. A visitor in 2018 could spot the Silver Dollar Saloon in a prominent position on Main Street. Outwardly, though, some features of the little town have stayed the same, including its population, which varied little over the past century and in 2018 stood at 272, according to a Census Bureau estimate.

* * *

Moving On

As with the Hagglunds' decision to leave Minnesota, it's not entirely clear why after a dozen years in Iowa they chose to move on. My guess is that John and Anna had stretched their scarce dollars – and perhaps their patience with Iowa farming – about as far as they could by the late 1870s.

The Everett account says John made the decision when "news of the chance to get good land in Nebraska under the 1862 Homestead Act reached him. He then decided to sell the Iowa farm and move to Nebraska; we find no record of what happened to the Iowa farm."

It was not that simple.

The availability of cheaper land in Nebraska under the Homestead Act would not have been news to John, although it certainly is possible that the writer of the Everett account meant John had caught wind of a particularly persuasive pitch about farming prospects in Nebraska. Land companies advertised aggressively in Iowa newspapers throughout the 1870s, so he would have heard and seen a lot of hype. The land commissioner's office in Omaha, for example, placed an ad in the Denison Review in 1874 proclaiming, "Rich Farming Lands in Nebraska NOW FOR SALE VERY CHEAP," and offering prospective buyers a pamphlet, "The Pioneer," containing a copy of the Homestead Act.

The Hagglunds' move, however, may have been more about Iowa than Nebraska.

Financial stresses on the family had piled up, perhaps worsened by John's apparent decision to buy a 40-acre parcel of land a short distance from the 40 on which they lived. County records are in seeming conflict on ownership of this second 40-acre parcel. I was unable to reconcile the differences but concluded that the Hagglunds had at least attempted to buy it – the northwest quarter of the northeast quarter of Section 25, lying just east of Otter Creek. Tax records list John Hagglund as owner from 1874 to 1879, yet other records contradict this.

This puzzle is a reminder that in the recording of public business, as in any human endeavor, mistakes are made and thus even the most carefully written history is imperfect. It also points up the hazards of interpreting fragmentary information from a distant era.

The set of county records generally considered the most authoritative on land ownership and land transactions are those held by the Recorder's Office. According to this set of original records, which I reviewed multiple times, the only portion of Section 25 in Otter Creek township (originally designated Township 85) for which John Hagglund held a deed was the 40 acres on which the family lived – the northwest quarter of the northwest quarter. Those records indicate that a railroad owned the second 40-acre piece in question until it sold it in 1879 to Olof Larson.

On the other hand, tax records kept by the county Treasurer's Office show that John Hagglund paid four years of taxes on the second 40-acre parcel. The Treasurer's 1878 "tax list" ledger, which shows the assessed value and the owner of each quarter section of property and the owner's tax liability for the year, says John Hagglund owned this second 40 in Otter Creek township, valued at $186, and paid taxes of $5.11 for the 1878 tax year. It says he made this payment in March 1879, and a short time later he also paid the 1876 and 1877 taxes on this property. The following March (1880) he paid the 1879 tax bill. Why would John have paid any of these taxes if he was not the owner of the property? And if he *was* the owner, why did he not start paying taxes until 1879?

My guess is that John had arranged in about 1874 to buy this second 40 acres from the railroad, probably by contract, as he had done in 1868 with the northwest 40. He then found himself unable to make the scheduled payments – including tax payments – and as a result the deal fell through in 1878 or 1879. If that was the case, the deed would never have changed hands, which would explain why it was not filed with the Recorder's Office in the Hagglunds' name. Perhaps John's payment of back taxes in 1879 was part of an arrangement to get out of the unfulfilled contract. An alternative explanation is that John leased the 40 acres from the railroad until 1879.

(Although John paid taxes on that property through 1879, records in the Recorder's Office say that in October of that year the railroad company sold it to Olof Larson, a Swede and neighbor of the Hagglunds. Larson already owned the east 80 in the northeast quarter of Section 25, abutting the boundary with Stockholm township; his place had been hit by the Easter Sunday tornado of 1878.)

Whether or not the Hagglunds ever owned that second 40 acres, the fact is that by 1879 they were landless.

The Hagglunds sold their original farm to Gus Anderson, a local farmer and Swedish immigrant, on December 11, 1878. On that same day, John paid taxes on that property for the last time – $6.64, based on the land's assessed value of $298 plus personal property valued at $134.[51] The combined value (land and personal property) was then cut nearly in half by a $225 credit the Hagglunds received for having trees on their property.

Gus Anderson paid $660 in cash and took over payments on the last $200 of the Hagglunds' $280 mortgage, which was held by Ira Davenport, a tightfisted financier from upstate New York who was something of a pioneer in his own right; he found innovative ways to lend in a farm mortgage market that was risky and raw.[52]

And when I call Davenport tightfisted, I mean he was careful with his money, not that he was cold hearted. He also cared about the less fortunate; in 1864 he established the Davenport Home for Female Orphan Children in his home town of Bath in Steuben County, New York, which provided free institutional care for destitute girls.

The Davenport mortgage was structured so that by December 1878, when they sold the property, the Hagglunds' initial obligation of $280 should have shrunk to $115. The fact that the buyer, Gus Anderson, took over payments with $200 still owed suggests that the Hagglunds had fallen quite far behind. Perhaps they had refinanced at some point, but the mortgage records give no indication of that.

Davenport was picky about who he would do business with, so his willingness to lend to John and Anna suggests they had a reputation as solid citizens and prudent farmers. Davenport seemed to loosen his business rules to accommodate the Hagglunds; he typically insisted a loan amount not exceed one-third of the value of the security. In the Hagglunds' case, I don't know what he judged to be their farm's value, but it would have had to be at least $840 – far above the assessed value – for his investment of $280 to stay within his one-third limit.

Davenport acknowledged in writing that the Hagglund mortgage was fully paid off on May 19, 1880. It remained in John and Anna's name until then, which seems to mean they had been legally obligated to ensure that Gus Anderson made the last $200 in payments. If he had not, the Hagglunds would have been left holding the bag, by my reading of the terms.[53]

This might explain why, after selling to Gus Anderson, John and Anna did not immediately join the wave of immigrants and others claiming homesteads in Nebraska.

The 1880 federal census, taken on June 7, shows the Hagglund family still in Iowa, somewhere in Stockholm township, one district east of Otter Creek. I was unable to pinpoint the date of their move (probably early 1879) or determine their exact location, but they likely were no more than several miles east of the original Otter Creek place. The census lists John and Anna and six children. Andrew, 23, was unmarried and a teacher; Lewis, 21, a farmer, and Christina, 17, "keeping house." The three youngest – Martha, 11, Oscar, 9, and John J., 6, – were recorded as "at school."

The Hagglunds were now tenant farmers. They operated an 80-acre farm for an absentee owner. I found no family records explaining why they quit the Otter Creek farm. Had it failed? "Failed" may be too strong a word, but my guess is that financial pressures forced the Hagglunds to sell. They must have figured their best option was a crop-sharing arrangement, perhaps as an interim step toward becoming Nebraska homesteaders.

I would not have known that they were tenant farmers in 1879 and 1880 if not for a supplement to the 1880 census known as an agriculture schedule, which spells out details of individual farm ownership and production. Most of the people listed in Stockholm township that year owned the farms on which they lived and worked, but some, including "J.A. Hagglund," fell into a category called "Rents for share of products." In that column on the official form, a "2/3" is written beside his name, indicating that in return for their use of the land, the Hagglunds "paid" the owner a fixed share of their farm products – two-thirds, in this case. This reminded me of the old "torpare" system in Sweden in which a family that had no farm of its own worked a certain percentage of the year on an estate owner's farm in lieu of cash rent for their cottage and small patch of land.

A Vanderbilt University history professor, Donald L. Winters, went to extraordinary lengths to study the practice of "tenancy," or farm leasing, in Iowa in the second half of the 19th century.[54] By reviewing farm lease contracts in 10 counties across Iowa (Crawford not among them), he found that tenants usually paid rent in cash, generally about $2 per acre. Others, like the Hagglunds, paid in crop shares – usually between one-third and one-half, with the percentage determined by whether the landlord provided farm implements and work stock like seed. Census records show that these arrangements grew in popularity in this period; in 1880, 24 percent of Iowa farms were operated by tenants rather than owners, and by 1900 the figure had grown to 35 percent.

Some county governments kept copies of these land leases. Crawford County did not. Even without knowing the terms of the Hagglunds' lease, I learned a good deal about their year-plus of farming on that property, thanks to the agriculture annex to the census. (Not included in the annex is the identity of the property owner.)

The value of the 80-acre Stockholm farm, "including land, fences and buildings," was listed at $1,300. Separately, farm equipment was valued at $200 and livestock at $500. It's not clear how much, if any, of the equipment and livestock was owned by the Hagglunds.

The Hagglunds grew wheat and corn and, as of June 1880, had on hand four horses, four milk cows, four "other" cattle, 25 chickens ("exclusive of spring hatching") and six sheep. The chickens produced 100 dozen eggs in 1879; the sheep surrendered 24 pounds of fleece ("shorn and to be shorn"), and the milk cows were credited with 250 pounds of butter. Also, three calves were born during the year.

The main crops for most area farmers in 1879 were corn and wheat. The Hagglunds had 40 acres in corn that year, producing

1,200 bushels. They grew wheat on 32, yielding 450 bushels. They also had eight acres of grassland that produced 10 tons of hay. Some farmers grew oats and harvested tree fruits; the Hagglunds did not, although they did grow fruit on their original 40-acre farm, according to county tax records that show their property value for tax purposes in 1875 was reduced by $50 for having one acre of fruit trees and by $150 for 1½ acres of "forest."

The crop-share farm's productivity in 1879 was about average for the area, with the value of "all farm productions sold, consumed or on hand" estimated at $615. If the Hagglunds were able to keep one-third under their "rent-for-share-of-products" arrangement, their income that year would have been a tad over $200.

It was the Hagglunds' only full year on the Stockholm farm.

In the latter half of 1880 they moved to Madison County, Nebraska, where they enjoyed a period of stability and progress and gained the first new branches of the family – the Mortons and the Tackstroms. But happier times would not last. Two tragic turns of fortune in the 1890s would change the course of family history.

III

The Nebraska Years

14

Starting Over

L ike an annoying house guest, winters on the Great Plains tend to arrive too soon and leave too late. Few came as early and lingered as long as the winter of 1880-81, the Hagglund family's first in Nebraska. Snow burst onto the prairie almost before summer's glow had faded, and as Lewis would later testify, it fell heavily, widely, and often — long overstaying its welcome.

This was a season of transition for the Hagglunds. In their path lay challenges, changes and disappointments they could not have foreseen in the gentler days of spring.

In May, just days after his 21st birthday, Lewis, the second-born surviving son, left the family farm in Iowa and made his way across the Missouri River to scout homesteading prospects in northeastern Nebraska. He may have made the trip by train; a few months earlier the Union Pacific had begun service to his destination, Norfolk, by way of Omaha and Columbus.

Lewis set his sights on a sparsely settled area where life and hope clung to the Elkhorn River, a meandering waterway skirted by groves of cottonwood and elm — a vein of vitality on a landscape touched but not yet transformed by westward migration. An East Coast writer later described this remote stretch of prairie as "unknown to the outside world" and a frontier "left to look after itself."

Being an enterprising sort, Lewis was undaunted by the unknown. But an adventure that started out smoothly soon jerked to a halt, owing to the power of winter's early surprise. This is revealed by his paper trail, which more than a century later enabled me to trace his footsteps and imagine his ambitions. Lewis left a more visible imprint than either of his parents or any of his siblings, allowing a glimpse of how the Hagglund family managed to start over in Madison County, Nebraska after a dozen years in Iowa.

* * *

'Poverty and Inclemency of Weather'

On May 13, 1880, a Thursday, Lewis walked into the federal land office in Norfolk, near the confluence of the Elkhorn's main channel and its north fork. (Norfolk is said to have gotten its name from a mangled reference to the river's north fork.) To know which parcels of land were not yet claimed, he probably consulted the land office's tract book. He then entered his claim for three adjoining parcels totaling 160 acres, the maximum allowed under the Homestead Act. His claim was several miles south of Norfolk, near a new rail stop called Munson.

Given its proximity to the Union Pacific line, this nearly treeless property may have looked to Lewis like the most promising available, but that's not saying much. Years earlier, government surveyors had deemed this part of Madison County unfit for farming, due less to its isolation and remoteness than to its seemingly ill-suited soil.

Whatever his reasoning, Lewis filed his homestead paperwork and hoped for the best.[55]

"I am a single person over 21 years of age and a citizen of the United States," he wrote above his signature on homestead application No. 7376. He had turned 21 on May 6. He did not become a naturalized citizen until March 20, 1884, but on April 13, 1880 – one month before he left home – he appeared in court in Denison, Iowa, to file what was known as a Declaration of Intent. This was the first step in the naturalization process and required him to renounce his allegiance to Sweden. This declaration was more than just words on paper; it's not an exaggeration to say it was a test of an immigrant's faith in his new country and in his own future. Having left his homeland, Lewis now was required to sever ties in the most final and fundamental way – "*... renounces forever all allegiance to any foreign prince, potentate, state or sovereignty whatsoever, and particularly to the King of Sweden of whom he was heretofore a subject.*" That was what Lewis signed up to in order to qualify for use of the Homestead Act.

At the land office he paid a $14 filing fee, and thus began the Hagglund family's search for better lives in Nebraska. Lewis led the way; his father followed with his own claim six months later. They and the rest of the Hagglund family would remain in Nebraska for the next two decades, scratching out a living as heavily mortgaged crop farmers.

By the time they left the Great Plains they had had their fill of hard times, including three national economic recessions that still rank among the four longest on record. According to the National Bureau of Economic Research, the official arbiter of business cycles, the longest recession by far was 1873-79, at 65 months. That was the Hagglunds' introduction in Iowa to the "bust" part of the boom-and-bust cycle in America in the second half of the 19th century, before the Federal Reserve system was created by Congress in 1913 to safeguard against bank panics. The second-longest recession was the Great Depression of 1929-33, at 43 months. No. 3 was the recession of 1882-85, which lasted 38 months. It began shortly after the Hagglunds arrived in Nebraska and before they could fully develop their farms. The depression of the 1890s, which finally pushed the Hagglunds off their land, was actually two separate downturns interrupted by a short reprieve: from January 1893 to June 1894, followed by December 1895 to June 1897, a combined 35 months of economic pain.

These radical swings in economic fortune were foreign to the Hagglunds. Back home in Sweden they had grown accustomed to the peasantry's immovable poverty.

The 1983 Everett account of Hagglund history is exceedingly thin on the Nebraska years. It sums up the period in three sentences, including this one: "We found very little information concerning Hagglund family activities in the state of Nebraska." It says correctly that John and Anna moved the family to Madison County in 1880. Nothing else from this period is recounted aside from declaring that John was "not too happy in Nebraska." If true, he had good reason.

This was a trying time, starting with Lewis' bumpy path from Iowa. His plan was to put down stakes immediately upon arriving in Madison County, but after paying the $14 filing fee he was broke. He could not afford materials to build a roof over his head, an essential step in converting his land claim to ownership. It turned out that earning a buck there was harder than he had figured.

"I was entirely without means and could not get any work to do in Madison County," he wrote nearly eight years later when it came time to explain in court why he had failed to fulfill a key Homestead Act legal requirement. His failure was that he had not moved onto the property within six months of filing his claim. As a result, his case — and, one could argue, his future — was submitted to the General Land

Office's Board of Equitable Adjudication, which eventually ruled in his favor.

Lewis' explanation for why he was slow to fully establish his property claim sheds light on the hardships and obstacles facing an entire generation of prairie pioneers. His words also offer a glimpse into a period of Hagglund family history that had drifted out of sight for many, if not most, descendants.

Lewis described his problem in a sworn statement in Madison County District Court on November 12, 1888. Judging by the wording, it appears to have been written by a clerk summarizing what Lewis conveyed verbally.

Lewis testified that he had been compelled to return to Crawford County, Iowa, to find work. He went back to his parent's place in Stockholm township, where census records show he was living as of June 30, 1880. Over the summer he earned enough money to buy a team of oxen to take him, his belongings and a load of supplies back to Nebraska in time to meet his November residency deadline.

But he was in for a surprise.

"On or about October 15th 1880 a severe snow storm set in and fell to such a great depth that I could not travel with the team I had purchased to improve my land with the money I had earned," he testified.

A full three months later he remained stuck in Iowa.

"Up to January 15th 1881 the snow was still deep on the ground, rendering travel by team impossible to haul timber for a house on my claim," he told the court.

The Great Plains winter of 1880-81 was bad, no doubt – even accounting for the possibility of some exaggeration in the retelling by Lewis and others. Numerous accounts of the suffering across Nebraska, Iowa, Minnesota, Wisconsin and the Dakotas say it did, indeed, start on October 15. It was so notoriously bad that it earned many names — "The Hard Winter" and "The Winter of Deep Snow," among others. It was bad for long enough to delay Lewis in his quest to become a first-time landowner.

An account of the history of Custer County, Nebraska, in the center of the state, called it the "Black Winter," with temperatures 10 to 20 degrees below zero "for days and weeks." The hardships it inflicted on ordinary families was described in Laura Ingalls Wilder's 1940 children's novel, *The Long Winter*. This was historical fiction, but she accurately depicted the severity of the winter, according to a University of Nebraska doctoral candidate who tested Wilder's words against a range of scientific data and other historical records and concluded in a 2014 dissertation that the winter of 1880-81 was and remains among the five worst on record for much of the Plains, including Iowa and Nebraska.[56]

Ranchers took the brunt of it.

"The snow came early in the fall and lay on the ground all winter," according to an account by the Nebraska American History and Genealogy Project. "It was so deep that the cattle could not travel, and at times a crust of ice covered the surface of it, making travel impossible as cattle sunk into the snow and thousands of head starved to death."

Lewis had to wait it out. In doing so he risked losing his homestead claim.

"Shortly after said 15th day of January 1881, the snow had thawed sufficiently to enable me to travel by slow stages," he said in his court statement. "Then I started for Madison County, Nebraska, where I arrived February 4th 1881, but the roads were blockaded so that I could not haul a load." (By "blockaded" he meant impassable due to snow drifts.)

I have no record of the route he took, but it's safe to say he did not go by train this time. He probably drove his team of oxen due west from Crawford County, crossing the Missouri River from the Iowa side near Tieville, a tiny mill town that owed its brief existence – and its name – to one enterprise: making rail ties for the Union Pacific. He would have reached the Nebraska side at Decatur, where flat-bottomed ferryboats, led by the "Queen of Decatur," operated before the first pedestrian and vehicle bridge spanning the Missouri opened at Omaha in 1888.

From Decatur, about 50 miles west of Lewis's starting point in Iowa, he had a nearly straight shot to Norfolk, another 70 miles west across a landscape of smooth-top hills that in a snowy winter might have resembled dunes. It took him nearly three weeks to cover those distances. It's hard to imagine, all these years later when we take highway travel for granted, how difficult Lewis' journey must have been, traveling solo in the dead of winter – just him and his team of oxen.

Once he arrived in the Norfolk area, Lewis had to wait out more storms. His team could not manage the snow-clogged roads or trails.

"It was impossible," he said, to get through the "snow blockades."

The pattern of wind-blown snowstorms continued well past January.

"Snowed in Again," said a Februay 23, 1881 headline in the Observer newspaper of Odebolt, Iowa, just north of the old Hagglund farm. "No sooner does our railroad get plowed out than it is snowed in again," the story said. A week later the Observer reported, "There is a snow drift in Early 10 miles long, 30 miles wide and 72 inches deep." (Early is a small town about a dozen miles north of Odebolt.)

Lewis did not mention exactly when he reached his claim, but it apparently was late March or early April. Even then, the snow pack was still accumulating. The Madison (Nebraska) Chronicle reported on April 14, "Last Sunday and Monday there was an average fall of about 12 inches of snow, on the level, in this vicinity." Shortly after that the snow melt triggered epic flooding along the Missouri and the Elkhorn.

Lewis forged ahead.

"As soon as the road became passable, I immediately procured lumber and built a house on my claim and moved into said house April 15, 1881," he wrote. There he remained.

Lewis's residency problem surfaced when it came time for him to show in writing that he had fulfilled all Homestead Act requirements for gaining his land patent, which is the term for the initial transfer of ownership of a parcel of public land. This process was known as "proving up" or "perfecting" one's claim. In simple terms it meant showing not only that he had established residency within six months of filing his claim, but also that he had lived on the property continuously for five years and cultivated a portion of it. Many claimants failed to do so.

Lewis's problem was first mentioned in a hand-written notation on a General Land Office form dated September 14, 1885 that suggests he was given conditional approval for his land patent.

"Residence not established within six months. Reason: Poverty and inclemency of weather," it reads. Elsewhere on the same form someone wrote, "Recommend for patent subject to confirmation by the Board of Equitable Adjudication under Rule 25 and request District C(ourt) for final action December of 1888."

(The Board of Equitable Adjudication is a story in itself – too tangled to fully explain here. The choice of name – not just adjudication but *equitable* adjudication – reflects what seems to have been the genuine aim of the officials who created the board in 1845. They argued that too many aspiring land owners had their claims "suspended," or temporarily denied, for minor violations or as a result of mistakes by the land office. The remedy was to create a board to separate true frauds from those, like Lewis, who deserved the benefit of the doubt.)

Another land office document in Lewis' file, dated October 26, 1888, included a hand-written notation: "After entry, returned to Iowa to earn means to build with when in Oct. 80 a severe snow storm and blockade prevented from returning in 6 months." That document, incidentally, put the value of Lewis's 160 acres at $500.

The Homestead Act had been amended in March 1881 to say a settler unable for "climatic reasons" to establish residence within six months could be allowed 12 months if he submitted an affidavit "setting forth in detail the storms, floods, blockade by snow or ice, or other hindrances" that made it impossible to do it in six. Thus, the Lewis court statement.

When the time came to "prove up" his claim in 1885, the sworn witnesses for him were his father and his brother-in-law, Lars Morton. His father vouched for Lewis having met the requirement for five years of continuous residence on the land, while acknowledging some temporary absences, which were permissible under the law.

"He was away sometimes to work about a week or a month at a time, claimant was single at the time," John wrote in his supporting testimony September 10, 1885, seven months after Lewis got married. (I don't know what kind of work Lewis was doing, or where he did it, when he left his property for as long as a month at a time. A fair guess is that he found some of this temporary work in Butler County, two counties south of Madison, since this is where he found his future wife.) John testified that Lewis had 30 acres "ploughed," and estimated the farm's value at $400. Nine years later Lewis sold it for a little over four times that amount.

John correctly stated that Lewis had established residence in April 1881. Lars, however, got his facts a little twisted. He said Lewis had established residence "in summer of 1880."

Residency was not Lewis's only problem. His claim also seemed to have been delayed by a paperwork glitch. In a sworn deposition in Madison County district court on September 10, 1885, Lewis said, "My Homestead papers are lost and after diligent search cannot be found." It's unclear whether they were lost by him or the land office, but the papers apparently were found, because he did manage to finish the process. Four days later, Lewis paid a $4 administrative fee to complete his paperwork, as documented by a "final receiver's receipt" issued at the nearest land office, which by then was at Neligh rather than Norfolk.

From start to finish, Lewis's homestead claim took almost precisely nine years.

His land patent was issued by the government on May 21, 1889. (Key details of the Homestead Act claims of Lewis Hagglund, John Hagglund and Lars Morton are in the Appendix of this book.)

* * *

Next Up, the Parents

John and Anna followed Lewis to Madison County, probably in the same year and with the same goal. Their timeline is less clear because their paper trail in this period is especially thin. Available evidence, supported by family lore, indicates they made the move from Iowa in late summer or early fall. One thing is certain: As of June 30, 1880, the entire family was still in Iowa, as recorded in the federal census. John was 52 and Anna was 50, but they were nowhere near reaching their empty-nester years. Andrew and Lewis were adults but still at home, as was 17-year-old Christine. Of the two youngest, Oscar was 10 and John J. was six.

At a family reunion in Everett in June 1983, Hazel (Tackstrom)

Booth recalled being told that her mother, Martha (Hagglund) Tackstrom — the youngest Hagglund daughter — was 11 when the family moved to Nebraska. By Hazel's account, Martha walked the entire way "and helped drive the cows." If Martha was 11, then the year of the move was indeed 1880. She turned 12 in December.

The distance they covered, by foot or wagon, was about 120 miles if they took the most direct route, which probably included crossing the Missouri at Decatur.

The earliest record of their presence in Nebraska is a federal land office receipt dated November 26, 1880. It shows John had gone to the land office in Norfolk and paid $2 to file a "declaratory statement," a legal note stating his intention to stake a claim for 160 acres under the Pre-emption Act of 1841. Pre-emption allowed a settler to buy up to 160 acres of public land directly from the federal government, "pre-empting" a public auctioning. Some called this a legalization of "squatter's rights," although that referred to people settling on land not yet surveyed by the government. This was not the case with John and Anna, whose land was "unoffered," meaning it had been surveyed but not yet offered for public sale.

I don't know why John chose to file under the Pre-emption Act instead of the Homestead Act, nor do I know why, nearly a year later, he switched gears and entered a new claim for the same property under terms of the Homestead Act. His entry, or application, number was 7779.

Claiming land under the Homestead Act had one big advantage over pre-emption: You paid nothing except two administrative fees. A claimant under the Pre-emption Act generally paid $1.25 per acre, or $200 for a 160-acre claim. John paid fees of $14 when he filed his Homestead claim in September 1881 and $4 when he completed the process in November 1886. The land itself was free.

On the other hand, a Homestead Act claimant – or "entryman" in the terminology of the day – was required to reside on and cultivate a portion of his claim continuously for five years before obtaining title to the land. The time requirement under Pre-emption was 12 months.

By either path – Pre-emption or Homestead – a claimant had to provide proof of American citizenship by the time he or she applied for title to the land. A copy of John's certificate of citizenship, dated September 11, 1885 and issued by the district court in Madison, is included in land office records at the National Archives.

Parts of John's homesteading chronology are murky, making it difficult to know for sure exactly when he and the family moved onto their land. In his declaratory statement of November 26, 1880, he said he had "settled upon" his claim six days earlier, November 20. That would appear to mean he had moved onto that piece of land on that date. This is consistent with the dates he cited when he filed his Homestead application nearly a year later, on September 7, 1881.[57]

"I claim residence from Nov. 26, 1880 under my DS filing No. 9866," he wrote in the Homestead Act application, swearing that he was head of a family and had stated his intention to become a U.S. citizen. ("DS" was a reference to his declaratory statement.) His handwritten declaratory statement was squeezed into a small space above his signature and below a printed section of the application.

But several years later, when he filed paperwork to "prove up," or legitimize his claim, he gave a notably different date. In those papers he said he and Anna had established their "actual residence" on that land on September 7, 1881, rather than in November 1880 – a difference of 10 months. "Actual residence" would seem to mean what it says – actually living there. But it might be a legal term of art referring to the date on which he filed his Homestead claim, since that started the clock ticking toward the five-year minimum residency required for attaining legal ownership.

John's claim was for two adjacent 80-acre tracts situated in what became known as Union Creek township, named for the predominant stream running through it.

On balance, it seems most likely that he and Anna settled on their Madison County property in November 1880. There is, however, one other puzzling thing about this scenario: November 1880 coincided with a long stretch of bad weather that began in mid-October and that Lewis said had made the roads from Iowa impassable until January. How could John and the rest of the family have made it to Norfolk in such conditions if Lewis could not? Had the family moved prior to the October onset of bad weather, perhaps renting a place in the town of Madison, about seven miles southwest of his claim, and then moving onto the claim in November? It is difficult to document the timing of their departure from Iowa because as tenant farmers they had no land or house to sell.

Andrew Hagglund, the eldest son, filed naturalization paperwork at the Crawford County district court in Denison, Iowa, on September 21, 1880, which suggests that he and probably the rest of the family had not yet moved to Nebraska by that date. Lewis filed his naturalization paperwork in Denison on April 13, 1880, and his father filed his on March 2, 1880. As best I could tell, the court retained none of their naturalization paperwork other than a notation of the dates on which it was filed. The fact that all three men filed their initial naturalization paperwork within several months of each other suggests they were planning the Nebraska move together.[58]

One other curious detail in John's Homestead Act paperwork is his statement that the house on his claim was built in March 1880. At that point he and the family were still living in Iowa and it would be another eight months before he filed for pre-emption. Might the house have been built by a previous settler who abandoned it between March and November, when John says he settled on the property?

It's possible – though unlikely, it seems to me – that John traveled to Madison County to build the house, returned home to Iowa, and then waited several more months before going back to file his claim.

In an affidavit recorded October 23, 1886, John responded to standard questions designed to prove that he had fulfilled all requirements of the Homestead Act. Among the questions: When was your house built, and when did you establish actual residence there?

His answer to the first part was "March 1880," without mentioning the builder. To the second part he responded, "Sept. 7, 1881 actual residence," which I suspect was the date used as the starting point for his required five-year residence prior to "proving up" his claim.

He described the house and other property improvements as follows:

"Frame house, 12 x 20, 2 doors, 5 windows, shingle roof, barn, granary, corn crib, cow shed, 2 wells, grove. Value $1,000." (The value of the place seems to have been a matter of opinion; a neighbor farmer, Stephen Stork, put it at $700 when he provided witness testimony to the General Land Office in support of John's claim. Another neighbor and witness, Charles Lodge, put it at $800.)

It's not clear whether the house was the same one John said was built in March 1880.

On November 8, 1886, John paid the $4 fee required to complete the "proving up" process. Two days later he filed the receipt with the Madison County Register of Deeds. The number of his final certificate, to be submitted to Washington for approval of his land patent, was 5106.

More than two years later, on March 27, 1889, John's land patent was issued. It includes the signature of Benjamin Harrison, whose inauguration as the 23rd U.S. president was so recent – March 4 – that the patent form used the signature of his White House predecessor, Grover Cleveland. The Cleveland signature was crossed out; Harrison's was entered above it. Until 1833, all land patents were personally signed by the president, but the number of government land grants had grown so rapidly that the Congress authorized the presidential signature to be written by a secretary – a legal forgery, you might say.

15

Lars Morton's 'Ordinary Prairie'

The other Madison County homesteader of special note at the start of the Hagglunds' second full decade in America was John and Anna's future son-in-law, Lars Gustav Morton, sometimes called Gus Morton, sometimes L.G. Morton. Like the Hagglunds, he moved from Crawford County, Iowa, to Nebraska in 1880, apparently with two related goals: to become a first-time landowner and to marry the Hagglund's eldest daughter, Christine.

In December 1880, Lars filed his claim for free land under the Timber Culture Act, which had become law seven years earlier as a complement to the Homestead Act. It was intended to promote forestation in tree-scarce Plains states. The law allowed a "timber claim," as it was known, only on "prairie land, or land naturally devoid of timber." Madison County certainly qualified on both counts.

A timber claim would be legitimized only if the claimant met certain exacting requirements. Five of the 160 acres had to be broken (cleared and plowed) within the first year, cultivated in the second year, and "planted to forest trees, or planted with the seeds of forest trees, four feet apart each way" within the third year. An additional five acres had to be broken the second year, cultivated the third year, and planted in trees the fourth year. Title to the land would be granted after eight years if at least 675 trees were "found in a growing condition" by then.

Lars seems to have given up on the tree-planting regimen, but not before he placed cottonwood seedlings in a semi-circle around his house. I did not find record of his actual timber claim, but in 1884 he converted it to a claim under the Homestead Act. "Ordinary prairie," he called it in his homestead paperwork.[59]

It probably was not a coincidence that Lars' tract was very near Lewis's. Both men would have wanted to be near a newly built rail line running north-south between Norfolk and Columbus, a bustling Platte River town about 35 miles south of Lars's place. The line, known as the Omaha, Niobrara & Black Hills, was a branch of the Union Pacific; it opened in December 1879, just months before Lars and the Hagglunds came onto the scene. The train, hauling mostly freight and mail, made two stops along the way, at Munson and at Madison, opening new possibilities for agriculture in an area previously isolated from major markets.

Both Lewis and Lars were about two miles south of the Munson depot. Lewis's place was a couple miles west of the railroad track; Lars's was a couple miles east of it.

John and Anna were about three miles southeast of Lars' place, near the Stanton County line.

* * *

On Antelope Run

In those days, Munson was not even a town; it was merely a post office at the rail depot, but it would become a landmark in Morton family history. All six of Lars and Christine's children were born nearby over a ten-year span, 1882-92.

The few people living in Munson apparently felt neglected, at least by the newspaper in nearby Madison. On July 1, 1880, the Madison County Chronicle published a letter signed by an anonymous reader; the headline read, "Munson Mince Meat."

"I notice you have but very little from Munson and vicinity," it began, referring to a lack of published news. "Would say, by way of introduction, that we are expecting a large immigration in these parts this spring, which has already begun." It said a Mr. Conway of Iowa had arrived along with his wife, ten children, livestock, farm equipment, seven "very fine work horses," and 12 of "Iowa's best cows."

"We are looking for others every day," the ever-hopeful letter writer added. The letter mentioned a "Mr. Rowlett" – perhaps referring to Ezekiel "Zeke" Rowlett, a disabled Civil War veteran; the letter said Rowlett "has had a little bad luck, but he looks brisk and is going to build on his homestead this spring." He was a friend or acquaintance of Lewis Hagglund, who provided written testimony in November 1884 in support of Rowlett's homestead claim. The two men were of one mind on a leading social issue of the day: alcohol use. In 1888 Rowlett announced plans to organize a "prohibition club."

The Munson letter writer had good intentions and outsized expectations. Even five years later the "large immigration" had not materialized, nor would it. The 1885 state census shows Munson had essentially no residents other than railroad workers. Even Mr. Conway, the 1880 arrival from Iowa, seems to have moved on. A handwritten notation in the margin of the page just below the census listing for Lewis Hagglund says, "Munson 13 inhabitants." The 13 were mostly Union Pacific workers: a section boss and his family, several section hands and a station agent.

Lewis and his wife at the time, Ella, as well as Lars and Christine Morton and their children, were just beyond the tiny limits of Munson – later called Warnerville, although the Morton children would consider Warnerville to be the place of their birth. For census purposes they were counted as part of Norfolk township. To confuse matters further, Warnerville was later carved out of Norfolk township and became its own township. So, like Norfolk, Warnerville was both a town and a township. John and Anna's place, though only a few miles away, was in another township, Union.

Set along a spring-fed creek called Antelope Run, Munson was named in honor of Civil War veteran and Madison County civic leader Henry Addison Munson, a descendant of veterans of the Revolutionary War. According to a Munson family history published in 1896, the site was renamed Warnerville when Orson D. Munson, a son of the original namesake, sold the land to another Civil War veteran, Hiram Warner.

Warner, a New York native, settled in Munson in 1887 and established several businesses, eventually including a creamery, a general store, a lumber yard and a vegetable cannery – the Warnerville Canning Co., whose product label boasted that its "goods are packed where grown and guaranteed first class and perfectly fresh." As of 1888 there was even a small hotel – the Samaritan.

At its peak in 1892 the town had roughly 100 residents. A land investment ad touting the virtues of Warnerville said it was attracting a thrifty and industrious class of people who enjoyed rising prices for real estate blessed with well water "as soft as rain water."

What Warnerville lacked was a future.

The post office was shuttered in 1917. The Methodist church later was moved to Norfolk – all, that is, except its concrete front steps. In 2018, Earl Reed, a retired minister who gave the final sermon in the church, led me into a grove of trees to rediscover those abandoned steps. They lay in a jumbled heap, surrounded by tiger lilies.

Even the rail depot was moved a few miles down the line to Enola.

By the time of my first visit hardly a trace of Warnerville remained. It had truly vanished.

In one of the few publicly available accounts of life in Warnerville, a former resident named Jane Sleeper Meyer recalled it in charming detail. She was born there in January 1898 to Oren and Iola Sleeper and remembered it in her memoir[60] as "a very small place" where the biggest thing that happened was the coming and going of the train – "the bell-ringing engines with their belching of black smoke." Times were tough. "It was cornmeal mush for breakfast," she wrote, "and fried mush for supper." Milk to wash it down was donated daily by a more prosperous neighbor.

Every building from the Munson/Warnerville era is long gone, save two. The exceptions are an older section of Earl Reed's house, which stands across the street from where Hiram Warner lived, and the schoolhouse, designated as School District No. 25. The owner of the school building, Timothy Miller, told me in April 2016 that he had been trying to sell it, offering to take a token $1 and help pay the buyer's cost of removal. He expected no takers and planned to "turn it into match sticks."

Although Warnerville faded away, memories remained. When I visited, Peg Timmer-Kathol, a retired school teacher, lived across the tracks from where the depot once stood. The train still rumbled down the line, virtually in her front yard. Peg didn't mind. She considered it a pleasant reminder of the town's lost history. To keep the memory alive, she arranged to have an official "Warnerville Drive" sign erected on the gravel road she calls her driveway — originally the town's Main Street.

These days, the main local attraction is an 18-hole public golf course. It stands not much more than a chip shot from the old Munson rail depot but light years from the world of late-19th century homesteaders like Lars and Christine Morton.

* * *

Lars Switches Gears

Lars apparently did not move onto his 160 acres immediately after filing his claim in December 1880. After he and Christine got married the following spring in Madison, they raised their first crops in 1882 and apparently moved onto the property in October 1883. Timber claims did not require residence on the land.

The following year, Lars switched gears and filed for the same land under the Homestead Act. His entry number was 9577.

"I have declared my intention to become a citizen of the United States, that I am the head of a family and am over 21 years of age," he wrote in his homestead affidavit dated October 6, 1884. He was 37 at the time. Nearly a year later, on September 10, 1885, he got his certificate of citizenship – one day before his father-in-law got his.

In sworn testimony to "prove up," his claim in November 1889 after satisfying the five-year residency requirement, Lars said he "made a timber claim entry" on December 7, 1880 "and turned it into this homestead."

In that testimony, he was asked when he first made "an actual personal settlement on this land." He answered, "23rd of Oct., 1883, as timber claim. Built a house, stable and dug a well." That means the

Morton's first child, Anna, was not born on the homestead, although the rest of the Morton children probably were.

Asked, "Where did you live before settling upon this land?" Lars wrote with an unfortunate lack of specificity, "Madison County, Nebraska, farming." It seems possible that after he married Christine in June 1881 they lived on her parents' farm or with her brother Lewis.

When asked, "By whom was your house built?" He wrote, "By myself in October 1883." (The question was put less pointedly to John in his homestead testimony; he was asked when the house on his claim was built, not who built it.)

Lars paid the $4 administrative fee to complete his paperwork on November 30, 1889. Notably, that same day he and Christine took out a $600 mortgage on their property from Omaha Loan and Trust, with a 6 percent interest rate. Four days later they signed for an additional $60 loan — likely to pay a 10 percent commission fee to the mortgage broker — with two promissory notes of $30 each. Mortgaging a homestead was common practice in those tough economic times. For many, there was no other way to afford the equipment, animals, seed and other essentials for turning unbroken prairie into viable cropland.

Lars gained permanent title with issuance of his land patent on February 18, 1891, a little more than 10 years after he filed his timber claim.

* * *

Lars and Christine

The backstory to the Lars-Christine romance is a blank page. Time erased virtually all details of their relationship and, for that matter, almost the entirety of their 11 years of marriage, beyond the bare threads of information in assorted official records. Sadly, the human side of their story – the courtship, the parenting and the rest – seems lost to history, although it is possible that enriching details will emerge, perhaps from a diary, letters or other personal items still to be discovered in a descendant's attic, dresser drawer or cedar chest.

Christine Morton and Lars Morton, in Madison, Nebraska, circa mid-1880s.

It seems likely that the two became acquainted before either moved to

Nebraska, since they lived within a few miles of each other in Iowa in 1880, when she was 17. Both were Swedish immigrants from similar backgrounds as children of peasants. The biggest apparent difference was their ages; he was 16 years older. He came to America in 1866 as a young adult, she a year later as a child.

Lars was born April 25, 1847 as Lars Gustav Larsson, the third son of Lars Mårtensson and Anna Cajsa Pehrsdotter, farmers in the Skaraborg area of southern Sweden. This area is rich in prehistoric ruins, including remnants of so-called passage graves that were built in the Neolithic period of the Stone Age, about 5,000 years ago. (In the late 1990s, Skaraborg was disestablished as a county and merged with others to form Västra Götaland county.)

In his decision to emigrate, Lars may have been influenced by his older siblings, two of whom moved to America in 1864. He and three other siblings followed two years later. In fact, all seven children in his family emigrated to America except the youngest, Sara Lotta, who died at home as a child in June 1860.

Lars Mårtensson, the father of Lars, was born May 31, 1804 to Mårten Andersson and Greta Jacobsdotter in a small Skaraborg parish called Broddestorp.

Anna Cajsa Pehrsdotter, the mother of Lars, was born December 13, 1808 in the parish of Falköping, about eight miles south of Broddestorp. She and Lars were married in 1832 and a year later they started a family that would grow to seven — three boys and four girls. The first two were born on a farm compound called Larsegården: Maja Greta in August 1833 and Pehr Magnus in October 1836. The year after Pehr Magnus was born, the family moved to a nearby farm called Storegården, perhaps to make room for Anna Cajsa's brother, Pehr Pehrsson, and his family, with whom they had shared the farmhouse at Larsegården.

At Storegården, another five children were born, starting with

Johan in August 1839. He was followed by Anna Christina in February 1842 and Inga Cajsa in October 1844. Lars came three years later. The youngest, Sara Lotta, was born in January 1851 and died at age nine. Their farm was in a medieval hamlet called Ostra Tunhem, in the parish of Gudhem, established in the 12th century.

In ways that sadly parallel the childhood years of his future father-in-law, John Hagglund, Lars Morton's family life was disrupted by the loss of his mother. He was seven when she died at age 46 on January 27, 1855. Ten months later, the eldest daughter, Maja Greta (later known as Marie), at age 22, and the No. 2 son, Johan (John), 16, left home and resettled in Falköping, which is both a parish and a small city a few miles south of Gudhem, the parish where Lars and all of his siblings were born. The eldest son, Pehr (Peter) Magnus, had moved to Falköping three years earlier, at age 16.

The rest of the children – three girls and Lars – ranged in age from 12 to four at the time their mother died.

Like his older brothers, Lars moved away from home at age 16. He went to work on a farm in a parish called Friggeråker, a few miles south of Gudhem. He stayed just one year, 1863, before moving back to Gudhem. When he set out on his journey to America, he was in Gudhem parish working as a farmhand at Ostra Tunhem.

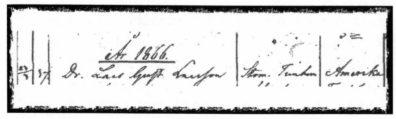

Parish records show Lars Morton, then called Lars Gustav Larsson, departed the village of Tunhem for America on March 23, 1866. The "Dr." before his name is an abbreviation for the Swedish term for farmer.

The first in the family to leave for America were Peter and Anna Christina. They made the trek together in June 1864, sailing from the German city of Hamburg to New York on a steamship called Der Nord.

Three other siblings – Maja Greta, Inga Cajsa and Johan – emigrated together, the same year as Lars but separately from him. They and six other Falköping parish residents are recorded on "utflyttning" (moving out) rolls as having departed for America on the same day – April 4, 1866. That was about two weeks after Lars left. The April group of nine included a man named Pehr Johan Johansson, who worked on the same farm as Lars' brother Johan.

Parish records say Lars began his emigrant journey on March 23, 1866, but I could not fully establish his path. He may have traveled aboard a New York-bound, German-flagged steamship, the Saxonia, built in 1857 at the Greenock shipyard in Scotland. A 19-year-old Swedish farmworker named Lars Larsson is listed among passengers aboard the Saxonia, but I have my doubts that this was the future Lars Morton. The Saxonia departed from Hamburg, in northern Germany, on June 23, 1866. That is three months after Lars Morton left home, which seems like a long interlude and a possible reason to doubt that the man aboard the Saxonia was the Lars Larsson from Ostra Tunhem. In fact, the Saxonia passenger list says this Lars Larsson was from Oskarshamn, a port city on Sweden's east coast, far from the area in Skaraborg where Lars Gustav Larsson was living at the time.[61] The Saxonia arrived in New York, by way of Southampton, on July 9.

Three of Lars' siblings – Peter, Johan, and Anna Christina – settled in western Illinois, which some call the cradle of Swedish America. All three lived in and around Princeton, the seat of Bureau County.[62] They joined a Lutheran church, raised families and died there early in the 20th century. I believe Maja Greta also lived in Princeton and changed her name to Mary Morton; that name appears in the 1870 census as a "domestic servant" in her sister Anna Christina's household in Princeton. I was unable to determine where Inga Cajsa settled.

For reasons left to the imagination, Lars and his siblings seem to have had trouble settling on a surname once they arrived in America. Instead of sticking with Larson, they went with not one but three Americanized versions of their father's patronym, Mårtenson. Some chose to use Mortenson, others preferred Martenson, but most went with Morton, a name of some note in Swedish-American history. One of the signers of the Declaration of Independence was John Morton, born in Pennsylvania of Swedish/Finnish descent.

Trying on new surnames was not unique to this family. There is an old saying: "Swedes changed their names as easily as they changed their shirts."

Johan initially called himself John Morton but by 1900 was going by John Mortenson. Like Lars, Johan married a woman named Christine; they settled initially in Princeton, about 100 miles southwest of Chicago and about 60 miles east of the Mississippi River town of Moline, Illinois. Dozens, if not hundreds, of Swedes had begun settling in and around Princeton at mid-century; some were from the group of Lutherans, including the previously mentioned Eric and Andrew Norelius, who set out to create their own Swedish colony in Illinois in 1850.

At the time of the 1870 census, John and Christine Morton had two children, Charles (sometimes called Carl), age 3, and August (Gustav August), age 1. Ten years later they were living in Peru, a town on the Illinois River about 15 miles east of Princeton, with five children ranging in age from 1 to 13.

John died in Peru in May 1906. Christine followed in April 1931, also in Peru.

Peter Morton also settled down. In 1866, he married Lisa Marie Svensdotter, a Swedish immigrant from the small village of Bäckaby in the Jönköping area of Småland province. She went by the name Mary. They had five children; the oldest, Oskar Albert, was born in Princeton in April 1867.

Mary died in 1909, and Peter followed in 1917; both are buried in Princeton.

Although Lars apparently chose not to join his siblings in Illinois at first, the Princeton group eventually produced a new connection to him through marriage. In 1868, four years after settling in Princeton, Lars' older sister Anna Christina married a fellow Swede, Mans (Marshall) Ekdahl, who had arrived in the U.S. one year before her. (The Ekdahls' children added a "c" to the surname to make it Eckdahl, spoiling the original name's meaning; "ek" is Swedish for oak, and "dahl" means dale or valley.) Many years later, one of their offspring would marry one of Lars' daughters.

Anna Christina died in July 1912 and Marshall in 1924; both are buried in Princeton.

Anna Christina's obituary in the local newspaper, the Bureau County Record, said her grown children had long since moved on to "business cares and their own home circles."

"They may have grown away from her, but she never from them," it said. "They were still her boys and girls. We know that years hence, the memory of her unselfish devotion will make them better men and better women and her precepts be their guiding star."

All seven Eckdahl children were born in Princeton, beginning with George Emil in 1869. The second son, Frank (born Frans Leo) is among Swedish Americans whose biography was included in a book published in 1908 called *History of the Swedes of Illinois*. It says that after studying at Princeton Business College, he began a career as a clothing merchant in the fall of 1897. He and his business partner,

F.E. Peterson, ran a clothing company called Eckdahl & Peterson.

Marshall and Anna Eckdahl's fifth child was Charles Oscar, born Carl Oscar on October 30, 1881. His life's path eventually would intersect with that of his uncle, Lars Morton. Charles moved west from Illinois as a young man, living for a short time in Colorado (where he and his first wife, Jennie, had their only child, Clifford P. Eckdahl in 1909) and then settling in Laramie, Wyoming, where he was a clothing store salesman and tailor.

In the mid-1950s Charles married a cousin, Clara Mae (Morton) Stanley, his uncle Lars' youngest daughter. At the time, she was a widow (her husband Grant Stanley died in February 1953) and he was a widower (Jennie died in Laramie in January 1933). Clara and Charles were married in Laramie and lived there for a few years before moving to Bellingham, Washington, where they remained.

The closest thing to a clue about when Lars met Christine is his mention in 1885 that he first encountered her brother, Lewis, in August 1880. He made that statement, without elaboration, in witness testimony years later in support of Lewis's homestead claim. In August 1880 Lewis was living in Crawford County, probably on his parents' farm in Stockholm township while earning money to build on his homestead claim in Nebraska. Lars at the time was a boarder on a farm a few miles south of the Hagglunds in the adjacent township of Milford. He was a 33-year-old bachelor living with Swedish immigrants Carl and Matilda "Tillie" Selander. Carl's brother Gust Selander would play an important role in Lars' life many years later.

Lars and Christine were married on June 7, 1881 in Madison, Nebraska, less than a year after moving from Iowa. The ceremony was officiated by a local justice of the peace, Erwin W. Sims, whose judicial credentials would play a role in Hagglund history several years later under less pleasant circumstances. The witnesses at Christine's wedding were her father and her oldest brother, Andrew.

Christine gave birth to six children in 10 years, all in Nebraska. She was two months shy of her 19th birthday when she had her first, Anna, on March 14, 1882. (Anna Morton was my grandmother; her youngest daughter Annabelle was my mother.) This made John and Anna Hagglund grandparents for the first time.

Precisely two years after Anna arrived, Christine gave birth to Mabel Florence on March 14, 1884. She was followed a little over a year later by Mary Blanche on May 10, 1885. John Albert was next, on December 14, 1886 and Harry Levi arrived on October 25, 1888. Last came Clara Mae, on February 9, 1892, which would turn out to be the start of a pivotal, tragic period for the Mortons, through no fault of Clara's.

16

'Nearly Worthless'

Madison County, especially the eastern part where the Hagglunds and Lars Morton settled, was populated mainly by Germans, eastern Europeans and native-born Americans transplanted from back East. There were few Swedes or other Scandinavians. There were, however, plenty of characters.

One of the more colorful locals was the grocer, O.H. Gillespie. He often placed notices in the newspaper begging customers to pay their bills. "I need money *very* much," he once pleaded. "Will those owing me *please* help me out?" At other times he was feeling generous; he once offered a pair of large vases "to the fattest baby under one year old."

In May 1898 Gillespie bought a front-page newspaper ad to announce he was putting his store in the hands of a caretaker because he was "going to war." Congress had declared war on Spain a month earlier, amid outrage over the sinking of the USS Maine in Havana harbor. He signed off, "Yours for Spanish scalps, O.H. Gillespie."

Another notable character was Francis E. Long, a country doctor who took his responsibilities seriously at a time when medical expertise was hit and miss, especially in remote frontier towns like

Madison. He wrote a book[63] about his times in Madison County, while Nebraska was, as he put it, "still in the making." He described colorful details of life in the prairie town where he set up practice in June 1882, two years after the Hagglunds arrived.

The Madison he described sounds more prosperous, or at least more vibrant, than the town I visited more than a century later. In Long's day, there was Charles Fritz's saloon, the Buettner & Zessin men's clothing store, Philip Bauch's cigar store, and Lewis Herr's meat market. The town also had two hotels – the Madison House and the Prince Hotel – two general merchandise stores, two banks, two hardware stores, one restaurant, a confectionery, two blacksmith shops, two farm implement stores, a flouring mill, two lumber yards, a coal yard, two livery stables, five attorneys, two doctors, four churches, one grocery store and two weekly newspapers, the Chronicle and the Reporter.

The Madison of 2016 had the look and feel of a place well past its prime, a time-worn replica of a once-busy frontier town. Main Street was partly deserted. The town's main employer was a nearby Tyson Foods pork processing plant whose immigrant workers were a source of social tension evident even to an outsider.

In Francis Long's day, Madison's population was said to be 1,000, but he was certain "it could not have had half that number." He may have been right. Nebraska's first business gazetteer, published in 1879, put the town's population at 300. In 2016, the year of my first visit, it was said to be about 2,400, but it seemed to me, as it had to Long over a century earlier, that someone was exaggerating.

Madison had no particularly outstanding features, but it managed to grow after the first settlers arrived from Wisconsin in 1866, led by a group of German immigrants.

Norfolk, about 15 miles north of Madison, was a larger settlement and the more naturally dominant town, given its position on the

Elkhorn river. (Norfolk's claim to fame is that talk show host Johnny Carson, an Iowa native, attended Norfolk High School in the early 1940s. His life and fame are celebrated in the Johnny Carson Gallery at Norfolk's Elkhorn Valley Museum.) Even though Norfolk was always more populous than Madison, the smaller town won a heated debate over which would be the seat of Madison County.

From a mere 140 settlers in 1868, Madison County's population jumped to nearly 9,000 in 1884. By 1890 it had reached 13,669 and twenty years later it approached 20,000. By the year 2000 the population plateaued at about 35,000.

Long, who called himself "just a plain country doctor,"[64] described a relatively primitive state of medical practice in Madison County in the 1880s. His home was his office. For a time, his kitchen table doubled as his operating table.

In those days, "doctoring" could require ingenuity. Long recalled a "medical friend of many years" – maybe a trained doctor, maybe not – who prided himself in keeping his personal penknife very sharp. One day this friend responded to a call for help at a house where a child was strangling from the effects of diphtheria. "He took his penknife, made a stab wound through the windpipe and the child at once breathed easier." He then used a household thread and needle and "passed a ligature through the skin on each side of the wound and tied the two behind the neck." Later, a tracheotomy tube was inserted. The child recovered.

Long also spun a yarn about one "so-called physician" named John Quincy Adams Harvey who served as the county's first coroner. As the story goes, a homesteader had been found in his cabin "frozen stiff." The coroner was summoned.

"On reaching the cabin he pushed the door ajar, looked in and in his staccato voice gave his verdict, 'Deader 'n hell!'"

The development of agriculture in these parts also was hit and miss.

Madison County is just west and north of those parts of Nebraska where the soil and climate were considered invitingly hospitable and where, consequently, the first waves of homesteaders had settled in the 1870s – along the Missouri River and in areas south of the Platte River.

If John Hagglund had been steered specifically to Madison County, it's unclear what led him or Lewis or Lars to choose their specific pieces of land. One wonders whether they were aware of observations recorded by the government surveyor team that charted each square mile of the county in 1866. The surveyors were under contract to the General Land Office, whose local office in nearby Norfolk kept track of all public land transactions, but I don't know whether the surveyors' field notes were available to walk-in homesteaders.[65]

In addition to laying boundaries for individual townships and dividing them into one-square-mile parcels, known as sections, the survey team leader recorded his assessment of the character and quality of the land as he walked it. These were unscientific judgments but were based on first-hand observation.

Here is what the lead surveyor, Chauncey Wiltse, wrote in his field notes August 19, 1866 about the land in the northeast corner of Township 22, where John later staked his claim:

"Sandy, nearly worthless."

Wiltse may have lacked imagination or innate optimism, but he did judge other areas of this township to be much more promising. Perhaps those areas had already been claimed when John came on the scene.

Wiltse's concluding observations about Township 22 were a mixed bag:

"The surface of this township is gently rolling with a fair share of bottom land along the streams on the Southern Boundary. The North Eastern part of the township is more or less sandy, averaging from 3rd rate to worthless." He called the central section "generally good second rate" and said the southern portion had "first rate soil" that was "well watered by small spring brooks and larger streams" and "well adapted to agricultural purposes." Wiltse would have been referring to Union and Taylor creeks, which converge at the town of Madison, several miles south of John's claim. Township 22 would become known as Union Creek township.

Two months after Wiltse recorded those notes, he led the surveying of the adjoining township to the north, Township 23, which includes what would become Warnerville. In his field notes he paid little heed to standard grammar but left no doubt about his view of the quality of land in the spots where Lewis and Lars later settled. His notes about Section 30, which included Lewis's claim, read in part:

"Sand slightly Rolling Prairie. Soil sandy 3rd rate."

Wiltse was enthused about the potential of the northern part of the township, which is traversed from west to east by the Elkhorn River. He noted that this area "has quite large groves of timber, both cottonwood and elm." He called the soil along the river "1st rate." Lewis and Lars settled several miles to the south, where the sandy soil, in Wiltse's view, was "not of much value for agricultural purposes."

Wiltse was proved wrong.

* * *

Uncle Sam's free farms

John and Anna probably were among a multitude who saw a move to Nebraska as a fresh start and a new opportunity after toiling for little gain in Iowa. Their move fit a pattern of westward migration among first- and second-generation Swedish immigrants – generally from

Illinois and Wisconsin to Minnesota and Iowa, then to Nebraska and Kansas as well as the Dakotas, and finally to the West Coast.

By the end of the 1870s, most arable land in Iowa had been spoken for, whereas Nebraska was still up for grabs. Iowa was practically bursting at the seams with settlers compared to its neighbor to the west. The Iowa population in 1880 was 1.6 million. Nebraska's was barely a quarter of that, although growth was accelerating.

In Nebraska, the Hagglunds could avail themselves of free land as homesteaders. In Iowa they had chosen a different path; their land had originally been granted by the state to a railroad company and thus was not eligible to be claimed under the Homestead Act.

The homesteading law, while not suited for every farmer's situation, was wildly popular. (The first applicant was a Nebraskan.)

President Abraham Lincoln signed the Homestead Act in May 1862, even as the nation was convulsed by the Civil War, its very future in doubt. The law took effect Jan. 1, 1863, the same day Lincoln issued the Emancipation Proclamation to end slavery.

Any adult homesteader who met a few basic requirements could claim 160 acres of unsettled public land. You had to be 21 years old or head of a household, but you need not be an American citizen so long as you had filed a declaration of intent to become one and swore to have never borne arms against the U.S. government. This last requirement meant that when the Civil War ended in 1865, veterans of the rebel army were ineligible. In 1867 Congress agreed to allow Confederate veterans to apply for Homestead Act claims, but only if they first signed an affidavit of allegiance to the U.S. government.

Why limit a homestead to 160 acres? As good an explanation as I could find was offered in 1873 by James D. Butler in a promotional pamphlet for the Burlington & Missouri River Railroad Co., aimed at attracting settlers to Nebraska. He wrote that 160 aces "forms as large a farm as a man with two boys, or one hired laborer, can properly till." Larger homesteads, he wrote, would lead to "a sparseness of population unfavorable to schools, churches and other civilizing institutions." The railroads had a financial stake, of course, in promoting the development of communities, but they were right about the importance of social bonds.

Qualifying for a homestead was simple – in some ways so simple that the law almost invited fraud. It contained loopholes easily exploited by land speculators and cheaters. For example, a claimant was required to build a dwelling on the property, but "dwelling" was not well defined. Connivers were quick to take advantage.

The law required a "12 x 14" house but did not specify whether that was to be in feet or inches. For some, imprecision equaled opportunity. They put up tiny "dwellings."

Imaginations worked overtime.

"Some wheeled portable cabins from claim to claim and hired witnesses to swear they had seen a dwelling on the property, omitting the fact the 'dwelling' would be on a neighbor's homestead the next day," a government archivist wrote years later.[66]

"Perfecting" a claim was straightforward but not always easy. In fact, fewer than half of the Homestead Act claims filed in Nebraska were completed. As of 1880, the most common reason was the one that temporarily tripped up Lewis: failure to settle on the land with six months of claiming it. Some settlers became discouraged, gave up and moved on. Others were disqualified for not providing proof they had lived continuously on their land for the required five years.

A lot of paperwork was involved. Much of it has been preserved and can be seen online in record holdings of the National Archives and the Bureau of Land Management, the successor agency to the General Land Office that managed implementation of the Homestead Act and was responsible for disposing of public lands.

From its headquarters in Washington, D.C., the General Land

Office gave extensive "advice" to field officers who collected witness testimony, sworn affidavits and other information required before a claimant could pass muster and be granted ownership.

The land office was on guard against enterprising land speculators. It required sworn testimony from the claimant as well as two witnesses who could vouch for the claimant having lived on the land without interruption and testify that he was using the land for his and his family's exclusive use.

Here is a sample of written guidance to the local land offices on asking the right questions:

"Elicit all facts that tend to show residence, such as smoke from chimney, light seen at night through windows, family washing seen drying, paths trod, piles of wood and other fuel, cats, dogs and other domestic animals and fowls seen about the place, farming machinery, tools and evidence of daily occupation and use of the land."

Although Lewis ran into some difficulties, John Hagglund and Lars Morton seem to have stepped lightly through the bureaucratic minefields. Like many other poor immigrants in the late 19th century, they used the Homestead Act to improve their lot in life.

In its centennial year, 1962, President John F. Kennedy called the Homestead Act "the single greatest stimulus to national development ever enacted." At the time of its passage, however, many Americans were hostile to the idea of encouraging immigration; some felt Europe was dumping its undesirables – paupers, criminals and prostitutes – on America, while others saw the foreigners as extra competition for jobs.

On the whole, however, immigrants were welcomed on the prairie.

Addison Erwin Sheldon, in his 1915 book, *History and Stories of Nebraska*, recalled a song that he said was "sung everywhere" after passage of the Homestead Act:

"Come along, come along, make no delay.
  Come from every nation, come from every way.
  Our lands they are broad enough, have no alarm,
  For Uncle Sam is rich enough to give us all a farm."

Despite its initial popularity, the Homestead Act was not a panacea. The government could give away land, but it could not assure its profitability. As Lewis Hagglund's early struggle showed, it was not cheap or easy to acquire the tools, plow teams, building materials and other resources required to develop a viable farm from scratch. Bank credit was tightest when you needed it most, in those first years of scratching out a living on unbroken land.

The climate added to the difficulty.

* * *

Nebraska's 'peculiarities'

Situated about as near the middle of the country as you can get, Nebraska is on the Great Plains, the flatlands that stretch from North Dakota to north Texas and from the Missouri River to the eastern approaches to the Rocky Mountains.

Nebraska does not usually come to mind when considering the more interesting or attractive states in the union. Until migrants began arriving in droves in the 1870s and 1880s, Nebraska had been largely ignored, overlooked or carefully avoided.

As novelist Willa Cather put it in *My Antonia* in a passage describing a seemingly endless train ride across the state in which she grew up, "The only thing very noticeable about Nebraska was that it was still, all day long, Nebraska."

It would, however, be wrong to think of Nebraska as entirely featureless. It is not all grasslands and not all flat. The central and eastern parts of the state are drained by numerous rivers, the largest being the Platte, which crosses the state from west to east, spilling into the Missouri south of Omaha. West-central Nebraska is dominated by the Sandhills, a semi-arid area of grassy sand dunes where cattle ranching thrives but the human population is in decline. Farther west are ponderosa pine forests as well as spectacular geologic formations, including Chimney Rock, a slender spire that towers above the North Platte River Valley.

No doubt the character of this land — its wide-open spaces, its relentless sense of sameness — shaped the thinking and outlook of the people who tended it and drew sustenance from its fruits. Far from the cities and their crowds, these plains farmers and their families confronted an isolation that was both liberating and lonely. They were free to find their own way, in whatever way they wished. This put a premium on individual judgment and family cohesion, and on competence and self-confidence, to a degree that outsiders were unlikely to understand.

White settlement of the state began in earnest in 1854 after John C. Fremont, a military officer who in 1856 ran unsuccessfully for the White House as the Republican Party's first presidential candidate, led a series of five map-making expeditions along the Platte River between 1842 and 1853. Fremont's effort was part of a federal plan to open new overland routes to the West and draw settlers beyond the Missouri River. He spent time with the Otoe Indian tribe living along a broad river that we know as the Platte but which the Otoe called the "Nebrathka," meaning "flat water." In 1854 the name became official when Nebraska was made a U.S. territory. Before that, maps typically labeled this part of the continent "The Great American Desert." It was widely considered uninhabitable — "an unproductive waste, suited only to occupancy by wild beasts of prey, the bison and the Indian," as one writer put it in a late-19th century account.[67]

In 1867, the year the Hagglunds arrived in America, Nebraska Territory became the nation's 37th state.

Prior to this period, Nebraska had been largely left to the Indians, white trappers and adventurers. Overland trails along the Platte River led hopeful hustlers to California in the 1849 gold rush. Similarly, this territory was the first long leg of the journey for Mormons following the same trails westward in the late 1840s in search of the valley of the Great Salt Lake after having been driven out of their Utopian commune in Illinois. Later, the railroads – and in the 20th century, the interstate highways – would be built along some of the same pathways to the Pacific slope.

Luring settlers during the great Western migration of the mid-19th century was a top priority for every state that saw its future tied to railroads and agriculture. Sometimes that required artful exaggeration.

J.M. Wolfe, editor of Nebraska's first gazetteer, or business directory, wrote in 1879:

"Nebraska has exchanged its traditional character as part of the 'Great American Desert,' and is now known as one of the most fertile countries of the earth." And if his "most fertile" claim was not close enough to exaggeration, Wolfe added: "Its situation is exceedingly fortunate, being midway between ocean and ocean and upon that line of latitude which bears supremacy over all other parts of the western world."

Boosters even bragged about the "peculiarities" of Nebraska's climate.

"Nearly everyone who comes to the state feels a general quickening and elasticity of spirits," one unidentified writer is quoted as saying in a 1912 portrait of the state.[68] The writer claimed the benefits didn't stop at elevating one's mood.

"The appetite and digestion improve wonderfully," he wrote. "Mind and body are lifted up. It must originate from our peculiarities of climate. I have myself felt in this state as I have never felt it elsewhere."

It's doubtful the Hagglunds were drawn to Nebraska by considerations of climate. Whatever their reason for moving, it could not have been an easy choice. In leaving Iowa they gave up the familiarity of a Swedish immigrant community where many shared a language and customs from the homeland. They also left behind the Swedish Baptist church of which they were founding members in Kiron.

In Madison County the Hagglunds were among many other European immigrants, mostly Germans. One of John and Anna's close neighbors was Vaclav Karella, possibly a Czech (known in those days as a Bohemian), who made his homestead claim in 1880 and was naturalized in 1885, the same year as John Hagglund.

One thing they would have found all too familiar in their new setting was the threat of disease. The 1885 state census offers a glimpse of the toll it could take. In the Union Creek township where John and Anna were homesteading, 23 deaths were recorded in the 12 months ended June 30, 1885. Seventeen of the 23 were children. Eleven of the 17 died of diphtheria. In addition, one Union Creek family lost four children aged 2 to 18 to diphtheria, but they were not counted in Union Creek's total because they happened to be in a neighboring township when they died.

Typhoid also was a prominent killer at a time when many did not recognize the risks of using shallow water wells.

This and other threats to life and limb did not stop the optimists.

The local newspaper, the Madison Chronicle, quoted an excerpt from an account published in 1883 by the American Agriculturist, a New York City journal, after its editor-in-chief, David W. Judd, paid a springtime visit to Madison.

"Here, 35 miles north of the main line of the Union Pacific railroad, we are surprised at finding a land flowing with milk and honey, a population equaling in intelligence that of the older states," he wrote, combining a bit of exaggeration with a tone of condescension.

The newspaper columns oozed with confidence that boom times were coming.

"Boom" was the one-word headline atop page one of the Madison Chronicle on Christmas Day 1879. "One Million Dollars," was the sub-head, followed by an explanation: The town was expecting to attract a million dollars of investment in local industries, based on a belief that the opening of the Union Pacific's Columbus-Norfolk branch line would vault Madison into prominence. The boom never quite arrived, souring those visions of milk and honey.

The reality of those times was that settler-farmers had to make do with little. As Willa Cather put it, they had to possess the "ingenuity of shipwrecked sailors."

One of those resilient pioneers was Stephen Stork, who emigrated from England in 1852 and arrived in Madison County in 1870 after stops in New York and Illinois. His homestead was a bit north and east of the town of Madison. A local newspaper account in 1932 said Stephen at times had been ready to give up and move on, but his wife Ann talked him out of it.

"No, we have a real home for the first time in our lives," Ann is quoted as saying.[69] "Let us stay."

And so, they did.

In 2018, in a stroke of luck, I met a great-grandson of Stephen Stork. He is Earl Reed, the retired minister I mentioned earlier as a longtime resident of Warnerville. I didn't know his ancestry when he graciously invited me into his home, a few miles from the original Stork homestead. In recounting his family history, Earl mentioned the Stork name, and it rang a bell. I had seen the name in John

161

Hagglund's homestead paperwork; Stephen Stork provided written testimony in support of the Hagglund land claim; he qualified as a witness for John because the Stork homestead was next door to John and Anna's, which almost certainly means the families were acquaintances, if not friends.

17

Subduing the Soil

The absence of written remembrances of the Hagglunds' years in the Midwest makes it difficult to know how they went about their daily lives. I know almost nothing of their habits, their hobbies or what they thought of their surroundings. Lewis was an exception in this regard, in part because he had a knack for appearing in newspaper columns in Iowa, Nebraska, and beyond.

On April 25, 1884, the Denison Review, the Hagglunds' former "hometown" paper in Crawford County, Iowa, published an item under the headline, "A Letter from Nebraska." It was from Lewis. The paper's editors summarized the contents of his letter rather than publishing his actual words, but it gives a glimpse of life on the farm.

"We are in receipt of a letter to the paper from a subscriber, Mr. L. G. Haggland, located in Munson, Neb.," it began. (The slight misspelling of his surname was a common occurrence, likely explained by a typesetter's mistaking Lewis's handwritten "u" for an "a.")

"He states that the crops in his locality last year were as good as could be expected for the season. Corn planted on low ground did not mature, but that on the high, was very good and sound, and yielded from forty to fifty bushels per acre."

Lewis reported that the wheat crop was "one of the best for many years," yielding 20 to 30 bushels per acre. Even so, he, like others in the area, struggled to make a go of it. That's not surprising, given that he started from scratch, with little or no start-up capital.

In his letter to the Review, Lewis said fruit trees were bountiful in 1883, with one Nebraska county (he did not say which) growing more than 3,000 bushels of apples.

"Mr. Haggland says that the country about him is fast settling up and that their [sic] is an excellent opening for an energetic man to start a dry goods store there," the article said.

"In the fall an elevator will be needed," he told the paper, referring to a grain elevator. Usually located along a rail line, elevators were an indispensable link in the farm-to-market chain. Farmers delivered their harvested grain to a local elevator where it was weighed and graded for quality. The farmer was paid based on a schedule provided by a major grain exchange. The grain was then transported by rail to a central terminal, which in Lewis' case would have been in Omaha, Chicago or Kansas City.

Lewis's farm was along the Union Pacific rail line. The fact that no elevator operated near the depot at Munson says a lot about how undeveloped the county's agricultural system was in the mid-1880s. Two elevators eventually were built there, according to a sketch of Warnerville drawn in the 1930s based on the recollections of Maud R. Pettitt, a former resident.[70]

The April 1884 Review article based on Lewis's letter ended with this: "He promises that the readers of the paper will hear from him again." And they did. Two weeks later, in its May 9 edition, the Review published a longer article titled simply, "From Nebraska."

"We are in receipt of a second letter from T. G. Haggland, which we are obliged to condense," it began, gently suggesting that their correspondent was long-winded. This time the paper misread or mistyped his first initial and again used the "Haggland" spelling.

Lewis was business-like in his choice of topics and tone. He offered an overview of soil types and conditions not only in Madison County, where he farmed, but also in five other counties – one just to his west, one northeast of him on the Missouri River and three counties directly east between Madison and the Missouri. It seems likely that Lewis passed through those three counties east of Madison – Stanton, Cuming and Burt – on his journey from Iowa in 1881. The town of Decatur, where he likely crossed the Missouri, is in Burt County.

Referring to Antelope, Madison and Stanton counties, he identified a "strip of eight or nine miles on the south side of the Elkhorn River" where the soil is sandy.

"This sand is black and will retain moisture," he wrote. "It does not drift by the wind as will white sand, and [it] will raise good crops. Beyond this sand is yellow clay and black soil." He probably knew what he was talking about, having farmed this land himself, although his description of the crop-raising potential of sandy soil is contrary to the "third rate" and "nearly worthless" assessment of parts of this territory by government surveyors who covered it on foot in 1866.

The entire area covered by Lewis's description, from the Missouri to the Elkhorn "offer good facilities for raising cattle, as they have an abundance of fine grass which grows from two to four feet high, and plenty of good water," he said.

He sounded eager to help attract new settlers. "Coal is being found in some portions of the State," he told the paper, adding that settlers were arriving from Virginia and Indiana.

"They are mostly well-to-do farmers. Railroads are being built in all directions, so that soon there will be few towns without a road. Creameries are being rapidly established. As there are plenty of cattle, cream is plenty."

He then veered into a discussion of Arbor Day, a Nebraska idea that has endured. He said Arbor Day was conceived as a remedy for the fact that "there is a great lack of timber in Nebraska."

"This is a day designated by the governor for general tree planting. ... It occurred this year upon April 16 and was very generally observed. For the largest number of forest trees planted by one man upon this day, the state board of agriculture offered a cash prize of $50, and $25 to the person coming second."

Nebraskans are especially proud of their claim to be originators of Arbor Day, which became an annual celebration of tree planting. (County government offices still close for Arbor Day.)

It apparently didn't take the early settlers long to realize that their barren territory was in dire need of trees.

"All the early speeches and the early newspapers are filled with the thought that the prairie must be plowed and trees must be planted and made to grow before the people would have homes where they would like to live and bring up their children," Sheldon, the Nebraska historian, wrote in 1915. "Out of these plans and thinking came the idea of Arbor Day."

* * *

Steady, Steady

By 1885, Lewis and Christine were the only Hagglund children to have left the family home. Not surprisingly, the three youngest – Martha, 16, Oscar, 15, and 11-year-old John – were still on the farm. But so was the oldest, 28-year-old Andrew.

Andrew by this time seemed to have some sort of cooperative farming arrangement with his father. For reasons not apparent from available records, the 1885 census listed Andrew as operating a

200-acre farm, possibly adjacent to the 160 acres owned and farmed by his father. This is puzzling because I found no record of Andrew ever owning farmland other than a 40-acre parcel[71] that he purchased from the government the following year, 1886. Perhaps he leased the 200 acres cited in the census records.

His land patent for the 40-acre parcel is on file with the Bureau of Land Management, the successor agency to the General Land Office of the Hagglunds' era. Madison County land records show Andrew paid $1.25 an acre, for a total of $50, for his 40, adjacent to his father's homestead. Andrew's payment was made May 29, 1886 and record of the transaction was filed at the county courthouse on November 1. The next day, on November 2, he sold the land to his father for $275. (The land patent, number 4576, was issued in Andrew's name on March 19, 1890.)

With their purchase of Andrew's 40 acres, John and Anna's holdings expanded to 200 acres. Four years later they added 80 more. This marked the peak of their accumulated holdings – 280 contiguous acres — and possibly the apex of their financial health.

The outlook for the family appeared promising, at least on paper. Even the teenagers were busy. The 1885 census listed 15-year-old Oscar as a home "servant," which I take to mean he was a farmhand. He might have worked for his father or brother, since John reported that he paid $150 in wages for 26 weeks of farm labor the prior year (1884), and Andrew paid $50 in wages for nine weeks of work. The workers are not identified.

The business relationship between Andrew and his father at this point is unclear. The tradition in Sweden in the 1800s was for the eldest son to inherit the family farm. Maybe this was an influence in Andrew's arrangement with his parents. (After both parents died years later, Andrew was the court-approved administrator of his father's will, and although each of the Hagglund children was given a portion of their parents' land holdings in Cedarhome, Andrew got the single biggest share.)

A remarkably detailed, though not complete, picture of the Hagglund farms at the midpoint of the 1880s emerges from the state census, thanks to its "farm schedule" supplement, which preserved a wealth of information about each farm in the state, including individual farm production over the previous 12 months.

Even so, it is hard to judge how well John and Andrew were doing based only on a census snapshot. John is listed as owner of 160 acres – 50 in cultivation as of June 1885 and 110 in unimproved land, including "old fields." Andrew was credited with 200 acres – 56 in cultivation, 10 in "woodlands" and 134 in other categories of unimproved lands. The legal description of the land is not included, so it is unclear which 200 acres Andrew was operating.

John apparently was the more efficient farmer. He reported an estimated value of all production – sold, consumed and on hand – of $485 for 1884. Andrew's total was $266, a remarkably precise number.

Their farms, including land, fences and buildings, were valued at $2,000 each. John also reported $350 worth of farm implements and machinery ($20 more than Andrew) and $700 in livestock, which consisted of four milk cows, seven "other" cattle, and five calves born in 1884. He reported buying one cow, selling two and losing one that year. He made 300 pounds of butter on the farm; Andrew made none.

Andrew reported livestock worth $355. He had no cattle but 14 sheep and two lambs that produced 34 pounds of fleece. John had 15 sheep and four lambs, of which two were slaughtered and two died of "stress of weather," which probably meant they froze to death. He reported 42 pounds of fleece from his small flock.

John had 11 hogs; Andrew had six. John had 36 chickens that produced 400 dozen eggs during the year; Andrew had no chickens.

John had six horses; Andrew had two.

Their farming fortunes were limited by economic conditions and by Mother Nature. They were at the mercy of the climate. As in Iowa, tornados were an all-too-often menace. In September 1881, a twister smashed parts of Madison and nearby farms. I don't know whether the Hagglund place was hit. Two photos I found in the collection of my mother, Annabelle (Freberg) Burns, indicate a Hagglund farm was, indeed, damaged in a tornado, but it almost certainly was not this tornado. On the back of one photo someone wrote: "Windmill on grandpa Hagglunds old farm in Nebr. blown down by cyclone." A notation on the other photo says: "Trees on grandpa Hagglunds old farm torn out by cyclone." Almost hidden in the second photo is evidence that this was not the 1881 tornado. Partially crushed beneath the trees is an automobile, perhaps a Model T, of early 20th century vintage. So, the "grandpa Hagglund" mentioned on the photos was not John; he and Anna left Nebraska well before the first Model T hit the roads in 1908. The only Hagglunds in Nebraska at that point were Oscar and his brother John.

Even if the photos are not from the 19th century, the Madison newspaper's description of the 1881 twister makes clear that it was ruinous for some. It arrived overnight September 28-29. Lewis Hagglund and his parents were by then living on their homesteads, but it's unclear whether they suffered damage.

"At twenty minutes past one last Thursday morning a tornado, coming from a direction a little south of west, struck this town, leaving ruin and destruction in its track," the weekly Madison County Chronicle reported that same day, September 29. It said two children were killed – a four-year-old boy and a one-year-old girl. A follow-up story in the next week's edition reported the twister "carried destruction to all farmers living in its course." It said that "almost every building in town" was damaged. It named 25 properties that were "totally demolished," including the Presbyterian Church and the Chronicle's office.

The report ended with this:

"Owing to the lack of time and type – principally type – we are unable to give a better and more complete account of the disaster."

The Hagglund homestead remained an active farm for more than 100 years after they left it. When I visited the property in 2016, a young family headed by Thomas and Shelli Hintz was raising several hundred head of cattle there and growing crops, including corn, soybeans and alfalfa. A short distance from the Hintz's home stood a grassy space beneath a gnarled maple tree. Shelli told me the Hagglund home likely stood on that spot, although no trace of it remained. She said others had told her it was a small, white, two-story wood-frame house.

* * *

Lewis and Luella

At the time Lewis wrote his second letter to the Denison Review, in May 1884, he had just turned 25 and was less than a year from marrying Margaret Luella ("Ella") Sherwood. I don't know how or when they met, but they tied the knot on February 15, 1885 at her parents' house in Ulysses, a Butler County town on the Big Blue River about 35 miles northwest of Lincoln, the state capital.

Ella was born in Marion, Indiana. Lewis thus was the first Hagglund to marry a non-Swede, a significant milestone in the family's assimilation. Ella's parents – Joseph H. Sherwood and Elizabeth Mary Sherwood – were Ohio natives, and their parents were from New York and Virginia, respectively.

Ella's parents were among a handful of original members of a Methodist Episcopal congregation organized in Ulysses in the spring of 1873. The town is about 70 miles due south of where Lewis was homesteading, which makes me wonder how he happened to cross her path. He could have made the trip to Ulysses by train; a line connecting Columbus and Lincoln ran through Ulysses, starting in 1880. Maybe this was one of the places he went to find work in the early '80s — the kind of temporary absence from his homestead that John Hagglund alluded to in his affidavit supporting Lewis's land claim.

Ella was 22 when she married Lewis, 25. A short article about the wedding was published in the Elkhorn Valley News of Norfolk, and republished by the Denison (Iowa) Review a month later with what sounds like a gentle jab at Lewis.

"Mr. Haggland is a young farmer, well known to many of the readers of the News, who will extend to him and his worthy bride a hearty welcome to these parts," the story said. "Mr. Haggland is also an old resident of Crawford County, Iowa, where he has a host of friends who will be somewhat surprised as well as pleased to learn that he has carried away one of the most popular young ladies of Ulysses."[72]

The 1885 state census showed the newlyweds living in Madison County, at his homestead near Munson. Of their 160 acres, 31 were cultivated, as of 1884. They had 24 acres in corn, yielding 750 bushels; six in oats, for 45 bushels, and one acre in potatoes, producing 50 bushels. Those were about average numbers for farms in the immediate area that year. For example, Ezekiel Rowlett, the previously mentioned neighbor who began farming on his homestead a year after Lewis, had 35 acres in cultivation in 1884. The value of his 160-acre farm, including buildings and the land, was estimated at $1,500, compared to $1,200 for Lewis' farm.

171

Most farmers in this part of Madison County raised mainly corn but also had wheat; Lewis had no wheat crop that year. Most also had more livestock than Lewis.

Lewis had four horses in 1884, one milk cow, three "other" cattle and a calf. He lost one of his cattle during the year. He made 100 pounds of butter – far less than most of his neighbors, who perhaps sold significant amounts to supplement their income. Lewis had one sheep and one lamb, yielding six pounds of fleece. He had five hogs, and his six chickens produced 10 dozen eggs during the year.

Lewis had 110 acres in grasslands, of which 25 were mown, yielding 25 tons of hay.

Taken together those are not bad numbers, considering that just a few years earlier he had arrived almost penniless.

The lay of the land on Lewis's old homestead did not change greatly over the years. In the 21st century it remained an active ranch. Doug Reigle, who was growing crops and raising cattle on a portion of the former homestead when I visited in April 2016, recalled that when he was growing up in the area, his mother would send him out to pick asparagus, plums and berries that grew wildly and in great abundance along dirt pathways. That is now only a fond memory, decades after pesticides became widely used on farms large and small.

* * *

The Mortons: poorer than most

Lars and Christine's farming prospects, meanwhile, looked dim. In 1882, his first year raising crops,[73] Lars had 10 acres in corn and oats, yielding a total return of $12. Even by standards of the day, that was precious little for a family of three. Lars may have earned extra money by working part time on other farms. This was the first year of a long and severe national economic recession.

In 1883 the Mortons' fortunes improved a bit. Production increased tenfold. Lars harvested 250 bushels of corn and 175 bushels of oats on a total of 15 acres, earning $120.

In those days, ordinary people managed with little, but the Mortons were poorer than most. Census data for 1885 show that blacksmiths in Madison, for example, made at least $600 a year; a shoemaker earned $800 and a hat maker reported earning $900.

In most subsequent years, Lars cultivated more acreage and earned more money, peaking in 1887 at $290 on a harvest of 700 bushels of corn and 280 bushels of oats on 34 cultivated acres. That was his best year of the decade. The following year he suffered a major setback. He harvested 475 bushels of corn on 20 acres, earning $85, but his 15 acres of oats was destroyed in a hail storm.

The Morton farm was less productive than most others in their part of Madison County. For example, their 1884 farm income, as cited in the next year's census, was $400, reflecting the estimated value of "all farm productions" – sold, consumed or on hand. That compared to values ranging from $600 to $800 for nearby farms. The market value of the Morton farm itself, including buildings and fences, as of 1885 was $1,000. Those of their neighbors were two to four times greater.

The 1885 census was taken in June, one month after Christine had given birth to daughter number three – Blanche, whose given name was Mary Blanche. Anna was three years old and Mabel had turned one in March.

Many of their neighbors were cattle ranchers; the Mortons raised mostly crops but had some livestock. In 1884 they had four milk cows and two "other" cattle, sold two and had one in a census category defined as "died, strayed, and stolen/not recovered." They reported selling no milk from their four cows, which apparently supplied family needs only. They also made 350 pounds of butter. They had three sheep and two lambs, yielding six pounds of fleece, which also was likely for the family's own use.

They had four pigs and 24 chickens that produced 150 dozen eggs for the year. They had three horses and no oxen.

Lars got by with $175 worth of farm implements and machinery – about one-half that of his neighbors.

On the spot where Lars built his house, it remained possible in 2016 to envision what it might have looked like in the early days. The house was gone, but a newer home stood on the same spot. The owner in April 2016, Duane Zechmann, told me the house had been encircled by 70-foot cottonwoods that probably dated to the Morton years. Duane had them removed because they had weakened severely over time. Standing just a stone's throw from Duane's house was a small, wood-frame barn that he believes was the original; when he replaced the barn roof, he found three layers of brittle wood shakes, one of which he gave me as a souvenir.

By 1889 the outlook for the Mortons had not improved significantly, judging from the information Lars provided in his homestead paperwork in November of that year. He had more of some types of farm animals, but he did not mention having any chickens or sheep. He had 30 pigs and four hogs, compared to four pigs and no hogs five years earlier, plus two horses, four yearlings and three cows.

Some details in Lars' 1889 homestead testimony give a sense of what farm life was like. For example, he said they lived in a frame house that he described as "12 x 16, wing 12 x 26," with four doors and eight windows. He put the value at $250.

He also listed a 28-foot by 24-foot frame stable worth $145; a tubular well (providing drinking water for the family and the livestock) worth $80; a hog pen, $10, and a corral, $4. He described a variety of farm equipment but didn't place a value on it – one each of the following: plow, cultivator, harrow, "mowing machine," hay rake, lumber wagon, corn planter and seeder.

"Owned most of them eight years," he wrote.

As an indicator of how thoroughly the government quizzed a homesteader to ensure that he truly was living on the land as required by the Homestead Act, Lars was asked to report "what articles of furniture of every kind you keep and use in your residence on this claim and how long have you had them there."

His answer:

"Three bedsteads and bedding, two bureaus, one table, one sewing machine, one clock, eight chairs, two stoves, one cupboard." These, like his farm equipment, he had owned for eight years, dating approximately to 1881, the year he married Christine.

As the decade of the '80s closed, the Morton and Hagglund families seemed on an even keel. Lars and Christine Morton were farming as a family of seven, having added John in 1886 and Harry in 1888. Lewis and Martha Hagglund were on their homestead, and Lewis's three youngest siblings – Martha, Oscar and John – were still at home with their parents on the Union Creek farm.

This period of relative stability, however, would not last long.

18

1890s: Dry Decade, Hard Times

Despite a few stumbles, the Hagglunds and the Mortons kept their footing on the farm throughout the 1880s, even during the depression of '82-'85. But in the next decade the bottom fell out – for Nebraska's small farmers and for the national economy. Some have described the economy's tumble in 1890s as an all-out collapse; until the 1930s this was what was referred to as the Great Depression.

On a national level, the triggering event was the financial panic of 1893, when the failure of the overstretched Philadelphia and Reading Railroad led to the collapse of hundreds of banks, bankruptcy for thousands of businesses, and other economic disasters that pushed unemployment to an estimated 12 to 18 percent by 1894.

The farm economy's slide began in the late 1880s with drought and a decline in prices. Money was so tight that corn cobs became legal tender; the Madison Star reported on January 15, 1887, "Nebraska merchants are accepting corn in exchange for goods." It had become a barter economy. No wonder, then, that this marked the start of steadily declining fortunes for the Hagglunds and the Mortons.

Conditions approached dire even before the 1893 collapse. By some accounts, a full-fledged depression gripped the Great Plains by late 1889. Many desperate settlers fled the region, and the next sustained economic upswing did not begin until the turn of the century.

Addison Erwin Sheldon, the Nebraska historian, called the 1890s "the dry decade of hard times."

A tipping point came in July 1894 when a searing wind blew across much of Nebraska, leaving crops dead in their furrows. Sheldon described "a furnace wind" that ruined farms weakened by years of poor yields and low prices.

In his memoir, Charles H. Morrill, a prominent Nebraska farmer and banker, wrote that drought and hot winds destroyed crops in 1893, and that the following year was equally bad. "Some farmers shot their stock hogs to prevent their starving," he wrote.[74] "The entire state was almost in the grip of actual famine." A common question for farm families, he wrote, was where in the United States they could move to escape the heartbreak. (This reminded me of the near-famine conditions facing many in Sweden at the time of the Hagglunds' 'escape' a quarter-century earlier.)

The devastation drew the attention of a famous East Coast newspaper writer, Nellie Bly (the pen name of Elizabeth Cochrane) of the New York World. She traveled across north-central Nebraska in January 1895 and sketched what she called "tales of destitution" based on interviews with near-starving farm families.

"I saw nothing but misery and desolation," she wrote.

From the small town of Butte, in Boyd County, about 95 miles northwest of the Hagglunds' homestead, she spoke to ruined settlers whose tales convinced her that many had been duped by what she called "flowery tales" of high times and easy living in the new West.

"It is a horrible and ghastly delusion," she wrote.[75]

The Hagglunds seem to have fared better than many, perhaps because earlier hardships had taught them how to weather tough times on the prairie. Also, the climate and terrain in the area they chose to homestead was a little more forgiving for startup farmers than those in central and western Nebraska. Even so, in 1895 farmers in Madison County were questioning why they were getting only a tiny share of state relief funds for the hundreds among them lacking seed grain.

My ability to reconstruct this portion of the Hagglund story is limited by the loss of the richest source of historical data for that period – the 1890 federal census. Virtually the entire set of records was destroyed in a 1921 fire in the basement of the Commerce Building in Washington, D.C. The blaze wiped out priceless information about late-19th century American life – not just population counts but details on farming, immigration and industrialization.[76] The National Archives has called the loss "a genuine tragedy of records" of unending anguish to researchers. (For the census records collected from 1790 to 1880, all or parts of the data were required to be stored in county clerks' offices, but this was not required in 1890, so the original – and presumably only – copies were forwarded to Washington.)

Some states did their own census in 1895, but Nebraska did not. That leaves a partial gap in information about the Hagglunds between the federal censuses of 1880, when they were still in Iowa, and 1900, when most of them were newly arrived in Washington state. I managed to fill some of that 20-year gap by consulting county and city directories and state census data for Nebraska in 1885 and Iowa in 1895. I also reviewed maps and newspapers, consulted historians and contemporary farmers, and reviewed church, land and county court records.

* * *

The Hagglunds and the Lawyers

During their years in Madison County, the Hagglunds had at least three legal entanglements. The outcomes may have further soured them on life in Nebraska.

The first was a lawsuit filed in district court in March 1888 by Lewis and his father. I could not determine the nature of the dispute or its outcome.[77]

The second case began in the same month, March 1888, although the timing seems to have been coincidental. District court files and online research revealed the following:

In November 1887, as a weakened farm economy pushed the Hagglunds to seek additional sources of income, Andrew and John Hagglund entered into what looks in hindsight like a risky business deal. They jointly signed a $150 promissory note to be paid four months later (March 1, 1888) to Thomas E. Hall, who the Hagglunds said had presented himself as an inventor and agent for a Kansas City, Missouri outfit called Hall & Co.

In the Hagglunds' telling, they gave Hall the IOU with the understanding that he would send them within 30 days a sample of his invention, which he called a "hydrocarbon burner." It's unclear whether this promise was put in writing. The Hagglunds were to use the sample device, or prototype, to replicate the product and to market and sell the devices in three Madison County townships: Union Creek, Warnerville and Battle Creek. The device was described in court papers as an "attachment to or for a stove," apparently for home heating. (In his application for a patent on the device in 1889, Hall said his heater had "especial qualities to recommend its use in connection with railroad-trains, since in the event of the overturning of the heater the water in the steam-boiler will rush through the jet-openings of the burner, and thus wholly extinguish the fire, and consequently prevent the cars from taking fire.") The Hagglunds said Hall claimed to have a patent for his invention and that they were purchasing exclusive rights to sell it in their county. (A sketch of the device, as published by the U.S. Patent and Trademark Office, is reproduced in the Appendix section of this book.)

The Hagglunds signed the promissory note November 12, 1887. Eight days later, Hall, the supposed inventor, sold the note to a Madison banker, James Stuart, for $100, a one-third discount.

The problem was, Hall never provided the sample device, so the Hagglunds had nothing to replicate or to sell, meaning their $150 investment would be wasted. To them, the proper response was a no-brainer; they reneged on the promissory note. Since Stuart, the banker, was now the holder of the note, he sued the Hagglunds to force payment. Erwin W. Sims, justice of the peace for Union Creek township in Madison County, heard the case on March 9, 1888. (This was the same Sims who officiated at Lars and Christine's wedding in 1881. By the time of the lawsuit against Andrew and John Hagglund, Sims also was in the farming and real estate businesses.) The Hagglunds were represented by a local attorney named William M. Robertson.

"After hearing the evidence in the case," Sims wrote, "I find in favor of the plaintiff [Stuart]."

Presumably, Sims explained the legal basis for his decision when he announced it in the courtroom. In his written summary of the case, however, he made no mention of his reasoning. He ordered the Hagglunds to pay $153.85 – combining the value of the promissory note and $3.85 for reimbursement of Stuart's costs. He also ruled the Hagglunds owed $4.85 in court fees.

Four days later, Lars Morton got involved on behalf of his brother-in-law and father-in-law. He provided "surety" in the amount of $318, which was almost exactly double the amount the Hagglunds owed under the Sims decision. This written guarantee for double the amount apparently was required to permit the Hagglunds to undertake an appeal in Madison County District Court. On a one-page legal form that Lars signed on March 13, he pledged his $318 as a guarantee that if the Hagglunds were to lose their appeal they would "satisfy such judgment and costs."

More than a year later, on May 1, 1889, the Hagglunds got their day in District Court. It was a bad day. The jury ruled in Stuart's favor and said the Hagglunds owed him $167.65.

That same day, May 1, the Hagglunds asked for a new trial. Handwritten on a single sheet of paper, the motion by Robertson, the Hagglunds' attorney, made three arguments:

1. "That the verdict is not sustained by sufficient evidence."
2. "That the verdict is contrary to law."
3. "For error of law occurring at the trial and excepted to by the defendants."

The motion was denied. The Hagglunds had lost again.

But that still was not the end of the story. The Hagglunds took their case to the Nebraska Supreme Court. The case, "A.J. Hagglund et al., v. James Stuart," was filed March 11, 1890. In an official summary of cases the court heard in its 1890 term, I found a detailed but not complete picture of how the affair unfolded.

The gist of the Hagglund argument was that prior to signing the $150 promissory note, John and Andrew had obtained an "express agreement and understanding" with Hall that he would ship the prototype to them within 30 days and that the $150 bought them the right to market the burner in the three Madison County townships. It also was payment for "royalties, or in part payment for royalties" to Hall for burners they expected to sell. They said they would not have signed the promissory note "had they not been induced to do so through and by" Hall's assurances.

They asserted that everything Hall had told them was "false and untrue in every particular." The sales territory they were promised in the deal was "a fraud and myth," they argued, as was the agreement to provide the prototype burner.

It seems that Hall did give the Hagglunds a written contract in exchange for the promissory note, but it does not appear in the court records.

The Hagglunds' argument to the Supreme Court included this curious sentence:

"These defendants [the Hagglunds] do not know whether the person who took the [promissory] note was Thomas E. Hall, or who he was, or whether there is such a person living, or such a firm in existence as Hall & Co." They added: "Whoever the person was, he represented himself to be Thomas E. Hall, and by his false and fraudulent representation aforesaid induced these defendants to give the note."

In other words, they believed they had been snookered, although it was Stuart the banker who was left holding the bag.

The Supreme Court, in a decision signed by the chief justice, Amasa Cobb, wrote that the facts presented by the Hagglunds, "although obviously difficult to prove, are, if true, susceptible of proof, and if proved would establish fraud" on the part of Hall. The judge said Hall's failure to ship the prototype burner was a breach of contract, but not fraud. On the other hand, if Hall had falsely claimed to the Hagglunds that his device had been patented, then the claim would constitute a fraud that would "vitiate," or destroy the legal validity of, the promissory note. Justice Cobb seemed to believe the Hagglunds had not been given sufficient chance to prove their case.

"The judgment of the district court is reversed, and the cause remanded for further proceedings," Cobb wrote.

It turns out that Hall did not, in fact, have a patent for his device at the time he made the deal with the Hagglunds. He applied for a patent on March 20, 1889, more than a year after he took the promissory note. The patent (No. 405,884) was approved on June 25, 1889. The paperwork, including professional-looking line drawings of the "hydrocarbon burner" and Hall's highly technical explanation of how it worked, is preserved in the archives of the U.S. Patent and Trademark Office.

I was unable to determine how the case turned out after the Supreme Court sent it back to the Madison County District Court to be adjudicated again.

The third lawsuit involving the Hagglunds was brought by Andrew in April 1892. He was trying to collect on a bill of $61.70 for work he had done for a man named S.J. Adair. I don't know the type of work involved, but at the time Andrew was in the windmill, plumbing and well-digging business. He petitioned the district court to compel Adair to either pay his bill or sell his property to raise the money owed. Adair owned 160 acres just south of the Hagglund homestead. Andrew asked the judge to foreclose on a mechanic's lien, [78] — a hold against Adair's property — which he had filed in court on January 30, 1891. I was unable to learn how the case turned out.

19

Real Estate Shuffle

I n early 1892, less than two years after John and Anna had expanded their land holdings by purchasing an 80-acre parcel from a railroad, the ground beneath their feet suddenly shifted, setting family history on a new course. They and their sons Andrew and Lewis, as well as their son-in-law Lars Morton, made a series of land deals that suggest their farming days were over, or nearly so.

It appears they were all but forced off their homesteads by unrelenting financial headwinds. This was not a rare occurrence in late-19th century Nebraska — a stormy, even devastating, time for small farmers. The trouble for the Hagglunds and the Mortons came on the cusp of a national financial panic and happened to coincide with their next great personal tragedy.

This sequence spans nearly 10 years and ends with John and Anna selling their homestead and moving to Washington state at the turn of the century. Not every detail of every land transaction is recounted here; the main points give a sense of how earnestly the Hagglunds and Mortons struggled to stay afloat as they transitioned from farmers to town dwellers.[79]

It began in January 1892 when John and Anna sold their land –

all 280 acres, including the original homestead – to their newlywed daughter Martha and her husband, August Tackstrom. The sale price was $4,000, with Martha and August assuming her parents' $2,000 mortgage "and taxes for 1890 and 1891." The fact that John and Anna were slightly behind on their taxes suggests they were struggling. However, just 10 months later they reacquired title to the property, paying Martha and August a token $1. Might this have been an arrangement in which John and Anna held title to the land while Martha and August farmed it? That seems likely, since John and Anna seem to have maintained a residence in the town of Madison from about 1892 until they moved to Washington state at the end of the decade.

Also in January, John and Anna made another curious transaction. They sold back to their son Lewis the 160-acre homestead that they had purchased from him in May 1887. It's unclear why Lewis sold it to his parents in the first place. John and Anna paid him $1,500 for the land; he bought it back five years later for $1,750. In the interim, Lewis apparently continued to farm there.

In February 1892, one month after selling the homestead to Martha and August, John and Anna acquired two town lots in Madison. The lots were on Block 53 of what was called the F. W. Barnes Railroad Addition, an area annexed by the city with the arrival of the Union Pacific line on the town's west side.

Land records show that a Madison widower, Francis E. Cramer, sold the two lots and a portion of a third to "Anna Haggelund" for $1 on February 17, 1892. Two oddities about this transaction remain a mystery: why John's name is not included on the land deed, which I reviewed myself at the country courthouse, and why Cramer, who died 11 months later, accepted a token $1 for the land.[80] These were not empty lots. Two days after the sale, a newspaper report made clear that a house stood on one of the two contiguous properties – or straddled the two.

"F.E. Cramer has sold his residence in west Madison to John Hagglund," it said.

The newspaper offered an update five months later that suggests the Hagglunds used the former Cramer house as their residence, not a rental. "Mrs. Annie Hagglund is having city water put in at her residence in west Madison," it said. So now, John and Anna were off the farm. The unanswered question is why.

I found it surprising that John and Anna became townfolk, given their rural background. Madison was no metropolis, but it was a significantly different setting.

The properties Anna received from Cramer were Lots 19 and 20 in Block 53 and the east 22 feet of Lot 5 in Block 11 of the original town limits. That last property – Lot 5 of Block 11 – seemed to be an especially prime location, but I could not determine how the Hagglunds used it. It was two blocks west of Madison's central street, which was called Pearl at the time and today is called Main. Pearl was lined with businesses and a diverse collection of small shops – a blacksmith and wagon shop, multiple banks, the Madison Hotel, a shoemaker's shop, a photo studio and others.[81]

One or both of the other two lots – numbers 19 and 20 – became their home. The street address was 510 West 3rd Street. An 1896-97 Madison city directory shows that John and Anna lived there with Andrew and his youngest brother, John. Anna was listed as a "carpet weaver," apparently putting to use the weaving skills she learned in Sweden. (The skill was so common among women in her home county of Jämtland that there is a term, "jämtlandsdräll," called crackle weave in the United States, that refers to weave structure of Swedish origin.)

John was listed simply as "resident," and Andrew as operator of a "pumps, wind mills, tubular wells" business located at 514 West 3rd

Street, which was near, if not next door to, their home at 510 West 3rd. Their son John was listed as "farmer," with a note that he was a boarder at 510. The household arrangements would have changed at some point in 1896; John got married that summer.

Andrew joined the Madison real estate action in March 1892, one month after his parents bought Lots 19 and 20. For $160 he bought Lots 16 and 17 on the same block. He apparently located his plumbing business on one or both of his properties. At the time, this block was divided into 24 narrow lots; later they were consolidated into five lots, so the house numbers on the block when I visited in 2016 did not correspond to those from the 1890s. As a result, neither street address – the Hagglund residence at 510 West 3rd nor Andrew's shop at 514 on West 3rd – exists today. My research and my visit convinced me those two addresses were slivers of what became a single parcel at 506 West 3rd Street.[82]

Standing on that space when I visited in 2016 was a narrow, wood-frame house built in 1890, which means it is possible that it was once owned by one of the Hagglunds.

Even after buying the two lots near his parents' place in March 1892, Andrew was not done dealing. Two years later, on December 20, 1894, he bought Lot 14 in the same block (Block 53, Railroad Addition) from George and Amelia Savidge for $225. Two days later he signed for a $479.39 mortgage held by George Savidge, using Andrew's three lots – numbers 14, 16 and 17 – as collateral. The mortgage was to be paid down in installments over three years.

These purchases suggest Andrew had given up on crop farming, although he later ran a seasonal grain-threshing business in addition to his plumbing services, sometimes called the "wells and pumps" business.

The series of land deals that began in early 1892 also included Lars and Christine Morton. On February 26, a little over two weeks after

Christine gave birth to Clara, they sold their 160-acre homestead to Thomas Malone for $2,400. Malone was a prosperous cattle and hog breeder, real estate broker and local Democratic Party bigwig. By one account,[83] he founded the nearby town of Enola and gave it its name by spelling his own backwards, minus the "M."

The Mortons' deal with Malone was structured as a "subject to" sale, meaning the buyer would make payments on the existing $600 mortgage but not assume legal liability for it – not unlike the arrangement John and Anna made when they sold their Iowa farm to Gust Anderson in 1878. Thus, the Mortons' mortgage remained in their name even though they gave up the land deed. This seems to have been a sign of financial distress on their part. Land records show Lars was released from the mortgage in November 1899.

I don't know why the Mortons sold out, but financial strain would seem a fair guess. This may also have coincided with the onset of a disease that apparently struck Christine as early as 1892 and that probably meant substantial medical bills. It seems likely they moved into Madison at about this time, but I have no direct evidence of that.

It may have been coincidence of timing, but on February 17, 1892, about a week before the Mortons sold their homestead, Anna Hagglund took ownership of the two town lots in Madison that she had received from Francis E. Cramer for $1. If it was not a coincidence, might this have been an arrangement meant to accommodate an ill or disabled Christine?

Anna and John retained all three of their town lots until November 1902, when they sold 19 and 20 to a Madison farmer named John C. Botts for $450. At that point the Hagglunds were living in Cedarhome, Washington; they signed the documents in nearby Stanwood, where they were notarized by Whitfield C. Brokaw.[84]

* * *

Mortgaged to the hilt

From county land records it is hard to judge how badly the three original homesteaders – John and Anna Hagglund, Lewis Hagglund, and Lars Morton – were burdened by their mortgage debt. They mortgaged their homesteads multiple times – not uncommon for farmers struggling in an era of extreme hardship.

John and Anna, for example, took out a five-year $800 trust deed (functionally the same as a mortgage but with a different process in the event of foreclosure), in November 1886, as soon as they had completed the "proving up" process for their 160-acre claim. In keeping with usual practice, they also had to take out a commission mortgage – $80, in this case – to pay the broker who arranged the farm mortgage.

This happened virtually simultaneously with their purchase of Andrew's 40 acres, which gave them a total of 200 acres to use as collateral on the $800 loan, which carried a 7 percent interest rate. The five-year term seems short by today's standard, but it was normal at the time.

Two years later, in November 1888, they took out a second five-year mortgage on the same 200 acres. This one was for $1,500, plus a commission mortgage of $153.33. They paid those off in full on January 9, 1894.

They were not done borrowing. In the summer of 1890 John and Anna bought 80 acres (North half of the southwest quarter of Section 1 in Union Township), adjacent to their original homestead, from the Chicago, Burlington & Missouri River Railroad Co., for $400. Using that land as collateral, they took out a $500 mortgage from Farmers Loan & Trust Co., to be repaid by June 1895. The commission mortgage on this was $50; it was paid off in ten semiannual installments of $5 each.

This brings us to the period in which the Mortons and some of the Hagglunds began selling off their farms, even as John and Anna kept borrowing. In 1894, John and Anna took on a $1,500 five-year mortgage and a $119 one-year loan,[85] followed by a $195 loan the next year, and in 1898 they borrowed $391 from a local attorney.

Finally, in April 1899 John and Anna took out the largest mortgage of this whole sequence, seemingly a sign that they had no plan to sell the farm and move away. And, yet, less than one year later they *did* sell and move away. This mortgage was a five-year trust deed for $2,400. The lender was New York Chemical Bank. The Hagglunds used their full 280 acres as collateral, and the mortgage was co-signed by Andrew. The full amount, $2,400, was due April 10, 1904, but they paid it off early, in March 1902 – more than two years after they had moved to Washington and one month after completing the sale of their homestead.

20

A 'Medical Ignoramous'

T he backdrop to the Hagglunds' real estate scramble was the economic depression of the mid-1890s, felt widely among farm families. For the Hagglunds and Mortons, the financial pain coincided with a more personal blow that resounded across decades and set in motion surprising changes.

The blow was struck on Wednesday, August 2, 1893. That evening, while in the care of three flawed doctors in Madison, Christine Morton died in anguishing circumstances. The doctors were not what they might seem at first glance. In trying to extend the life of the 30-year-old mother of six, they may have hastened its end. At the least, it appears Christine could have been spared some of her distress as she lay near death with husband Lars and other family members probably waiting in fear.

Hindsight being imperfect and documentation incomplete, it is impossible to know exactly what happened.[86] I found no family records about this, but there is reason to believe the episode was exceptionally upsetting. One version of events was told in a Hagglund family letter to the local newspaper, the *Madison Chronicle*. The letter was never published in full and no copy is known to have survived, but in two years of research I found telling snippets that give a more detailed understanding of what happened than was revealed in initial news reports.

The day after Christine died, the tragedy was recounted ever so briefly by the *Chronicle*. A day after that, on August 4, a longer, more detailed account appeared in a rival newspaper, the *Madison County Reporter*, whose editor and publisher, J. H. Mackay, happened to be one of the three doctors present at her death.

It seems reasonable to think the *Reporter*, as the paper was commonly called, framed the story in a way that undercut any idea that Mackay might be at fault, if there was in fact blame to be assigned. Mackay very likely wrote the story himself.

The *Reporter* story began with the dubious assertion that Christine had been "a semi-invalid for a number of years." Depending on what was meant by "semi-invalid," this seems an exaggeration; she had given birth to Clara just 18 months earlier.

Further setting the stage for the fatal outcome, the story said Christine had been "hovering upon the borders of the eternal land for several days" before the operation.

"Her trouble was blood poisoning from internal inflammation which caused a form of abscess to gather, and the absorption from this disturbed her system so as to cause death," it said.

The story summarized the surgical operation: "The abdomen was opened and the cyst containing the poisonous matter removed. The parts were cleaned of all poison and the diseased tissue removed. She stood the operation well, but her general condition remained unchanged and the poison already in her system did its fatal work."

The article then presented what amounts to a justification of the doctors' actions, perhaps knowing or anticipating that some in her family would find fault with them. It said the operation was performed at the "urgent request" of Christine, with the consent of her husband and relatives and upon the advice of several unnamed physicians "as the only thing that could offer any possible hope for the patient who had only a day or two to live at best without an operation."

"The result showed that it was but a hope – a grasping at a straw, but it was justifiable under the circumstance."

The story said Christine "some time ago" had undergone an operation in Omaha with no resulting improvement in her condition. Perhaps she had gone to see Dr. Dellizon A. Foote. He led the ill-fated surgical procedure the night of her death; his practice was based in Omaha.

"All will sorrow with the brave woman who endured her long term of suffering with such patience and fortitude, waiting for her change to come," the story said.

The town's other newspaper, the *Chronicle*, published only a brief account but mentioned a more specific illness.

"Mrs. L.G. Morton has been very ill for some time with an ovarian disease," it began flatly, "and yesterday Dr. Foote, of Omaha, assisted by Drs. Mackay and Hutchinson, of this city, performed an operation upon the lady." Before publication the *Chronicle* apparently received a late update, and to the sentence above it added this: "LATER – Mrs. Morton died last night at 9 o'clock."

The holes in both stories are obvious. What was the nature of the "internal inflammation" that had led Christine to her death bed, as described by the Reporter? What was the "ovarian disease" cited by the *Chronicle*? Why were those three doctors involved? We may never know the answer to those and other questions, but we know enough to question the accuracy or completeness of the newspapers' accounts and to wonder whether the doctors made mistakes of judgment or procedure. It certainly is possible Christine would have died no matter what the doctors had done, and yet something about this episode seems amiss.

Christine's eldest child, Anna, who was 11 at the time, recalled many years later that her mother died of appendicitis. That may be true, or it may have been what the adults told the children to avoid a more gruesome, complicated truth. But if the fatal illness was appendicitis, then the "ovarian" surgery may have been aimed at the wrong problem. In any case the circumstances were suspicious.

Lars and the Hagglund family wanted answers. They tried to press the issue publicly, as reflected in an article that appeared in the following week's edition of the *Chronicle*.

"We have received a lengthy communication, signed by every member of the Hagglund family, telling their side of the story in connection with the operation performed upon their relative, Mrs. Morton, who died last week, shortly after the operation," it said. Hutchinson, one of the attending doctors, later claimed the letter had been written by Lewis Hagglund and that he had added the names of other Hagglund family members without their permission. It's hard to imagine how Hutchinson could have known this unless he had discussed it with Lewis or other family members. At any rate, the letter's authorship is not the main point.

"The article particularly censures Drs. Mackay and Hutchinson," the *Chronicle* said of the family's letter, "but as the unfortunate lady is dead and beyond recall, we do not see how any good can be accomplished by publishing it at this time. Anyhow, we haven't space for it this week."

In that same edition of the paper, August 10, 1893, the *Chronicle* also published a note from Lars Morton thanking community members for their support and sympathy.

"We desire to extend our thanks to neighbors and friends, who so kindly assisted us during the illness of our late wife and mother," it said. "Also, for the floral offerings, words of sympathy and assistance rendered at the burial of our loved one." It was signed "L.G. Morton and Family."

That was a gracious gesture, given the family's distress and apparent anger. Christine was buried at Crown Hill Cemetery (known at the time as the Clausen Cemetery) at the south end of Madison in one of eight plots purchased by "A. Haggland" (apparently Andrew) for $20. The undertaker was a Norwegian immigrant named Jacob Henderson who also was a furniture and cabinet maker. When I first visited in 2016, I found that Christine's grave is unmarked; it is noted in cemetery records as "Grave 1, Lot 6, Section 9," which is toward the front of the cemetery, just south of the circle driveway. The only personal information recorded in cemetery records is the surname of the interred – Hagglund – her last residence, Madison, and her "social state," married. I was shown the original records by their keeper, Eugene Trine, president of the Madison cemetery association.

Since the Hagglund letter to the *Chronicle* amounted to a "censure" of two of the three doctors involved, it's clear they found fault with them or their methods. Less clear is whether Lars or the Hagglunds contemplated legal action. My review of county court records and local newspapers turned up no sign of a lawsuit.

The Hagglund letter seems to have been lost to history, and with it a fuller understanding of Christine's death. But I did find additional, revealing clues, including an excerpt from the letter.

Of the three doctors involved, only the two criticized by the Hagglunds – William F. Hutchinson and J.H. Mackay – seem to have had anything to say publicly about the episode. On August 17, two weeks after Christine's death and one week after the *Chronicle*'s mention of the Hagglund complaint, the *Chronicle* ran this one-sentence note:

"Dr. Hutchinson informs us that he had nothing whatever to do with the operation performed upon Mrs. Morton, and was simply a spectator, at the invitation of the other physicians."

Was he really just a bystander? The first *Reporter* account of August 4, which was certainly not unsympathetic to Hutchinson, said he was "present and assisted Dr. Foote," who performed the surgery. It also said Mackay administered anesthesia. That sounds as if all three men were actively involved.

Hutchinson advertised himself as an expert in women's illnesses, or, as he put it in one-line blurbs published frequently in the Chronicle during the 1890s, "Dr. Hutchinson, female diseases a specialty." He seemed to have peculiar non-medical interests; the June 19, 1896 edition of the *Madison Star* newspaper said he "has decided to place his eight-legged calf on exhibition July 4th in our city."

Several months after Christine's death, Hutchinson announced plans to convert his home to what he called a "Private Hospital for Women and Children." This was not a hospital of the kind we commonly think of in the 21st century. In rural Nebraska at the time, hospitalization simply was not considered necessary or even desirable. The Madison newspapers made mention of Hutchinson's expansion plans in late April 1894. The *Reporter* said he planned to build a two-story addition to his residence and use it to "receive chronic and surgical patients and treat them and furnish rooms and board." It said he had arranged with an Omaha doctor to do "surgical operations." The *Chronicle* reported that Hutchinson simply put a new sign on his home reading, "Private Hospital for Women and Children."

The 1896 edition of the Polk Medical and Surgical Register of the United States said Hutchinson's facility opened for business in 1895 and advertised a capacity of 14 patients. Hutchinson billed himself as "physician-in-charge."

A deeper look at Hutchinson's background gives reason to doubt his record and reliability.

Hutchinson is included in a set of biographical sketches of Madison's earliest doctors written in 1930 by Francis A. Long, the doctor mentioned earlier as author of a book-length memoir, *A Prairie Doctor of the Eighties*. Long was a local physician who rose to become president of the Nebraska State Medical Association in 1906. In his 1930 sketch of local doctors, Long offered a less-than-flattering view of Hutchinson's credentials. He said that before coming to Madison, Hutchinson had been a "fulminate mixer" for an ammunition company in Bridgeport, Connecticut, meaning he helped prepare chemical ingredients for explosives.

Long said Hutchinson claimed to have earned a diploma from a college in Keokuk, Iowa, "which was afterward found to be bogus."

In his memoir, Long again took aim at Hutchinson without mentioning his name. He called him a "medical ignoramus" and said he had claimed to have been physician to the Queen of England. I am certain Long was referring to Hutchinson because he mentioned that the object of his scorn had been "fulminate mixer for the Union Metallic Cartridge Company at Bridgeport, Conn."

"He had not the slightest claim to being a physician," Long wrote.

One day after the Chronicle published Hutchinson's note denying he had played any role in Christine's surgery, he made it known he was not going to let the matter rest. He wrote a blistering rebuttal to the unpublished Hagglund family letter, which he seemed to have read. In his broadside, published by the *Reporter* on August 18, he not only denied the *Chronicle*'s report that the Hagglunds had aimed their criticism at him, he also threw barbs at the Mortons, the Hagglunds and the *Chronicle*'s editor and publisher, Carl T. Seely.

Hutchinson's letter was a mixture of calm self-defense and full-throated attack. He got highly personal, although his main purpose seemed to be to dispute the *Chronicle*'s characterization of the

Hagglund letter, which he said was written by Lewis.

"It [the Hagglund letter] simply stated that I was invited to be present at the operation without the Hagglunds having been consulted, which was no reflection on me as I was ignorant of that fact," he wrote. (In fact, that was not the main point of the Hagglund letter, as I will show shortly.) Hutchinson added sarcastically, "And anyhow, Mr. and Mrs. Morton and the physicians in charge would scarcely be expected to consult the third cousins of the unfortunate woman away back in Sweden before having the operation performed."

He went on to belittle the Mortons and Hagglunds by saying they should never have made a public issue of Christine's death.

"This was not a matter of public concern, but some addle patted people seem to be possessed with a mania scribendi, and rush into print with their family tittle tattle on every possible occasion," Hutchinson wrote. (A "mania scribendi" is an uncontrollable urge to write regardless of the quality of the composition.) He added that the Chronicle editor was "malicious" and guilty of a "disgraceful abuse" of his responsibilities as a newspaper publisher.

"If the Hagglunds had a grievance one would think they could find yourself [Mackay] or myself at our offices, and failing to get satisfaction the courts are open to them, and the public will wonder why they should rush into a newspaper."

An unsigned note, probably written by Mackay as the paper's editor, was placed after Hutchinson's sign-off. It said, "We ... endorse every word he says," and closed with this line: "Further, if Carl T. Seely or the Hagglund family have a personal grievance against the editor of this paper they can find him at his place of business 313 days in the year, and they can thus avoid inflicting upon the public another eruption of their ideas about the Morton operation."

The Hutchinson volley was not the end of the story. Seely's *Chronicle* returned fire.

In its August 24 edition, the *Chronicle* said it did not want to "jump on a sick man" but felt compelled to answer Hutchinson's claim in the Reporter that the Hagglunds had not "censured" him.

"The only reason we did not publish the Hagglund letter was simply because it did reflect upon Dr. Hutchinson, and we thought he had had enough trouble since coming to Madison, but it appears the gentleman wants a little more free advertising, and we herewith publish that portion of the Hagglund letter referring to Dr. Hutchinson:"

(Seely seemed to forget that two weeks earlier he had said the Hagglund letter was not published because it would do no good and because of a lack of space in the paper.)

What followed were two paragraphs quoted directly from the letter – the first one starting mid-sentence:

> *"... that when she (the patient) learned that Dr. Hutchinson had been called by the other physicians to assist, she told the other physicians that if they could not operate upon her without the assistance of Dr. Hutchinson she did not want an operation; that she had no confidence in Dr. Hutchinson."*

> *"Why did not Dr. Hutchinson, in the name of honesty, withdraw from the case when he learned that the patient did not want him? Then the operation would have been POSTPONED, which certainly would have been the proper thing to do with a dying woman. Then she could have died in peace."*

The *Chronicle* closed with this comment aimed at Hutchinson: "Now, if that isn't censure, we will confess that we were wrong in saying that the Hagglund letter censured Dr. Hutchinson."

The newspaper never published the rest of the letter, so it's hard to know what else the family found objectionable beyond the unwanted participation of Hutchinson. What was their complaint about Dr.

Mackay? Given the generally reserved nature of the Hagglunds, I can only imagine the depth of anger and sense of injustice that drove them to seek a public airing of the matter.

Four months later, Hutchinson was still seething. An unsigned item in the December 29 edition of the *Reporter* said Hutchinson was "after some of the people with a club who have been damaging his reputation, and he promises to make it interesting." In words that sounded like they came from Mackay, the item went on to say, "We don't blame the doctor; he has been a butt of some parties' malice ever since he came to town, and he says he is going to make it hot for people who attempt to damage his reputation." No names were mentioned, but it's hard to imagine this did not refer at least in part to the Hagglund matter.[87]

The other two doctors involved in Christine's surgery were practitioners of homeopathic medicine. Mackay was a graduate of Hahnemann College of Chicago and advertised that he held a "certificate" from the Illinois State Board of Health, which may have given him legitimacy in those days but did not necessarily mean, in today's terms, that he was fully qualified to practice medicine.

An advertisement for his services, published in his newspaper the same month Christine died, said "Special attention given to surgical and obscure cases." A year earlier his newspaper ad said he "treats the medical and surgical diseases of mankind."

Mackay was a vocal crusader for homeopathy, which at the time was considered a radical alternative to conventional medical practices. Some saw homeopaths as quacks, although many were graduates of reputable medical schools and later became generally accepted in medical societies. Mackay, however, espoused ideas that today sound like something well beyond quackery.

During his tenure as superintendent of the State Hospital for the Insane, which began in May 1895, Mackay gave a speech that was stunning in its presentation of mental illness as a byproduct of physical deformity, and shocking in its prescribed solutions.[88]

"A unique fact in connection with the insane is that any injury producing pain, such as a scald, burn or corporeal punishment, as well as shock or fright, has a remarkably salutary influence in brightening up the minds of the insane," he said. "It would be interesting," he added, "to try the results of scorching the soles of the feet or of ... bloodletting, fright and shock in some of the chronic cases of insanity and confirmed melancholia and mania."

He flatly rejected the idea that these should be considered barbaric acts.

"No treatment is barbarous that benefits a patient and releases his mind from the fog and gloom of insanity, however painful that treatment might be," he said.

He seemed proud of his institution's unorthodox methods, which he said included "a very large number of orificial operations," and "radical operation for cure of hernia." Each of the 350 patients there was treated medically or surgically, he said.

Six times in the past four months, he said, patients with misshapen skulls, which he believed were the root cause of insanity, had undergone reshaping operations – "with the happiest of results" – using a trephine, a surgical instrument with a cylindrical blade used to cut bone.

Two-thirds of his patients, he said, were "scrubs," which he defined as "driftwood, biped animal toadstools; flat-chested, thin-legged, lop-shouldered, sway-backed ... bow-legged ... anthropoid allies without energy, ambition or prospect."

His solution: "abridge the life" of these unfortunates, quarantine others, and "prevent, as far as possible, the birth of such." This sounds a lot like the eugenics movement, which aimed to improve the genetic composition of the human race through selective breeding and involuntary sterilization of those with "inferior" traits.

How and why Mackay was involved in Christine's surgery on the night she died is unknown. Long, the local doctor who compiled the 1930 sketches of Madison-area doctors, called Mackay brilliant but erratic. He said Mackay had resigned his position as superintendent of the insane asylum in Norfolk "under some pressure," which was a gentle way of putting it. Mackay had been accused of professional misconduct but was cleared after a contentious investigation.

The allegations, mostly by employees at the insane asylum, were summarized as follows:

"Dr. J. H. Mackay is and ... has been cruel, unjust, foul of speech, neglectful of duty, coarse and ungentlemanly to visitors, rude and insulting with some employees but unduly and improperly intimate with others, grossly partial, quarrelsome, vulgar, incapable and licentious."[89]

The Mackay case, which played out in April 1896, was such a big deal in Nebraska that the governor, Silas Holcomb, felt compelled to attend a public hearing in Norfolk. He personally questioned all who testified. The *Norfolk Daily News* filled nearly two full pages with its report under the headline, "The Asylum Row."

Mackay testified in his own defense, and the governor – whose most vocal supporters in the 1894 election included Mackay – ultimately ruled in his favor. Mackay later called his accusers an "unscrupulous and malicious gang of traitors." A brief item in the *Madison Star* on January 15, 1897 said he had "resigned as superintendent of the Norfolk asylum and will open an office in Norfolk for the practice of medicine." The news item made no mention of the legal case.

In the year following Christine's death, Mackay made a name for himself in Madison and beyond with a crusading form of journalism. As editor and publisher of the *Madison County Reporter*, he pushed hard to stamp out vice crimes, including prostitution. (His newspaper noted in May 1894 that Madison had attracted too many prostitutes. Lock them up, he wrote, "and the city will cease to be such an El Dorado.")

Mackay paid a price for this crusade. In May 1894 his paper reported that a local man, Peter Oberg — who years later would buy a piece of Madison property from John J. Hagglund — was arrested after police "discovered a female of easy virtue domiciled and receiving company" in Oberg's plumbing shop. The following month Oberg sought revenge. In Mackay's telling, Oberg attacked him with an 18-inch steel file used to sharpen plow blades; Mackay suffered a broken rib and seven stab wounds, one of which cut an artery in his left leg, "and his shoe was overflowing and his pants crimson in a few seconds with his life-blood."

The article was unsigned, but the word choices – "toadstool," for one – suggest it was written by Mackay. It went on:

"An item in the Reporter chronicling the arrest of Oberg for maintaining a lewd resort and harboring a woman of ill-fame in his place of business probably stirred the otherwise lethargic and phlegmatic animal toadstool to give vent to his latent viciousness and murderous inclinations."

This was not the first time Mackay had been targeted by people he had embarrassed in print. Earlier in 1894 a saloon keeper's wife and son came at him with horse whips after the Reporter published a story accusing the saloon keeper of "selling liquor to drunkards."

The third doctor involved in Christine's surgery was Dellizon A. Foote, a native of Ohio and the son of a Civil War veteran. His medical practice was in Omaha, about 100 miles southeast of Madison. The fact that he traveled such a distance to attend to Christine strongly suggests that he had been involved in her earlier treatment; this may align with the mention in the *Reporter*'s August 4 report that Christine had previously undergone an operation in Omaha. It also suggests that Lars Morton, perhaps assisted by the Hagglunds, had to put up significant sums of money for Foote's services and travel.

Foote had credentials. He was an 1887 graduate of the Chicago Homeopathic Medical College and interned at the Chicago Homeopathic Hospital before starting his own practice in Omaha in 1888 as a general practitioner. In 1891 he attended Martin's Course of Operative Gynecology in Berlin, Germany.

His writings indicate that he had extensive experience in gynecology. He wrote an article titled, "Uterine Fibroids," published in the January 1903 edition of the *Medical Forum*, a professional publication. Apropos of Christine's case, he also seems to have had some expertise in handling appendicitis; he wrote an article in 1903 titled, "Surgery of the Appendix," although I could not find a copy.

Nothing I found in Foote's professional record suggests quackery, although one wonders about the implications of the story that follows.

In March 1892, just 17 months before Christine's death, Foote and Hutchinson were involved in a surgery that led to both being sued for malpractice. The suit was filed by John C. Griswold, a Madison tinner, a trade also known as a tinker or tinsmith, who made and repaired tinware such as cups and candleholders.

Griswold accused the doctors of negligence in misdiagnosing his wife, Elizabeth Griswold, as suffering from an ovarian tumor, and of lying about having removed it.

According to two independent summaries of the court case, plus a news account, John and Elizabeth traveled to Omaha, where Foote operated on her with Hutchinson and other doctors present. Afterward, Foote proclaimed success. He collected his $200 fee and told the couple that a large tumor had been removed.

The *Madison Independent Reporter* (later renamed the *Madison County Reporter*), spread this version of events, taking Hutchinson at his word when he told the paper a tumor weighing nearly 20 pounds had been removed from Elizabeth and that she had emerged no worse for wear. (At the time, Mackay had not yet taken over as the paper's editor.)

"Dr. Hutchinson states that of all operation(s) ... of which he has taken part, or which he has witnessed, this was the most carefully and skillfully performed," the story said, adding that he called the operation a "happily successful one."[90]

The problem with this story was not just the exaggerated weight of the tumor. The problem was that there was no ovarian tumor to begin with, and Foote knew it.

The owner of the hospital testified that shortly after the surgery, Foote insisted she (the owner) not reveal the true outcome. The hospital owner said Foote informed her – but not the Griswolds – that the only tumors found during the operation were "immovable fibroid tumors of the uterus." Mr. Griswold claimed that the doctors did not reveal they had found fibrous tumors until after he had filed suit.

Elizabeth survived the surgery, but her husband claimed she was permanently injured. He sued for negligence.

Documents in the archives of the Madison County District Court show John Griswold filed his suit May 26, 1892. A Madison newspaper note about his case in early June said he sued Hutchinson and Foote for $10,000 on grounds that their treatment of his wife was "careless, negligent and improper." For some reason, Griswold's wife, Elizabeth, filed a separate, similar suit against the two doctors.

Shortly after the Griswolds filed their suits, a medical journal called the *Omaha Clinic* published a short article highlighting the main arguments in the case. It said Foote performed the operation at Omaha's Methodist Hospital "in the presence of a number of the Homeopathic fraternity." It described Foote as the homeopathic staff surgeon at the hospital. Two months after the surgery, the case was "brought to the attention" of the hospital's board of trustees, which held a hearing to consider what had happened. The medical journal's report said the hospital's chief of staff, Dr. B.F. Crummer, "gave as his opinion" that both Foote and Hutchinson were guilty of gross deception and that their actions were detrimental to the interests of the hospital and the medical profession. It's not clear what, if any, punitive action the hospital took against Foote.

In the John Griswold lawsuit, Madison County District Court Judge E.T. Allen ruled in favor of the two doctors. Griswold appealed to the Nebraska Supreme Court, which partly reversed the ruling. The higher court found Foote to be negligent, but it upheld the lower court's ruling in favor of Hutchison, largely on the argument that he was not liable because Foote had been the lead surgeon. (Echos of Hutchinson's assertion in Christine's case that he was just an observer.)

In its April 1896 ruling, the state supreme court said doctors cannot be required to use "the utmost degree of care" or to possess "the highest attainable skill in their profession." Instead, the standard to which they should be held is the exercise of "such necessary and proper care and attention as may reasonably be expected from members of their profession under like circumstances."

On the face of it, the Griswold case suggests incompetence or poor judgment on the part of Hutchinson and Foote. The state supreme court confirmed, with ever-so-delicate phrasing, that both doctors had been negligent in their examination of the woman and in "the unfortunate result thereof." It said she was given only a cursory examination by each doctor, yet Foote, who examined her the day before he operated, told the woman and her husband after the exam, "It is an ovarian tumor; no doubt about it."

There should have been doubt about it, according to the court's finding, since Hutchinson and Foote did not use what other medical experts told the court were standard exam procedures in a case like this where a suspected tumor could not be explained by pregnancy and where her life was not in immediate danger. They should have used uterine sound, or dilators, to examine the vaginal cavity, according to Dr. Crummer, the hospital chief of staff, who testified at the trial.

From this and other testimony the court concluded that the doctors had been negligent. On that basis, the court reversed the lower court's ruling for Foote, meaning it found him liable. The court agreed, however, that Hutchinson was not liable. The judge credited Hutchinson with having shown generosity in lending the Griswolds the $200 for Foote's surgical fee, noting that Hutchinson had "intimate personal and church relations" with the Griswolds. (John Griswold and Hutchinson's wife, Tillie, were officers of the Madison Baptist church.)

The circumstances and outcome of the Griswold case, while not directly applicable to Christine's, suggest the possibility that her fate may not have been placed in the best hands. It's unclear how much she and her family knew about the Griswold lawsuit before they agreed to enlist Foote, but they probably were at least aware of it since the case was reported in the local newspapers.

In sum, the passage of time has made it impossible to know for sure whether Christine was served well or poorly by Foote, Mackay and Hutchinson, but two conclusions are clear: Medical practice in Nebraska was not sufficiently advanced to save her, and the episode created an unusual amount of public acrimony and private agony. The Hagglund letter excerpt published on August 24, 1893 strongly suggests she was beyond saving by the night of the surgery, yet one wonders whether something more could have been done for her earlier.

Christine was the fifth of John and Anna's offspring to die young but the first to live long enough to bear children of her own, and so her legacy endured.

21

Keeping On

I t's easy to imagine that the burden of Christine's medical expenses played a role in the real estate decisions by her husband and her parents. The emotional weight of her death is harder to figure; I found no first-hand account of how the families coped. Eventually the loss would lead to big changes that would play out later in the decade, particularly for the Mortons.

In the short term they all got on with their lives, as they had after previous tragedies.

A year after his sister's death, Oscar Hagglund married Bertha Anderson, a Nebraska native of Norwegian descent. Bertha, 17, and Oscar, 24, tied the knot on September 16, 1894 in Stanton County, where she was living with her parents, Gilbert and Inga.[91]

The town of Stanton, which is the seat of the county by the same name, is situated on the Elkhorn River, about 15 miles southeast of Norfolk and a similar distance east of Warnerville. Stanton was originally called Pleasant Run when a post office was established there in 1867. For a period in the early 20th century, Stanton County would figure prominently in the lives of not just Oscar – who would return to the area and remarry shortly after Bertha died in Washington state

– but also his younger brother John.

The official witnesses at Oscar and Bertha's wedding were the couple's fathers. The marriage certificate, on file at the county courthouse, says the officiating minister was H.G. Myers. The ceremony was performed at "Mrs. Halverson's," which almost certainly referred to Sarah Halverson, a Norwegian immigrant and mother of four who lived near Bertha's family in Stanton County's Elkhorn township.

Oddly, the marriage license lists Oscar's mother as Anna Henrickson. That is the first and only time I saw Anna's maiden name in a form that refers to her father's surname, Henriksson, rather than his given name, Lars. She grew up as Anna Larsdotter, using the traditional Swedish patronymic form in which children were given their father's first name as their surname, with the -dotter suffix for girls. At times she used Larson as her maiden name.

Oscar and Bertha made Stanton County their first home. It's where their first two children were born – Clarence Andrew on May 20, 1896 and Leonard Dewey on June 29, 1898. (The boys would become the first Hagglunds to serve in the U.S. military — both of them as infantrymen in France in the final months of World War I.)[92] During this period Oscar apparently hired himself out as a farm hand; an 1899 Madison city directory includes mention of Oscar as "thresher and laborer."

* * *

The Tackstrom branch

Like her older sister, Martha Hagglund married a Swedish immigrant. His name was August Tackstrom. He arrived in America as a 21-year-old bachelor, probably with little idea that he would find the love of his life in the farmlands of Nebraska.

The eighth and youngest child of Johan (Jan) Hansson and Stina Ersdotter, August was born March 20, 1861 in Domnarfvet village along the Dal River in Dalarna county in central Sweden, about 50 miles south of John Hagglund's parents' hometown of Färnäs. Domnarfvet is situated in the parish of Stora Tuna, whose church dates to the 15th century and is one of the largest in rural Sweden.

August was the family's second son born by that name; the first August was born May 29, 1856 and died two days later. The next child, Carolina, also died young, succumbing to rheumatic fever in 1871 at age 14.

August emigrated alone. He left Domnarfvet on July 17, 1882 and made his way to the southern port city of Gothenburg.[93] There, details of his ship passenger contract, No. 9987, were recorded at the police station, in line with usual practice. The next day he stepped aboard a newly built steamship, the SS Romeo, for a 40-plus hour journey to the English port city of Hull. The ship's manifest listed his final destination as New York. From Hull, he would have taken a train across England to Liverpool to catch another steamship for the Atlantic crossing. I could not find a record of his trip from Liverpool, but he likely arrived in New York in the first days of August.

The following summer, in August 1883 in Castle Rock, Douglas County, Colorado, August formally declared his intention to become a U.S. citizen, but he did not complete the process until he filed his petition for naturalization in 1917 in Everett, Washington. The petition was approved after a judge in Douglas County verified for the Snohomish County Superior Court in Everett that August had formally renounced his allegiance to Sweden on August 16, 1883.

Castle Rock, named for a castle tower-shaped butte, is about 30 miles south of Denver. In the 1880s, it was a thriving town. Swedish immigrants were drawn to it by the promise of employment in quarries that produced rhyolite, a pinkish-gray volcanic lava stone widely used at the time in building construction.

August seems not to have stayed put for long. A search of the 1885 Colorado state census for Douglas County turned up no sign of him. His brother Andrew, who emigrated before him, was living in Creighton, Nebraska that year, but I could not determine August's whereabouts.

It's unclear when August moved from Colorado to Nebraska or how he happened to meet Martha, but I found some broad clues. Andrew, the brother, seems to have moved from Creighton to Madison, Nebraska in the late 1880s. Perhaps August joined him there. Soon after that, probably in 1891, Andrew went his own way – to a riverside village called Stanwood in the Puget Sound area of Washington state, where his own family tragedy later changed the direction of Hagglund history.

August remained in Nebraska and married Martha Hagglund on July 2, 1891 in Madison County.

The witnesses for August's bride were recorded as "Mr. and Mrs. Morton" – presumably her brother-in-law Lars and her sister, Christine. August's witnesses were "Mrs. and Mr. Shultz." The ceremony was held at "Mortons residence," according to the certificate of marriage issued by a Madison County judge.

The Tackstroms' first three children were born in Madison – Anna in April 1892, Lawrence in June 1894 and Harry in October 1897.

* * *

From Sweden to Nebraska via "Alaska"

In the sequence of Hagglund marriages – Christine in 1881, Lewis in 1885, Martha in 1891 and Oscar in 1894 – the "baby" of the family, John J., came last. (Andrew, the oldest, was a lifelong bachelor.)

John's bride was a Swedish immigrant, Hattie Granlund, born Hedvig Sofia Granlund. She was 15 years old when she arrived in New York harbor on September 14, 1891 aboard the steamship *SS Alaska*.

Like most immigrants from Sweden at the time, Hattie made the journey in three stages, first sailing aboard the *SS Cameo*, which departed Gothenburg in southern Sweden on September 1 and dropped her on the east coast of England at Hull. From there she would have taken a train to Liverpool, where she boarded the *Alaska*. She arrived in New York three and a half months before Ellis Island was established as the main immigrant point of entry; thus, she would have been processed at the Castle Garden depot on the southern tip of Manhattan island, at what later became known as Battery Park.

On the *Alaska's* hand-written passenger manifest, Hattie's destination is noted simply as "Nebraska." No other Granlund is among the listed passengers. The record of her departure August 28 from her home at Stora Skedvi, a parish on the Dal River, says she emigrated alone, which was a brave undertaking for a teenager.

John and Hattie were married June 7, 1896 in Newman Grove, the main village in a township in southern Madison County known as Shell Creek, named for a stream that runs through it. The witnesses for John were his father and his brother Andrew. No Granlunds are listed as witnesses; I don't believe her parents, noted on the marriage application as Gilbert Granlund and Margrita Johnson (maiden name), ever emigrated from Sweden, although two of her brothers did.

Hattie was born February 25, 1876 in a village called Ytter-sätra

213

in Stora Skedvi parish, Kopparberg (Dalarna) county. The village is about 60 miles southeast of the home village of John Hagglund's parents and about 15 miles downriver from where Andrew and August Tackstrom grew up.

Hattie's father was Gustav Granlund, born Gustav Andersson, the son of a corporal in the Swedish army. Gustav followed his father's footsteps into the military, which probably is where he got the surname Granlund, since soldiers were assigned new names to avoid a multiplicity of common names like Andersson in a military unit. He later earned a living as a shoemaker. Hattie's mother was Greta Stina Jansdotter, a surname that would correspond in the U.S. to Johnson. Thus, the Margrita Johnson listed on Hattie's marriage application was an Americanized version of her mother's name.

Before John came into her life, Hattie lived in Shell Creek township, along with two of her brothers. One brother, Gustav Ulrick Granlund, was a harness maker in Newman Grove, the town where Hattie was married. He emigrated from Sweden in 1890, one year before Hattie, and was two years older than her. Gustav married a woman named Hannah in 1898, and two years later they had a daughter, Ellen.

The other Granlund brother in the Shell Creek area was Carl August, who was the oldest and became known as Charles A. Granlund when he emigrated in 1888. Charles is listed in the 1900 census as a 31-year-old bachelor and day laborer.

Hattie had two other siblings, neither of whom seem to have emigrated: Anna Maria, five years older than Hattie, and Erik Axel, the baby of the family.

When John married Hattie, he was 22 and she was 20. I found no record of how they met, but an 1896-97 Madison city directory suggests a clue. It lists Hattie as a waitress at the Prince Hotel, which stood on the corner of 4th and Pearl and was owned by a prominent Madison businessman, E. F. Prince. John at that point was living a few blocks away in his parents' home.

John and Hattie's first daughter, Anna May, was born in Madison County in May 1898. An 1899 county directory lists John J. Hagglund as "farmer, stock raiser and thresher" in Union township, Section 1, which is where his father's homestead was situated.

* * *

A Second Martha Hagglund

Lewis, the second of John and Anna's children to marry, was the first to remarry. His marriage to Ella went sour and she sued him for divorce in Butler County District Court in June 1890. She won the case by default four months later. Lewis did not answer a court summons presented to him by the Madison County sheriff, George Losey. Since he chose not to appear in court or provide a written response, his side of the divorce story has gone unrecorded, as far as I know.[94]

In a hand-written decree issued in October 1890, the judge ruled that Lewis had "wholly abandoned the plaintiff without just cause for a term of two years prior to" her filing a divorce petition. The judge dissolved the marriage, declaring it "set aside and wholly annulled and the parties released from the obligations of the same." The decree made no mention of there being any children from the marriage or of a financial settlement, although it said Ella – "hereby restored to her maiden name, Luella Sherwood" – would pay the court costs.

(Oddly, Lewis is recorded in these court documents as George Lewis Hagglund. In no other record in Nebraska or elsewhere did I ever see him referred to as anything other than his original Swedish name, which was Lars with no middle name, or his Americanized

215

name, Lewis Hagglund, which was sometimes spelled Louis, or by the initials, L. G. Hagglund. It's possible the "G" was meant to stand for George, but I never saw evidence of that.)

Ella remarried in 1891. Her new husband was Samuel Masten, a farmer. They had at least four children together. As of 1910 they were living in Logan township, Knox County, Nebraska, two counties directly north of Madison County. She died in March 1923 in Independence, Missouri, and was buried in Nebraska.

During the course of Lewis's divorce proceedings, his next wife appeared on the scene. She was Martha Olson (originally Olsdotter), the eldest daughter of Lewis's uncle, Olof Larson, who was Anna Hagglund's younger brother. Thus, Martha and Lewis were cousins.

Martha, like her parents and her aunt Anna, was born in central Sweden in Hammerdal parish in the county of Jämtland. In July 1890 at age 24, she emigrated unaccompanied by family members just days after Ella sued Lewis for divorce. Her destination was recorded by the parish minister as "Nebraska in N. Amerika." I can only wonder whether her more specific "destination" was Lewis, or whether their Nebraska romance was simply a coincidence of timing.

Martha's parents chose not to emigrate until one year after she left, a decision that may have been connected to an illness of another daughter. Declaring Nebraska their destination, the parents, Olof and Christina (originally Kerstin and sometimes spelled Christine), left home on July 4, 1891 with four children – 17-year-old Brita Christina, 9-year-old Elin (Ella) and two sons, Olof (Ollie), 12, and Elias (Eli), 7. The two oldest sons – 23-year-old Måns and Lars, who was turning 20 that month — stayed behind. Lars remained on the family farm. Måns moved in 1892 to another farm in Sikas, where he worked as a farmhand.

Tragically, a daughter who also remained behind, Anna Catarina, died just days after her parents left. Parish records say she died of tuberculosis on July 31, two weeks shy of her 15th birthday. Olof and Christina and the four children sailed from Liverpool to New York aboard the SS Nevada, departing July 18 and arriving in New York harbor 11 days later. Having left home so soon before Anna Catarina's death, the parents must have been staggered by the news.

Once in Nebraska, the Larsons lived in Madison County for one year (perhaps with John and Anna Hagglund) before resettling in Stromsburg, a small town on the Big Blue River in Polk County, about 60 miles south of Madison. Christina died in June 1930 and is buried at Stromsburg Cemetery, East Side block, Lot 15. Her husband Olof died in December 1915. His death certificate says he also was buried in Stromsburg Cemetery, but I did not locate the plot.

Olof was a devout Baptist, judging by an obituary published in the local newspaper. It may have been written by his wife, Christina, or at least based on information she provided, such as the fact that he converted to the Baptist faith in 1861, at age 29, in Hammerdal.

"Mr. Larson possessed a keen insight in the Scriptures and dwelt much, in his mind, on spiritual matters," it said. "He was never satisfied with shallow views concerning religious matters, nor was he ever afraid to express his own views in the face of opposition" — possibly a reference to his willingness (like that of his sister Anna) to break with the Lutheran Church in the 1860s.

"He seemed to possess something of the rugged character of the mountains surrounding his early home," the obituary said.

When Lewis and Martha married on June 27, 1891, he was 32 and she was 25. Eleven months later they had their first child, Anna Carolina. By apparent coincidence, they obtained their marriage license in Madison County on nearly the same day as August Tackstrom and Martha Hagglund. Thus, in quick succession the original Martha Hagglund became Martha Tackstrom and Martha Olsdotter became the next Martha Hagglund.

Lewis's Martha listed Madison County as her residence on the marriage license application in June 1891, so she probably was living with her uncle and aunt, John and Anna Hagglund. This might explain why Lewis was on the tax rolls that year as a resident of Union Creek precinct, which is where his parents' farm was located. He is listed as Louis Hagglund, owing 20 cents in combined state and county taxes on a mere $11 in personal property, which perhaps reflected Martha's belongings. Oddly, Lewis didn't pay that year's full tax bill, which totaled $3.43, until March 22, 1894, the very month when he and Martha moved to Stromsburg.

Shortly after arriving, Lewis and Martha joined Stromburg's Swedish Baptist Church.[95] Records from that period, handwritten in Swedish, include mention of Lewis and Martha having been recommended for membership by the Baptist congregation in Madison. I found little information about Lewis and Martha's church activities during their years in Madison, beyond mention in the *Norfolk Daily News* on September 29, 1893 that they were enrolled as "delegates" at the introductory meeting of the Loup & Elkhorn Association of Baptist Churches.

* * *

Lewis and the Book of John

The depth of Lewis's religious devotion – and his outspoken nature – is evident in a letter he wrote during this period to the editors of *Hemlandet*, the oldest Swedish-language newspaper in America and since 1855 the voice of the Swedish-American Lutheran community. For at least half a century it was considered the most influential paper of its kind, but Lewis was not a fan.

Lewis's letter from Warnerville, Nebraska was published March 23, 1893, one year before he and Martha moved to Stromsburg. He was sharply critical of the paper's editors, accusing them of selling out to commercialism and forsaking the opportunity to use the newspaper's influence as Lewis believed it should – to spread the word of God. Proselytizing was, in fact, the aim of *Hemlandet's* creators; among its first editors was Eric Norelius, the legendary Swedish Lutheran minister. Over the years, the paper became more secular, more political and, to some, more controversial. The paper frequently attacked the Baptists.

It's unclear what triggered Lewis's critical letter, but he asserted that the paper had strayed from its original evangelical mission. Noting that the paper had been publishing for 38 years, he accused its editors of losing their moral compass.

"I say its mission during these 38 years has been vanity, not to mention harmful," he wrote, according to my own translation. "I say harmful because it is quite natural that *Hemlandet*, as well as other newspapers and publications, naturally have an influence on readers. And yet, publications (like this one) do not contribute to the propagation of the kingdom of Christ, to spread the empire's kingdom on Earth, for Christ himself says, 'He who is not with me is against me,' and, 'He who does not collect with me steals from me.'"

Lewis deftly drew a parallel to the Biblical story of Jesus miracu-lously healing a paralytic who had been infirm for 38 years. As told in the Book of John, the man was lying on a mat beside Bethesda Pool near the sheep market in Jerusalem. The pool was said to have healing powers; the first person to enter when the waters were stirred would be cured. The paralytic told Jesus that he could never get into the pool quickly enough to benefit from the healing powers. Jesus told him, "Get up and walk." He did so and was instantly healed.

"Thirty-eight years!" Lewis wrote, noting the newspaper's long life. "Let's see. That's as long as the sickness mentioned in the Bible. There a man had been sitting at the sheep gate in Jerusalem to whom Jesus said, 'Get up, take your bed and go.' Would it not be time for *Hemlandet*, as well as for all other political newspapers, to 'get up and go' and act for the widespread distribution of the kingdom of God after acting on the 'market of vanity' for 38 years now?"

"Choose today who will do the will! Whatever you do, do it soon, for time is short, 'and soon he will come and will not delay.'" Lewis closed with, "Bring this in prayer to God!"

My translation of his Swedish probably missed nuances of Lewis's message, and may even have missed some of his meaning. But his concern is unmistakable, as is the consistency of his religious fervor, which remains on record not only in Nebraska but also in his later years in Washington state.

Carefully preserved membership records at the Swedish Baptist Church in Stromsburg say a "Mr. L.G. Hagglund" and a "Mrs. Martha Hagglund" joined in 1894 and note for the record that Lewis began in the Baptist church at Kiron, Iowa.

Martha's parents, Olof and Christina Larson, became members in 1892. Beside each of their names in the church's membership records is a note dated October 1, 1892 and handwritten in Swedish: "från Hammerdal, Sverige" —from Hammerdal, Sweden. Hammerdal was their home parish in Jämtland. The year originally was recorded as 1893 but someone changed the "3" in both notes to a "2." Olof's funeral service was held at the church.

Many years after Lewis and Martha had moved on from Stromsburg, he shared vivid and fond memories of supporting the church and local campaigns against alcohol.

"It was my pleasure and privilege to try to do my 'little bit' to cooperate with those who worked hard to keep Stromsburg dry," he wrote in a letter to the editor of the local paper in February 1931.

He added: "You show me a community without a church and I will show you a community where the devil has full swing."

It's not clear what prompted Lewis and Martha's move out of Madison County, but this happened after a series of land transactions that beg explanation. In May 1887, two years into his marriage with Ella, they sold their 160 acres to his parents for $1,500. Why? Had Lewis gone broke again? Might this have been related to an estrangement or separation leading to their eventual divorce?

Nearly five years later, in January 1892, shortly after he had remarried, Lewis bought the property back for $1,750. Two years after that, in February 1894, he and Martha sold the farm to a local man, Jacob D. Horner, for $1,700. The buyer also assumed a $600 mortgage and agreed to pay back taxes for 1892 and 1893, according to the warranty deed.

A further curious tidbit that is hard to fit into this sequence of events is a note in the Norfolk Daily News on January 6, 1894, the month before Lewis and Martha sold the homestead. A list of approved expenses by the Madison County Board of Commissioners included this notation: "Ann Hagglund, taking care of Annie Hagglund, $25." That would appear to be Anna Hagglund caring for Lewis and Martha's daughter Anna, who would have been five months shy of her second birthday. Perhaps grandma looked after the little girl during her parents' transition to Stromsburg. I don't know why she would have received payment by the county unless the family was considered some sort of hardship case.

Stromsburg was one of the most predominantly Swedish communities in the state. Founded in 1872 by a group of Swedish immigrants from Galva, Illinois, it remained a farming town well into the 21st century, advertising itself as the "Swede Capital of Nebraska."

Aside from the familiar Swedish character of Stromburg, it's possible that Lewis and Martha were attracted by the presence of her parents.

The 1900 census shows Olof, a painter and paper hanger by trade, and Christina residing on Fourth Street in Stromsburg. Fifteen years later, shortly before he died, Olof signed over the property to his wife.[96] I discovered this in an unusual and charming entry in Warranty Deed Book 40 on file at the Polk County courthouse. On page 446, it says Olof sold his Stromsburg property to Christina in August 1915. On the line where the sale price is entered, it says he received from the buyer, "One Dollar and Love and Affection."

Fifteen years later in an obituary for Martha's mother, a local newspaper, the *Headlight*, mentioned several of her children. It said one son, Eli, was living in Stromsburg, and Martha was noted as "Mrs. Hagglund of Blaine, Washington." It said two daughters, cited as Bertha and Elin, and one son, Olof, preceded her in death. (Bertha may have been a reference to Brita Christina, born in January 1874. Elin, the younger daughter more commonly known as Ellen or Ella, moved west and married Earl D. Nims in Mt. Vernon, Washington on January 18, 1903 and died three years later.)

Very shortly after arriving in Stromsburg, Lewis got into the draying business, meaning he hauled goods by dray, or flatbed wagon, to and from the rail station for businesses, farmers and others. The wagon was pulled by horses or mules. The local newspaper once referred to Lewis's wagon as "that old, antiquated pile of Michigan lumber," while giving him credit for having fixed it up in 1896 so that it was capable of carrying "all most any kind of a load put on it" and able to "run as easy as a $300 phaeton" — a reference to the horse-drawn carriage popular at the time.

Draymen, as they were known, were much in demand in Lewis's time, before the arrival of the combustion engine ended the era of horse-drawn transport in towns and cities.

"At one time there were as many as eight trains a day in and out of

Stromsburg, making draying a good business," says a 1997 history of Stromsburg. Indeed, Lewis recalled late in life that his dray line, which he bought from a local man named Pete Anderson in March 1894 and operated for six years, was only modestly successful "by reason of too much competition – the draying business being overdone for a small town at that time." He sold the business at public auction in 1900.

Never shy with newspaper editors, Lewis in 1931 responded to a call from the Stromsburg *Headlight* for memories of the town's early years. He said he didn't have much to offer the remembrance project but was sending his thoughts "just to be doing something," adding "and probably that was about all my business amounted to, too – 'just to be doing something.'"

If he failed to make a good living as a drayman, it was not for lack of trying. During the summer of 1894, his first year in the business, Lewis regularly advertised what he called his "General Dray Line" in the *Headlight*.

"All kinds of Draying and Team Work done on short notice," his small ad said.

Lewis made many other appearances in the *Headlight*. In June and July 1894, amid a national economic depression, he regularly put a notice in the paper indicating he was hawking corn cobs to make extra pennies: "Cobs for sale. Inquire of L.G. Hagglund."

An item in the May 17, 1894 edition said, "I have a good work horse to trade for cows. L.G. Hagglund, Stromsburg, Neb." This sort of blurb was a common form of quasi-advertising offered by many local newspapers to merchants and other as "complimentary notices." A blurb published directly above Lewis's said, "H.W. Brash has added a new peanut roaster to the many improvements at his lunch room."

In April 1895, Lewis bought a parcel of land from a local widower named John Wilson for $300. The legal description of the property

Lewis bought from Wilson, as recorded by the Polk County Register of Deeds, is so convoluted that even the staff in the Office of the Register of Deeds could not pinpoint the location when we reviewed the records together in April 2016 and attempted to match the description against maps of that era. The property was near a rail line, perhaps the Omaha & Republican Valley, which came to Stromsburg in 1879 as a branch of the Union Pacific.

I found no official record of Lewis selling the property, but the Stromsburg Weekly News reported on March 8, 1900 that a local man, Axel Lindholm, bought it for $250 – $50 less than Lewis had paid five years earlier. Another item in the same edition said Lewis and his family would be moving to Washington state in four days (March 12), "and will be missed by a great many."

Lewis and Martha had their share of trouble in Stromsburg. In December 1894, the entire family, which by then included 2-year-old Anna and 3-month-old Dora, was nearly killed in their own beds. A newspaper reported they "came near being asphyxiated" by coal gas, which was used to light and heat homes and businesses before electricity became widely available.

"The family had retired and were awakened by the strong smell of gas, which had been escaping for some time," the story said. "Mr. Hagglund and wife were quite sick for some time afterward."

Despite this and other setbacks, Lewis held fond memories of Stromsburg for the rest of his life. He kept close tabs on Stromsburg by subscribing to its newspapers by mail. In September 1905 he wrote a short letter to the Stromsburg *Weekly News*, which printed it under the headline, "Word From An Old-Timer." He instructed the editor to change his mailing address from New Whatcom to Bellingham – "as Whatcom is no more and Bellingham has taken its place" – and expressed his fondness for Stromsburg.

"To receive the paper is just like 'getting a letter from home,'" he wrote. In this and other letters to the paper, Lewis praised his former neighbors' stance against alcohol.

"I am glad that the good people of Stromsburg have banished the saloon from their midst and that a Y.M.C.A. has taken its place for the elevation of young men," he wrote.

Ten years later, on March 7, 1915, he wrote again to comment on one of his other favorite topics — the weather.

"It seemed almost like a dream for us to read your accounts of the snow storms you have been having in old Stromsburg, Polk county, and Nebraska in general, while we have not had any snow here yet this winter and now it is March," he wrote. "The nearest thing we had to snow is a little white frost."

Lewis was outspoken about more than the vagaries of weather and the evils of booze. He was a man of strong views and not shy about sharing them. In the heat of the 1896 president election, he chimed in on the No. 1 national issue: the gold/silver debate between those who argued for backing the dollar only with gold and those who believed the currency should be redeemable in silver as well as gold. This was the "battle of the standards," between the "gold bugs" and the "silverites." Though arcane, this was not mainly a debate about monetary technicalities. The issue was argued as a matter of basic economic fairness, with farmers generally favoring "free silver," or the unlimited coinage of silver, on grounds that the demonetization of silver in the 1870s had been a ploy by the rich to tightened credit for the benefit of banks and merchants. Farmers relied on credit for economic survival.

Lewis was on the side of the "silverites," and in September 1896 he was invited to express his view in the Stromsburg *Weekly News*. The editor showcased Lewis as a counterweight to a man the editor detested, a local druggist and real estate broker named Albert B. Hedbloom, an outspoken advocate for the gold standard.

Setting aside the merits of the competing arguments, it's notable that the newspaper editor saw Lewis as an effective spokesman for the "free silver" crowd. "Though being a common Swede drayman," the editor wrote, Lewis was sufficiently well informed and wise to help lead this important public policy debate. (The editor employed an archaic expression, writing that Lewis could "give [Hedbloom] cards and spades and beat him at his own game," which in this context meant Lewis, seemingly disadvantaged as a commoner, could prevail over a member of the merchant class because he was on the right side of the argument.)

In introducing Lewis's letter, the editor made another reference to Lewis being an unlikely spokesman. The wording suggests a mixture of contempt for Lewis's commoner status and admiration for his intelligence. "We must admit we were astonished" by the content of Lewis's letter, the editor wrote, adding that it reminded him that you cannot "judge a man as to what he knows or thinks by his looks."

As to his actual arguments for monetizing silver, Lewis posed a series of questions, some of which touched on the underlying issue of economic fairness for farmers. He noted, for example, that bankers and the so-called monied interests had blamed farmers' overproduction for the collapse of farm prices in 1873. Now that same crowd, in opposing the coinage of silver, was arguing that it was the overproduction of silver in the early 1870s – before Congress discontinued the minting of silver coins in 1873 – that had depressed the farm economy. They argued that this would be repeated, and the economy destroyed, if the "silverites" prevailed in their backing of Democrat William Jennings Bryan against Republican William McKinley in the 1896 presidential election.[97]

"It was always claimed that it was over-production of wheat, corn, oats, etc., that caused a fall in the market prices of the same," Lewis wrote. "How is it now that you begin to lay it to the increased production of silver, will someone explain? Did not the market price of farm products begin to fall in 1873 and did not the difficulty in money matters begin then? What caused the decline in the price of silver? Do not tell us that it was 'over production.' There is no such thing as over-production of silver in this country! My idea is that it was the demonetization of silver that caused it to fall, but how do you explain it? Make silver a legal tender once more and silver will be in demand and consequently advance in value."

In Lewis's view, the talk of silver coinage leading to a collapse of the economy was an election-year scare tactic, or as he put it, "only blank shots to scare the voter."

Over the next decades, Lewis kept busy with pen and paper. In December 1926 the *Headlight* reported that he had written from Bellingham to say he was "still an invalid caused by an accident that happened five years ago." He didn't elaborate on his condition or its cause, but his daughter Esther later recalled that he had suffered a compound leg fracture in a fall from a ladder at his home and that a long recovery left him largely immobile.

"He needed crutches to walk," she wrote in a 1989 letter to a niece, "and there was nothing he could do except sit and read and have the grandchildren sing the old songs of the church to him."

In his 1926 letter to the *Headlight*, Lewis lamented the recent "passing to the great beyond" of many old Stromsburg friends. "May God, who is the only real source of comfort in His wonderful mercy comfort the bereaved ones," he wrote.

He and Martha suffered their own period of grief during the Stromsburg years.

After giving birth to two daughters in Stromsburg – Dora Mabel on September 25, 1894 and Elvera Christine on August 25, 1896 – Martha had a son on May 16, 1899. He lived only several weeks. His name was Arnold Raymond. On July 20, the *Headlight* published a very brief note of the death, reporting, "A two months old infant of Mr. and Mrs. L.G. Hagglund died on Wednesday night of last week." In the same edition of the paper, Lewis and Martha placed a note of appreciation for friends' expressions of sympathy. "Also," they wrote, "for the bountiful and beautiful floral offerings with which you covered the form of our little loved one."

Just a month earlier, relatives from Madison County had visited Lewis and Martha.

"L.G. Hagglund and wife are enjoying a visit from his brother John J. Hagglund and brother-in-law August Tackstrom, with their families," the *Headlight* reported on June 15.

August and Martha Tackstrom and their three young children and John and Hattie and their 1-year-old daughter might have made the trip to Stromsburg to see the Hagglunds' newborn. They might also have been in transit to an even more distant destination and the beginning of a new phase of the Hagglund family journey.

IV

The Final Steps

22

More Like Home

B y the turn of the century the Hagglunds were headed to western Washington, to a different climate, lifestyle and landscape some 1,600 miles from the frustrations of farming in northeastern Nebraska. Up the North Platte River Valley they went, across the Rocky Mountains and onto the shores of Puget Sound.

These were the final steps of an immigrant family's journey.

In a span of 33 years, John and Anna had crossed an ocean and a continent, by trail, by sail and by rail. They spent the prime of their lives on the sparse prairies of Iowa and Nebraska and by 1900 had reached the far side of their dreams, comforted by the moody skies of the Pacific Northwest and the modest charms of a village called Cedarhome.

Paradoxically, the farther they got from the homeland the more like home the surroundings may have seemed – the lakes, the wildflowers, the cool summers, the towering evergreens.

Much had changed for the Hagglunds since they uprooted themselves in Jämtland. Three had died young: Märet at age six aboard a steamship approaching Quebec; Olof, 12, on the family farm in Iowa, and Christine, 30, under a surgeon's knife in Nebraska. Five had married and made John and Anna grandparents many times over. All were now American citizens but still Swedes at heart.

Their adopted country had changed, too. From the Hagglunds' arrival in the early post-Civil War years through the boom-and-bust cycles of the 1880s and 90s, the country had industrialized and modernized. A headlong rush to riches had left many behind, deepening a social divide felt acutely by small-time farmers.

Looking west in search of a path to stability for the generations to come, the Hagglunds found it in Washington state, where they would live out their years and rest their souls.

Why Washington? Given all they had gone through since arriving in America in 1867 with little more than hope, faith and each other, one wonders what prompted the Hagglunds and then the Mortons to make yet another move to yet another new and distant frontier.

The answer comes in two essential parts. The first involves a cry for help, the second a lucky encounter. Each is a timeless lesson in the power of family cohesion.

* * *

Tragedy Strikes Again

The cry for help came from a corner of the country where growing numbers of Scandinavians were arriving for work in the woods, mines and fish canneries. The person in need was Andrew Tackstrom. He was the brother-in-law of John and Anna's only surviving daughter, Martha, the first U.S.-born Hagglund and wife of Andrew's younger brother August.

Andrew and his wife, Hannah, and their three children were living in Stanwood, Washington, a small riverside town in the big shadow of the Cascade Mountains. Andrew made and repaired boots and shoes, a trade he learned as a teenage apprentice in Sweden.

Fittingly for a man who worked in footwear, Andrew was a wanderer – not an aimless tumbleweed, but a bit of a rolling stone. From Stanwood, in the northwest corner of Snohomish County, he had set his sights on the remotest of frontiers – Alaska Territory, where gold prospecting tempted men's imaginations. That adventure had to wait, however, because during Christmas season 1898 his life took a sudden turn.

"Andrew's wife and both of his daughters were stricken with diphtheria and all died within one week," the 1983 Everett account of Hagglund family history says. "Andrew urgently needed someone to be with him in his sorrow and asked August and Martha to move from Iowa to Stanwood." Once the Tackstroms decided to accept the call, it says, Anna Hagglund talked John into following.

It was not quite that simple. With the benefit of better hindsight in the 21st century Internet Age, I found that the Everett account has some of the facts skewed. Death records cite diphtheria in just one of the three Tackstrom losses, although it is true that official records can be misleading and even wrong. And the Tackstrom deaths, while unspeakably tragic, did not happen within one week. Still, the gist of the story is correct: Andrew suffered sudden, life-changing losses, and this marked the start of a Hagglund migration to the Pacific Northwest.

* * *

Swedish Roots

The Tackstrom place in Hagglund family history has its roots in central Sweden. The two families almost certainly did not know each other, but they shared a destiny.

Andrew and August were sons of a sawyer, or wood cutter, named Johan Hansson and his wife, Stina Ersdotter. The brothers came to America separately – Andrew in July 1879 at age 28 and August three years later at 21.

Andrew's path to Stanwood is described briefly, with significant gaps and numerous inaccuracies, in *An Illustrated History of Skagit and Snohomish Counties*, published in 1906. One of the questions it leaves untouched is why the Tackstrom boys used a name with seemingly no relation to that of their parents.

With Swedes, names are not always what they seem. "Tackstrom" is a case in point. It is an Americanization of a Swedish name, Tägtström, which some members of the family adopted, starting with Andrew and August's generation. The name does not appear in parish records associated with the family until the 1870s.

August and Andrew's original family name was Jansson (son of Jans), in Sweden's patronymic tradition. The boys' paternal grandfather was Hans Hansson, born in May 1795, and thus Hans' eldest son Johan (Andrew and August's father) was called Johan Hansson – son of Hans. Johan was later shortened to Jan. Thus, Andrew was known as Anders Jansson, and his brother was August Jansson.

In the 1870s the boys switched to the Tägtström surname, and when they got to the United States it became the less foreign-looking Tackstrom. Some of their siblings in Sweden also used the Tägtström name, while others stuck with the patronym. One sister, Stina, used both. She was known as Stina Jansdotter Tägtström.

In September 1873, Andrew married Johanna Olsdotter, daughter of Olof Anderson and Brita Persdotter. Johanna gave birth to Oscar (born Oskar Eugene) on December 16, 1878, in the parish of Stora Tuna in Kopparberg county (now known as Dalarna county), one county south of Jämtland, where John and Anna Hagglund had been living when they emigrated a decade earlier. Oscar would turn out to be even more of an adventurer than his father, with tragic results.

When Andrew (recorded by parish clergy as "skomakare Anders" – "Andrew the shoemaker") left for America on July 12, 1879, his wife and infant son stayed behind for nine months in the village of Tjärna in Stora Tuna parish. On March 22, 1880, Johanna (recorded as "hustru Johanna Tägtström" – wife Johanna Tägtström) and 1-year-old Oscar set off for America with a group of 30 other Stora Tuna residents. Their destination is recorded simply as "Amerika."

August left next, in July 1882, arriving in New York by way of Liverpool. He likely set off immediately to find Andrew, who may have been in Colorado at that point.

The 1906 *Illustrated History* says that upon arrival in the United States, Andrew set up shop as a shoemaker in Chicago for six months before moving to an unspecified part of Nebraska sometime in 1882. That chronology is at least partly wrong, however, because Andrew, Johanna and Oscar were already in Nebraska by June 1880. That year's census lists them as living in a township in Saunders County called Mariposa, heavily populated by Swedish immigrants, including some from Dalarna. Andrew worked on a local farm. (Several years later, the first village to sprout in Mariposa was named Malmo, no doubt in honor of the city on the southern tip of Sweden that lies across the Oresund strait separating Sweden from its Scandinavian neighbor, Denmark.)

It certainly is possible that Andrew spent the latter half of 1879 in Chicago before resettling in Nebraska the following spring to receive his wife and son.

The not-entirely-reliable 1906 account says that during the 1880s Andrew worked on a railroad in Nebraska and then in Colorado before returning to Nebraska, where he "opened a shop" – presumably a shoemaker's shop. It says the shop was in Creston, a small town in Platte County a dozen miles southeast of Madison, the area where Andrew's future sister-in-law was living. More than a year after I visited tiny Creston in hopes of picking up signs of Andrew's trail, I discovered the 1906 account had led me astray. His town was not Creston. It was Creighton, in Knox County, about 60 miles northwest of Creston.

Andrew appeared in a Nebraska Business directory[98] as a Creighton shoemaker each year from 1884 through 1889. Also, he and Johanna and are in the 1885 Nebraska state census as Creighton residents, a family of four with 6-year-old Oscar and 3-year-old Mabel. Johanna was now called Hannah. Andrew was employed as a cobbler, but it's unclear what drew him and Hannah to Creighton, hardly an obvious destination for a Swedish shoemaker. Maybe his railroad work brought him there; an extension of the Sioux City & Pacific Railroad reached Creighton in the early 1880s.

The 1906 account says Andrew later moved to Madison, Nebraska, and "opened a shop there." No dates are cited, but this likely was about 1889 or 1890. August's trail was harder to track, but he apparently joined Andrew in Madison around this time. That would explain how he happened to meet Martha Hagglund; she was living with her parents and three brothers on the family farm a few miles northeast of Madison.

In 1890 or '91 a still-restless Andrew Tackstrom moved his family to Stanwood.[99] This would prove a fateful decision; it redirected the course of family history – for the Hagglunds as well as the Tackstroms.

August stayed in Madison and married Martha.

I don't know for sure why Andrew and Hannah moved to Stanwood, and I doubt I ever will, but I have a strong hunch that he saw the Puget Sound as a launch point – in a general sense, if not literally – for adventures in Alaska. He had shown throughout his adult life a yearning for new frontiers — first America as an immigration destination, then the hinterlands of Nebraska and Colorado and the transient life of a railroad hand. Much later he lived in Oregon and in southern California. Despite or perhaps because of its remoteness, Stanwood fit this pattern.

Whatever Andrew's reasoning, the little town at the mouth of the Stillaguamish River seemed to suit him.

"At first, he worked at making and repairing shoes, giving his whole time to that, but in 1898 he opened a harness shop in connection with the shoe business and he has since continued to operate both lines," the 1906 account says. "He is one of the prosperous men of the city, deservedly popular and influential."

Andrew served two terms as a member of the town council. As testament to his local prominence, he is mentioned briefly in other books.

In *Scandinavians on the Pacific, Puget Sound*, published in 1909, author Thomas O. Stine offered a minimalist compliment: "A. Tackstrom, the genial postmaster, was born in Sweden, and has been of practical usefulness to his city."

He also was mentioned at least twice in Swedish-language U.S. newspapers. A December 22, 1900 dispatch from Seattle published in the *Svenska Amerikanska Posten*, a Minneapolis paper, referred to him as the preeminent shoe and harness maker in Stanwood and one of very few Swedes in town. The writer, N.F. Olson, also offered observations about nearby Cedarhome, whose smaller farms he said grew mostly hay and fruit and looked more like farm country in New York state or Pennsylvania than in Minnesota or the Dakotas. Olson marveled at a surrounding forest thick with cedars, which he said were felled by loggers to create *de präktigaste bräder* – "the most magnificent boards."

An item in the January 23, 1903 edition of the Swedish-language *Westerns Tribun* mentioned Andrew as "a Swedish saddler" who "has been here 12 years and done well," suggesting he arrived in 1891. In a reminder that Swedes were not the dominant Scandinavian group, the article called Stanwood "more Norwegian than anything else."

Andrew became Stanwood's postmaster in April 1897. It was an appointment he owed to his Republican party connections, which paid off when William McKinley was elected president in 1896. In that era, unlike today, the Postmaster General was a member of a president's Cabinet, empowered to dole out postal service jobs as political patronage. Local postmasters earned not only a salary – Andrew was paid $488.57 in 1899 – but also commissions from the sale of stamps and other services.

Later in 1897, he was mentioned in a Seattle newspaper. It said an "A. Tackstrom" was among "arrivals" at Seattle's Diller Hotel, which at the time was a sort of way station for people heading to and returning from the Alaska gold fields.[100] Andrew may have been in Seattle for other reasons, but gold likely was on his mind.

Many Stanwood men did seek their fortunes in Alaska. Some cashed in, went back home, bought land and started new businesses. One of them, Henry C. Anderson, came to be called "Klondike" Anderson[101] when he returned to Stanwood after striking it rich in the Klondike gold rush, which started on Bonanza Creek in Canada's Yukon River Valley in 1896.

The 1906 account says Andrew resigned his postmaster commission with the intention of moving to Nome, Alaska, where gold fever had struck, "but circumstances altered his plans." This may have been a reference to the sudden deaths of his wife Hannah and their two teenage daughters, Mabel and Nellie.

Snohomish County's deaths registry says Hannah died on Christmas Day, 1898. She was 49. The handwritten "cause of death" entry is illegible, but it is not diphtheria.

As an official record, the county deaths registry is authoritative but imperfect. It says 17-year-old Mabel died on November 10 and her 13-year-old sister Nellie on December 10. However, a stone obelisk that stands near Nellie's grave in Cedarhome cemetery, memorializing Hannah and the two daughters, has both girls' date of death engraved as November 10. Either the death register got it wrong, or the engraving is wrong. I don't know which.

Mabel died of diphtheria, the often-fatal infectious disease of the upper respiratory system in which a thick membrane invades the throat. Nellie is listed in the death registry as succumbing to "lung fever," which may have been pneumonia. Small headstones mark the side-by-side graves of Hannah, Mabel and Nellie. The daughters' given names are engraved on the stones, so worn by weather that the lettering grew faint. Hannah's stone is engraved with just one word: Mother.

Only four months before her death, Mabel Tackstrom was mentioned in the August 20, 1898 edition of the weekly *Stanwood Press*, a forerunner of the *Stanwood/Camano News*. The newspaper made two references to Mabel having spent time at the beach – apparently near Utsalady, a community on the north end of Camano Island whose once-booming sawmill had closed earlier in the decade.

The first was a one-sentence item mentioning that she and three others "returned from the beach Monday." Separately, the paper ran a remarkably long and rambling account of the beach trip, which it called "a week of unalloyed pleasure." Mabel, who would have been about 17, was among the beach-goers.

"Bathing, boat riding, hunting, picking up agates, and swinging in hammocks were the principal amusements of the fun-loving crowd," the story said. "Several trips were made to Utsalady for supplies, and Pearson Hobson camp was called on."

The gaiety stands in stark contrast to the gloom that soon befell Andrew. By Christmas, all that remained of his immediate family was his son, Oscar, who had marked his 19th birthday just days before his mother died. So, it is understandable that Andrew would call on his brother to help fill the void and ease his pain. August and Martha moved to Stanwood six months later, on June 10, 1899, according to a naturalization petition August filed in court years later. This aligns closely with the Stromsburg (Nebraska) newspaper report that said the Tackstrom family had been visiting Lewis and Martha Hagglund in Stromsburg in early June 1899. They probably were on their way to Washington.

Although the 1983 Everett account of Andrew's losses is largely correct, one part remains a puzzle. That is the reference to Martha and August and their three children being in Iowa when they made the move to Stanwood to console Andrew. Available evidence suggests the Tackstroms were living in Nebraska, not Iowa. The Stromsburg news report of the Tackstroms visiting Lewis and Martha Hagglund in June 1899, for example, called them residents of Madison, Nebraska. A year later, in June 1900, the census shows the Tackstroms living in Stanwood; August worked as a mill fireman, meaning he fed the boiler fire that powered the saws.

It seems possible that after moving to Stanwood the Tackstroms reversed course a short time later to resettle in Iowa. This scenario is based on is a one-line blurb published in the Denison (Iowa) Review newspaper on October 14, 1903.

"Aug. Tackstrom and family near Kiron left Friday for their new home in Stanawood [sic] Wash.," it said with no further details. The language is ambiguous but seems to indicate the Tackstroms were moving their place of residence rather than merely returning to

Stanwood after a visit. I could find no other newspaper references to them in Iowa during that period.

It seems peculiar that the Tackstroms would have made three long-distance household moves in such a short period – from Nebraska to Washington in 1899, then to Iowa sometime after June 1900, only to return to Washington in 1903.[102]

23

The Rush to Alaska

Washington grew rapidly after gaining statehood in 1889. Over the next 20 years its population tripled, from 357,200 to 1.14 million, and Scandinavians were in the vanguard. Three counties in western Washington — Whatcom, Skagit and Snohomish — were among the biggest draws for Swedes and Norwegians, many of them second-stage immigrants from what was called the old Northwest – especially Minnesota, Wisconsin, Iowa, Illinois and the Dakotas.

On a wider scale, America at the turn of the century was experiencing rapid change that had only begun to touch the lives of the Hagglunds and their extended families. Telephones were coming into wide use, the automobile age was dawning, and cities were being electrified. The Puget Sound area enjoyed an economic boom led by fisheries, mining and the timber industry, which created jobs as well as social friction. The boom times attracted immigrants from Asia – some tolerated, others not. (In September 1907, some 200 "Hindu" lumber mill workers were forcibly run out of Bellingham – "hounded" out of the city, as the *Bellingham Herald* put it.)

This turn-of-the-century wave of newcomers included another

member of the Tackstrom clan, Carl, an older brother of August's. Carl emigrated with his wife and their four children in 1904, first to Pittsburgh, Pennsylvania. Later they resettled permanently in Bellingham, where he remained until his death in 1922. Interestingly, this was Carl's second immigration go-around. He initially came to the United States in May 1887, settling near Marquette, Michigan, and returned to Sweden in 1890.

Washington state has long attracted adventurers and dreamers, notably the thousands who were lured in the late 1890s by talk of striking it rich in the Klondike gold fields in Canada's Yukon River Valley. Seattle enjoyed its own bonanza as the outfitting center for most of the mining companies and individual "stampeders," supplying everything from food, clothing, maps and super-duper sleeping bags ("right to 80 degrees below zero," one Seattle newspaper ad claimed) to portable sawmills and collapsible canvas riverboats. Puget Sound was not the final frontier, but it was getting close.

In June 1900, Andrew Tackstrom's son Oscar headed to Alaska on his own, perhaps fulfilling his father's ambition. He was aboard the steamship SS *Olympia* on its way from Seattle to Nome at the time of the federal census, which is how I happened to discover his whereabouts. Two years earlier, a discovery of gold on Anvil Creek by prospectors who became known as the "Three Lucky Swedes" (although one was a Norwegian) set off a gold rush, giving rise to a tent city that became the town of Nome on the south coast of the Seward Peninsula. Oscar's ship arrived in Nome on June 17; on a return voyage many years later, he would be counted again, in a gravely different circumstance.

* * *

Alaska and 'Peril of the Sea'

Andrew Tackstrom eventually made it to Alaska. In late 1909 or very early in 1910 he moved into a boarding house in Fairbanks, where he worked as a cobbler. He is listed in the 1910 federal census, taken in January, as a "lodger" among a couple dozen others – mostly miners, joined by bartenders, a restaurateur, a machinist, and others apparently drawn to the little town on the Chena River that launched the gold rush of 1902. The census shows Andrew's son Oscar living separately in Fairbanks with his wife Christina and their son George, born in Alaska in April 1908.

Oscar seemed to have inherited his father's fascination with Alaska and adventure. He spent a dozen years or more living that rugged life, from the central Yukon River Valley in Alaska to the Klondike on the Canadian side. For his father, however, the attraction of the High North did not last long. Immigration records show Andrew arrived in port at White Rock, British Columbia, just south of Vancouver, in April 1910. From there he probably took a train across the border.

Snohomish County land records show Andrew owned 80 acres in Cedarhome in 1910 (the north half of the southwest quarter of Section 5), but he was not living there. He was running a saddle and harness business in the southern Oregon city of Medford. "Harness made to order," one of his Medford Harness Co. ads said in August 1910. He sold light and heavy harnesses, saddles, tents and other goods. For a brief time, Oscar also owned a business in Medford, even while he was spending most of his time in Alaska. His women's clothing store, The Emporium, was on East Main Street, apparently close to his father's shop. After less than a year of operation, Oscar sold the business, explaining in a December 1910 newspaper ad that he was turning his energies full time to his "extensive mining interests in Alaska," which required his "undivided attention."

In September 1911, Andrew remarried. His bride was Emma Zetta Hobbs. An Iowa native, Emma died in Medford in 1922, and by the following year Andrew had moved to Bellingham. Soon thereafter he was on the move again. The 1930 census shows him in Montebello township in Los Angeles County, California, where he lived in the home of his stepson, Bertrel L. Hobbs, and Bertrel's wife, Helen.

Andrew died in May 1942 in the Los Angeles area at age 91. He had outlived everyone in his immediate family, including two wives. In fact, his entire personal bloodline had been extinguished – all three of his children and his only two grandchildren – even before he reached old age.

Personal tragedy stalked Andrew well into the 20th century. In Medford in October 1918, he got word that a Canadian passenger liner, the SS *Princess Sophia*, had sunk off the coast of Alaska. Among the missing were Oscar, age 39, and Oscar's 29-year-old wife, Christina, as well as their two young children, George and Margaret.

After a decade in the High North, Oscar and Christina had given up their home in Ruby, Alaska, a gold-rush town on the Yukon River where he managed a lumber company. They planned to resettle in the Lower 48 before winter set in.[103]

From Ruby, the Tackstroms made their way by riverboat down the Yukon, past Tanana and Dawson City to Whitehorse, where a train took them to the port of Skagway. There they boarded the *Princess Sophia*, their escort to a new life. They may have intended to resettle in Alameda County, California, where Christina's sister, Margaret Pfrang, lived.

What Andrew would eventually learn is that at about 2 a.m. on October 24, as much of America awaited word of an armistice ending the First World War, the *Princess Sophia* went aground on a submerged rock called Vanderbilt Reef in Lynn Canal, in Alaska's Inner Passage about 30 miles north of Juneau. The pity of it was that all aboard —

353 by most accounts — were alive and waiting to be rescued, but the captain judged it too dangerous to attempt to move passengers onto rescue ships standing by in a blinding snowstorm. The ship's hull seemed fully intact, so they waited. "For a while there was some excitement but no panic," one passenger wrote in a letter to his mother as the drama unfolded.[104] Daybreak came, but the storm persisted. So they waited still longer. The next afternoon, some 40 hours after going aground, the ship broke up and quickly sank.

The only survivor was a dog.

It took more than two months to find the body of 10-year-old George Tackstrom.[105]

An official inquiry concluded that the ship, which was making its final scheduled trip of the season from Skagway to Vancouver and Victoria, British Columbia, was lost not by criminal negligence but "through peril of the sea."

The Alaska tragedy is notable for more than the stunning loss of life (six years after the sinking of the Titanic) and its nearly hidden place in American history. It also compounded the pain Andrew had suffered two decades earlier in Stanwood with the deaths of his wife and two daughters.

Alaska turns out to have influenced not just Tackstrom family history but also, less directly, that of the Hagglunds, even though no one in the Hagglund family is known to have ever set foot in the High North. I believe that Alaska's allure was the reason Andrew came to Stanwood in the first place. Had he not made that move and subsequently suffered his sudden losses of 1898, August and Martha Tackstrom would not have come, either. Had they not come, the Hagglunds would not have followed. Had the Hagglunds not made the move, the Mortons and their offspring would not have joined them, in which case some of the faces of succeeding generations would have looked much different – including my own.

If not for Andrew's cry for help, would August and Martha have remained in Nebraska? Or would some other circumstance have drawn them and the Hagglunds away from the prairie to resettle in another part of the country? Family legend says John and Anna were unhappy in Nebraska. But I have no reason to think that, absent the Stanwood tragedy, they would have ended up in Washington.

Lars Morton and his six children followed the Hagglunds to Washington, although not immediately, not directly and not all at once. The Mortons brought with them new additions to the extended family and, in Anna Morton's case, a new connection to the old homeland. And therein lies a story of its own: the lucky encounter.

* * *

Anna meets Carl

To answer the question of how Anna Morton, born and raised in Nebraska, happened to meet Carl Freberg, an Iowa farmhand fresh off the boat from Sweden, we must consider again the passing in 1893 of Anna's mother, Christine Morton. Her death had far-reaching consequences, some blurred by the passage of time. It changed the life paths of Anna, her siblings, and their father.

Suddenly a widower at age 46 with a need to keep working and the responsibility for raising six young children, Lars Morton faced a dilemma that would bedevil any father in his shoes. Should he count on 11-year-old Anna to be a surrogate mother to her two brothers and three sisters – one just 18 months old – to keep the family intact? Or should he break it up for the sake of placing the children with people better positioned to care for them?

He more or less split the difference. Some of them were separated, but not for long periods.

His decision might have been influenced by an event that, if portrayed accurately in a local newspaper, illustrated the hazards of keeping all six young ones together in a single-parent household. Two of the four Morton girls (the news report did not say which ones) came close to real trouble, either through mischief or mishap.

"What might have been a fatal accident occurred to one of L.G. Morton's children yesterday morning," the brief story began, referring to January 25, 1894. "Her clothes caught fire and she ran outdoors enveloped in the blaze. Her sister started after her with a pail of water and succeeded in throwing the water on her and extinguishing the fire before any injury was done."[106]

It probably was some weeks or months after this that Lars began moving some of the children from their home in Madison County to west-central Iowa, where their maternal grandparents once farmed and where Lars himself once lived. Just as Iowa had provided a fresh start for John and Anna Hagglund as immigrant parents in the late 1860s, it now offered a new beginning for the Mortons.

From this followed an unlikely series of events – sketched out here by relying on official records and deductive reasoning – that carried Anna, like a storm-tossed ship saved by a favorable current, to her future husband and eventually to Cedarhome. Like so many life-changing events, misfortune was reversed by a lucky encounter.

In the absence of personal records or recollections from those involved, my reconstruction of the Mortons' turn-of-the-century path from Nebraska to Iowa amounts to a circumstantial case and is thus susceptible to error. Piecing it together was a little like connecting badly faded dots on a crumpled canvas. It was more art than science.

The story starts with the girls.

In 1894 or early the following year, Lars sent Mabel, his second-born, to live with Gust and Amanda Selander, Swedish immigrant farmers in Crawford County, Iowa, near where the Hagglund family had lived years earlier. Gust and Amanda's grown children were no longer at home, according to the 1895 state census, which lists Mabel Morton, age 10, as a member of the household. She probably earned her keep by doing household or farm chores.

The Selanders were not a random choice for Lars. He had lived on a Crawford County farm operated by Gust's older brother Carl before Lars and the Hagglunds moved to Nebraska. The 1880 census lists Lars, age 33, as a boarder in the home of Carl A. and Matilda A. Selander, both Swedish immigrants. I don't know how long Lars lived with them, but it seems reasonable to conclude that he got to know the Selanders well enough to believe, 15 years later, that he could trust Carl's brother to look after young Mabel.

Carl and Matilda Selander's farm was in the northeast quarter of Section 16 of Milford township, which leads to one clue about how Anna Morton's path crossed Carl Freberg's.

For some or all of 1880, while living with the Selanders, Lars was a near neighbor of a 23-year-old farmhand named Gustafson A. Brown. (Brown was not his original surname; he was born Gustaf Alfred Eriksson.) As of June, Gust, as he was generally known, was a boarder in the home of John C. Robinson, whose farmhouse was about one mile east of the Carl Selander home. Like Lars, Brown was a Swedish immigrant and a bachelor; he arrived in the U.S. in April 1879. Two years later he married a fellow Swede, Louise Johnson, and the very next month Louise gave birth to a son, Harry.

I cannot prove that Lars was a friend or even an acquaintance of Gust Brown, but a connection seems likely, which suggests an explanation for the facts that follow:

More than a decade later, in the mid-1890s, Gust and Louise Brown were living in the Iowa township of Wheeler, in Sac County, a short distance north of the old Hagglund farm in Crawford County. Wheeler was virtually all farmland at the time; the nearest town of any note was Odebolt, a burg a bit to the north in Richland township. The 1895 state census shows that Gust and Louise had two non-family members living with them. One was a 9-year-old girl. Her name was Blanche Morton. The other was a 22-year-old farmhand, an immigrant who could read and write Swedish but not English. His name was recorded in the cramped handwriting of the census-taker as Elmer Friedberg.

Elmer Friedberg, I believe, was Carl Freberg. At first glance this seems a stretch, but on closer examination it looks like nearly a cinch. Here's why.

Official records show that when he left Sweden in March 1893, Carl told local authorities he was headed for Odebolt, Iowa, the little town near the Brown home. He likely was in search of farm work, and he almost certainly went there directly after arriving in New York harbor on April 11.

Also, the name Elmer Friedberg is not as far off the mark as it might look. Carl Freberg was known during his first years in the United States by several variations of his name. (Swedes tended not to put much stock in picking a name and sticking with it, and Americans tended not to care much about correct spelling.) Although he began life in Sweden as Karl Emil Härj, and then Karl Emil Gustafsson, he later took the surname Friberg. His younger brothers Set and Victor took the same new surname but did not emigrate. In the United States, Friberg evolved to Freberg and over time was subject to inventive spellings.

Government documents from the 1890s and early 1900s list Carl by a variety of surnames and given names. The Crawford County courthouse record of his marriage in February 1900, for instance, has him as Elmer Freeberg. That's remarkably close to Elmer Friedberg, the name in the 1895 census. The Denison Bulletin newspaper, in its wedding report the next day, also called him Elmer, which may have been an Americanization of "Emil," the name he answered to in Sweden.

There were other variations. The 1900 census taken a few months after his wedding lists him as Emil Freberg. At times, he was called Charles, not uncommon for a Swede named Carl. One census recorded his surname as "Freeborg," and a directory called him "Freborg." Even in death the spellings varied. The Stanwood funeral home that supplied his casket in 1963 called him "Freeburg."

The "Friedberg" spelling could be explained as the Iowa census-taker's interpretation of what he was told verbally by another member of the Brown household; in those days, census-taking was a door-to-door affair. It's clear from the record that the nose counter was told the Swedish immigrant knew little or no English. At any rate, there is no available evidence of an actual "Elmer Friedberg" in Sac County census records before or after 1895. This suggests a strong likelihood that the spelling was in error, as happened often in census-taking.

Also, of the two family members living with Gust and Louise Brown in 1895, one was their teenage son, Harvey "Harry" Arthur Brown. The other was a nephew of Gust's. His name was Adolph Brown, age 17, who five years later would be recorded as an official witness at Carl and Anna's wedding, suggesting a friendship that developed while he and Carl lived together on the Brown farm prior to 1900.

The only other details about "Elmer Friedberg" reported in the 1895 census were his country of origin (Sweden), his religious faith ("none"), and his age (22). The listed age aligns with the May 13, 1873 birth date Carl claimed incorrectly throughout his life in the United States. (Multiple Swedish records, including his official birth record, say he was born one year earlier, May 13, 1872. When he left Sweden in March 1893, he gave his age as 20, which was correct.)

So, while I have no proof, it seems reasonable to conclude that the man called Elmer Friedberg in the 1895 census was Carl Freberg. If correct, this suggests the likelihood that Carl met Anna Morton through her sister, his housemate Blanche. (Coincidence or not, Anna and Carl named their first-born daughter Edith Blanche.)

Exactly when Carl first set eyes on Anna is a matter of guesswork. One could imagine Blanche alerting her older sister to the presence of an eligible bachelor in their midst. Maybe Anna joined Blanche as part of the Brown household sometime after June 1895. Unraveling this mystery might be easier if I could have determined where Anna was living in the several years before she married Carl in 1900. Alas, I could not.

Anna, her younger siblings Harry and Clara, and their father probably were not in Iowa in 1895. I reviewed the entire Sac County section of that year's state census, name by name, and found no mention of them. They may have remained together in Nebraska until later in the decade; Nebraska conducted no census in 1895.

So, I do not know exactly when Anna met Carl or how the relationship developed. Once together in Iowa, the romance seems to have blossomed quickly. They were married on February 28, 1900 in Denison, the seat of Crawford County.

The *Denison Bulletin* published a brief account.

"Elmer Freberg and Annie Morton of Boyer were married in Denison Wednesday afternoon at the Baptist parsonage by Rev. Bateson. A dozen or more of the friends of the young people were present to witness the ceremony," it said without naming any. "The Bulletin joins in wishing them every joy from married life."

(Rev. Bateson was Frederick W. Bateson, an immigrant from Chester, England. He emigrated in 1885, attended college in Iowa and divinity school in Chicago, and was ordained a Baptist minister in Denison in February 1898. He and his wife, Ada M. Bateson, later moved to the Puget Sound area. He is buried in Tumwater, Washington.)

This Baptist parsonage no longer stands, but the church itself does, as of this writing.[107]

Only from Carl and Anna's marriage certificate do we know that her uncle John Hagglund attended as a witness for her. Carl's official witness was Adolph Brown. It's unclear why the wedding was held in Denison rather than Kiron, which was a bit closer to Carl and Anna's home in Boyer. The Kiron Baptist church held special family meaning; years earlier, Anna's parents had been founding members. One possible explanation: the Kiron church was moved from its original location to the new Kiron townsite in late 1899, probably in December; it might not have been back in operating condition by February of the new year.

As a side note that may be just a coincidence, Anna and Carl got married on the final day of February – as did Anna's grandparents, John and Anna Hagglund, a half century earlier in Sweden. Unlike in John and Anna's case, however, 1900 was not a Leap Year. Why get married in February? Not for the weather, especially in Iowa. Two weeks before Carl and Anna's wedding, a cold snap knocked the temperature to 25 degrees below zero.

"Plenty cold enough to freeze up the microbes and any other deadly things in the atmosphere," the *Denison Review* reported cheerily on February 15. "There being no wind, however, people did not feel it badly."

Fifty years later, Carl and Anna celebrated their golden wedding anniversary in Stanwood. A lengthy story, with photo, appeared on the front page of the *Twin City News* on March 9, 1950 below the headline, "Honored Pioneers Feted on 50th Wedding Anniversary." Nearly 200 friends and relatives attended, and "messages of congratulations were also received from Mr. Freberg's relatives in Sweden," the story said.

24

Odebolt or Bust

The story of Carl Freberg's first years in America is largely unrecorded. He arrived in New York harbor in April 1893 and made his way — likely by train — to Odebolt, the little town surrounded by famously rich Iowa farmland. Thereafter his trail goes cold until 1900.

The most remarkable fact I found about Carl's emigration is that even before he left the southern port city of Gothenburg on March 28, 1893, he had declared Odebolt his destination.[108] This is intriguing because Odebolt was remote and tiny, like a grain of sand on a vast beach. The town's obscurity is hard to exaggerate; it stands in contrast to the more common, well-known destinations listed on the ship's passenger manifest – places like New York, Denver and Minneapolis.

Carl and dozens of other Swedes boarded a steamship called the *Argo* for a two-day crossing of the North Sea from Gothenburg to Hull, England. The *Argo* had been plying the rough waters of Northern Europe for more than 30 years and was among numerous ships that fed immigrants to trans-Atlantic shipping hubs in England like Southampton and Liverpool.

Karl Gustafsson, as Carl Freberg called himself at the time, was one of two *Argo* passengers who listed Odebolt as their destination. The other appeared on the manifest as K.A. Ekberg, 22, of the Skaraborg area of southern Sweden. Ekberg was among a group of passengers who disembarked at Grimsby, England, rather than Hull. They may have been making the Atlantic crossing via Liverpool, whereas Carl and others were going by way of Southampton. I found no sign of Ekberg in Iowa records, so I could not determine whether he made it to Odebolt or had a more direct connection to Carl Freberg.

Of the innumerable places in America that Carl Freberg might have chosen to resettle, why Odebolt? How in the world did he even know of the existence of Odebolt, population 1,100 at the time? He left us no answer, but the fact that he had picked this spot even before he left Sweden suggests at least two possibilities. 1.) He had a friend or relative in Odebolt, or 2.) He had seen or heard mention of – or perhaps advertisements for – one of the two large and hugely successful crop and livestock farms near Odebolt. He might have focused on them as a ticket to a better life. Odebolt had nothing else to distinguish itself. (A fun footnote: later the little town would tout itself as popcorn capital of the world, since it was the main supplier of raw popcorn for the Chicago manufacturer of Cracker Jack, the molasses-coated treat that became a national rage after the little ditty, "Take Me Out to the Ballgame," with its "... buy me some peanuts and Cracker Jack" line was introduced in 1908 and later became inseparably associated with major league baseball's seventh inning stretch.)

Odebolt enjoyed what the local newspaper described as a mini-boom in 1891-92, even as much of the country's farm economy was tanking. Local newspaper reports bragged of new building – a grain elevator, a creamery, a Swedish Lutheran church and parsonage, among others. From Carl Freberg's perspective, the real attraction probably was farm jobs. The Odebolt area boasted of two especially big farms – the Cook Ranch, also known as the Brookmont Farm, and the Wheeler Ranch, which shortly after Carl's arrival changed ownership and was renamed the Adams Ranch. The 7,300-acre Cook Ranch was such a phenomenon that the Saturday Evening Post wrote a lengthy story about it in May 1910. The writer called it "farming on an industrial scale" – unusual for those times but perhaps a forerunner of today's corporate farming.

I can't rule out that Carl had a personal connection in Odebolt, possibly even in the Brown family, but I've seen no indication that he had a relative in Iowa. Adolph Brown, who emigrated in 1889, four years before Carl, was from the Falköping area of Sweden, roughly 20-30 miles east of where Carl grew up in the 1880s. Carl's future father-in-law, Lars Morton, also was from the Falköping area.

Once Carl arrived in Hull aboard the *Argo*, he would have remained there about long enough for a cup of coffee. The port at Hull was a common intermediate stop for Scandinavian emigrants. Here, Carl boarded a train for Southampton, 200 miles south. In naturalization papers filed many years later, he said the ship that brought him to New York had departed from Southampton, but he could not remember its name. He did not mention the Gothenburg-to-Hull leg, but the *Argo* passenger list is on file at the Gothenburg branch of the Swedish National Archives.

It appears that Carl sailed from Southampton aboard a trans-Atlantic steamer called the *Berlin*, but the available records make it hard to know for sure.[109] Two passengers named Karl Gustafsson, one age 19 and one age 20, are listed as *Berlin* passengers departing Southampton on April 1. That date would align with Carl Freberg's travel timeline, since he would have arrived in Southampton about three days earlier. The ship's passenger manifest says both Karl Gustafssons were laborers but provides no additional information about them. I suspect there was only one Karl Gustafsson, mistakenly counted twice.

Of the 618 passengers aboard the *Berlin*, 230 were Swedes. The rest were a mix of Danes, Norwegians, Russians, Brits and other nationalities. The ship pulled into port at New York on April 11. The arrivals included just one Karl Gustafson, with a small twist: he was listed with two middle initials added – Karl A.G. Gustafsson, age 19. This person's destination was listed only as New York.

Almost certainly this was Carl Freberg. Some of the Swedes who had been with him aboard the Argo from Gothenburg also were passengers on the *Berlin* from Southampton. They included a young man who likely was a friend of Carl's. His name was Arvid Virgilius Good and his family lived almost next door to Carl's in Trässberg parish. Arvid was three years younger than Carl; both boys' fathers were career soldiers. Arvid's given surname was God, the Swedish word for good. He probably figured, with good reason, that "Good" was preferable to being called "God" in his adopted country.

Parish records show that Arvid left Trässberg on March 14, 1893, the same day as Carl. They probably traveled together by train to Gothenburg. There, both registered for the *Argo*, departing March 28. Arvid listed his destination only as New York; he wound up in Minneapolis, where he married a girl named Anna, whose personal history included being born aboard a ship on the Atlantic Ocean.

Arriving in New York after 10 days at sea, Carl would have been taken with other steerage passengers to Ellis Island, the gateway to their new world, in the shadow of the Statue of Liberty. Ellis Island had opened a year earlier as New York's main immigration portal, replacing the Castle Garden station that had served the purpose since 1850 but had become overwhelmed by a rush of European immigrants.

At Ellis Island, Carl would have undergone medical and legal inspection and been sent on his way.

Carl waited more than 20 years before starting the process of becoming a naturalized citizen. In April 1917, more than a decade after moving to Washington state, he went to Skagit County Superior Court and took the first formal step by filing a Declaration of Intention, in which an immigrant states his or her intention to become an American citizen and forswears allegiance to a foreign power — in Carl's case, Gustavus V, the King of Sweden. This was step one in a two-step process for becoming a naturalized American.

For some reason, Carl waited longer than the allowed seven years before taking the next step of submitting a Petition for Naturalization. As a result, his original declaration lapsed, and he had to start over. In August 1933, at age 61, he filed a new Declaration of Intention in Snohomish County Superior Court in Everett. Three years later, in September 1936, he returned to court to file his Petition for Naturalization, which was granted. An interesting side story: although his wife Anna was born in the United States, never lived abroad and never held citizenship in a foreign country, she also filed a Petition for Naturalization. This is because she had, in effect, lost her citizenship by marrying a foreign national. In those days, a woman's status was governed by that of her husband, and courts generally ruled that a U.S. citizen woman forfeited her citizenship by marrying a foreigner. That changed with the Married Women's Independent Nationality Act (also called the Cable Act) of September 22, 1922, which said citizenship could not be taken away from a U.S.-born woman who married a foreign national who was eligible for naturalization. Anna filed her Petition for Naturalization in Everett in March 1936, six months before Carl.[110]

In the long interval between the start and finish of Carl's quest for naturalization, his memory seemed to falter. In his 1917 declaration, he said he arrived in the U.S. on about the 15th of April 1893 – very close to the actual date of April 11. In his second declaration years later, he said incorrectly that he had arrived on August 15, 1896. In neither instance could he remember the name of the ship.

Carl Emil was the fifth-born child, behind one brother and three sisters. (The first, Mathilda Christina, was born in December 1862 and lived only one month.) Carl also had three younger brothers and one younger sister. I could find nothing more than tidbits in the historical record to shed light on Carl's personality. His grandchildren remember him in his late years as a man of few words. As a child, however, he apparently earned a reputation as a yakker. In a letter to Carl in 1914, his older sister Anna Mathilda filled him in on life in Sweden and gave him a brief update on her four children. The youngest, 7-year-old Knut, she wrote in Swedish, is "a real talker, even worse than Uncle Emil."

Carl was the only member of his immediate family to leave Sweden. Given that he was descended from three generations of soldiers whose service spanned more than 80 years, the idea of abandoning the homeland may have been frowned upon.[111] Carl's father, Gustaf Svensson; his paternal grandfather, Sven Andersson, and his paternal great-grandfather, Anders Skjön, were career soldiers in Skånings company of Skaraborg regiment, an infantry unit that traces its origins to the 17th century. At least two of Carl's brothers also served in the military.

Military service in Sweden in those days was based on an "allotment" system that dated to the late 1600s. Each county was required to allot, or designate, 1,200 men fit for military duty – enough to fill one regiment. Groups of about four small farms, which together formed what was called a "rote," would provide one soldier each. The rote gave their soldier use of a small home, a patch of land, a cow and perhaps a few hogs and chickens, and paid his salary. He would work on the farms in the rote when he was not away for military training or at war. If he died or retired, the home would be returned to the rote. This might explain why Carl's father, Gustaf, entered service at nearly the same time Carl's grandfather father left it, thus enabling the family to remain in the home.

Carl's father was born in the Saleby area of Skaraborg in 1839 and spent 31 years in uniform, retiring in April 1890. He had joined the military in September 1859, just before his 20th birthday and three months after his father, Sven, retired. Sven was born in 1812 in the Ryda area of Skaraborg, about a dozen miles from Saleby; he was 19 when he joined the army and served for 27 years. Sven's father (Carl's great-grandfather), Anders Skjön (sometimes spelled Skön), was born in 1790 and served in uniform for 24 years, retiring in 1837.

Military service adds a further twist to the already complicated Swedish naming conventions. Carl's father Gustaf and his grandfather Sven were assigned the surname Härj, possibly because their home parish was called Härjevad, which originally referred to a church and its village. It was military custom to assign a soldier a short and distinctive name so that it would be easy for a commander to say and avoid confusion in the ranks that would come with having too many common names like Andersson or Gustafsson. The assigned name was sometimes a military-related term, like Svärd (sword) or a warrior characteristic like Stark (strong); other times the name would be derived from the soldier's home village.

The Härj name applied to all of Gustaf's children, as was customary. At some point, probably after their father left the military in 1890, Carl and some of his siblings dropped the name; Carl and his younger brother Set took the patronym Gustafsson, and later they switched to Friberg, combining "fri," meaning "free," with "berg," meaning "mountain," which combined as Friberg might best be translated as "mountain view."[112] Their older brother Johan Alfrid, who also served in the army, also switched but added another name. He became Johan Alfrid Gustafsson Lindqvist.

Carl chose not to follow in his father's military footsteps. At age 18 he hired on as a laborer at a farm called Sjötorp in or near the village of Järpås in Trässberg parish. He then appears to have switched to a farm a short distance away but still in Trässberg parish, which by coincidence was only about 20 miles northwest of Tunhem, the farm town where his future father-in-law, Lars Morton, was raised in the 1850s.

Parish records say Carl left Trässberg for "N. Amerika" on March 14, 1893. Two weeks later he was aboard the Argo and on his way to a new life.

The only other member of Carl's extended family who emigrated was a nephew, Gustaf Sixten Johansson, who made the move much later.[113] Sixten, as he was known in the family, was a son of Carl's older sister, Ida Kristina.

At age 27, Sixten left the port of Gothenburg on November 4, 1922 aboard the SS *Stockholm*. When he arrived in New York 11 days later he told authorities he had $25 in cash on hand and that he planned to find work as a farmhand, become a citizen and stay permanently in the United States. He said his American contact was Carl Moline of Dixon, Illinois, a small town on the Rock River about 90 miles west of Chicago. At the time, Dixon's population included a boy who would grow up to be the 40th president of the United States: Ronald Reagan.

Carl Moline was an acquaintance or possibly a personal friend of Sixten's in Sweden, where he was known as Karl Molin. He was four years older than Sixten and from a hamlet called Askjum, about a dozen miles from Sixten's birthplace at Trässberg. Karl emigrated in October 1913 with a couple of neighbors; they sailed together from Liverpool aboard the *Lusitania*, the British ocean liner that less than two years later during the World War 1 was infamously sunk by a German U-boat, killing more than 1,100 civilian passengers while en route from New York to Liverpool.

In an April 1960 letter to Carl Freberg, Ida Kristina's daughter Berta Svensson (Carl's niece) mentioned Sixten.

"Sixten, the next brother in order, has been in Illinois 13 years and stays right there," Berta wrote, according to a handwritten translation, perhaps by Carl Freberg. Her reference to 13 years is curious, since Sixten had been gone nearly 49 years.

Contrary to his initial plan, Sixten did not stay permanently in America. He returned to Sweden and died there in August 1978.

One additional mystery about Carl Freberg's early years in Iowa is a photo from a Freberg family album in which two unidentified, dark-haired young men posed together in the Ellsworth S. Frey studio in Odebolt. One is standing with his left hand on his hip, his right hand clasping a book that stands atop a small table. The other, who appears a bit older, is sitting with his hands clasped and his right arm slung over the back of his chair. There is no date or other writing on the photo, but below it someone wrote on the album page: "Two friends of C.E. Freberg who came with him to America." The faces are not recognizable from other Freberg family photos of that era, but one of the men may be Arvid V. Good, the former neighbor in Sweden who sailed with Carl aboard the *Argo* and the Berlin. Perhaps he came to Odebolt with Carl and continued to Minneapolis later.

Neither of the two in the photo was Adolph Brown, since he had come to America four years before Carl.

* * *

More name puzzles: Eriksson/Brown

I researched Adolph Brown's personal and family history because he and several relatives played a role in the Morton saga. One of the biggest obstacles to understanding those connections was his name.

Adolph Brown was born Adolf Eriksson. It's unclear when or why he abandoned the patronym, Eriksson, but as we have seen from the Hagglunds and others, name changes were common. He is listed in Swedish church records as Adolf Erik Ferdinand Eriksson, born February 22, 1877 in Falköping, which is both a city and a "municipality," or district, not far from Lidköping, the municipality that includes the villages and farms where Carl Freberg lived and worked while growing up, including Trässberg and Saleby. This area was known at the time as Skaraborg county but is now part of Västra Götaland county.

A descendant of Adolph Brown told me in 2016 that family legend says Adolph felt compelled to change his name upon arriving in Iowa because his cousin – presumably Harry – already had done so. The change started with Harry's father, Gust, while Gust was still single.

What could be called the "Brown factor" in Morton/Freberg family history spreads far and wide and touches many relationships that are hard to sort out in the absence of more detailed personal records. Clues reach across decades – from Adolph's role in Car Freberg's wedding in 1900 to the appearance of Adolph's sister-in-law in Anna Freberg's personal address book a half-century later.

Adolph was 12 when he emigrated in August 1889, leaving behind his parents, Klas Frederik Eriksson and Amanda Kristina Johansdotter, and several siblings with spectacular names. A younger brother, Henry Birger Arkadius Eriksson, followed Adolph to America in 1902. Henry, too, changed his name to Brown. Their sister Anhild Elvira Cecilia Eriksson made the move in 1904, declaring her destination as Council Bluffs, Iowa. Five years later, using the name Anhild E. Brown, she married a Norwegian immigrant, William Paulson, in Kiron.

Brothers Henry and Adolph are listed in the 1905 Iowa state census as living with their Uncle Gust and Aunt Louise in Wheeler township, Sac County. By this time Gust and Louise's son, Harry, had moved out; he married a Crawford County girl, Maud Belle Shives, in January 1904 and they lived out their lives in North Dakota.

Harry, like his cousin Adolph, was friends with Carl and Anna Freberg; the Freberg family photo collection includes at least three that I believe depict Harry. In one photo, he posed with three readily identifiable people – Carl, Anna and Anna's sister Mabel – and an unidentified young man and teenaged girl. The photo, taken in Denison, has no date designation but probably is from about 1900.

Sometime between 1905 and 1910 Adolph Brown moved to Dickey County in southeastern North Dakota with his Uncle Gust and Aunt Louise. He married a local woman, Jessie Gamber, in November 1912, and they remained in Dickey County. He died there in 1936 and she in 1942. Harry and Maud Brown, who lived several miles from Adolph and Jessie, also died there — he in 1954 and she in 1971.

The "Brown factor," however, was not finished.

25

The Mystery of John Morton

For reasons that eluded me, Lars and Christine Morton's eldest son, John, became the mystery member of the family. Even his sisters lost track after he left Nebraska and moved about, living for periods in Iowa, South Dakota, California, Missouri, Washington and perhaps Wyoming. I could not determine when, how or where he died. He seemed to vanish.

John was six when his mother died in 1893. By age 13 he was living on the Madison County farm of Charles and Mary Elizabeth Clark, about two miles from his parents' old homestead. I learned nothing of the relationship between the Clarks and the Mortons, but it seems possible that Lars placed John with the Clarks for the same reason he sent Mabel and Blanche to live with families in Iowa: It seemed like the best thing for them under the circumstance. When Charles Clark died in May 1902, a local newspaper called him "one of the best known and most respected citizens of this community."

John is listed in the 1900 census as the Clarks' "adopted son," although I found no court papers confirming an adoption. The Clarks farmed on 80 acres in the northwest corner of Section 8 of Union Creek township, next door to a schoolhouse (School District No. 41) and beside the Omaha, Niobrara & Black Hills rail line.

John seems to have moved to Crawford County, Iowa, for a short time starting in about 1902, and he apparently later moved to Washington state, or at least visited. In her November 1906 petition in Snohomish County Superior Court for probate of her husband's will, Anna Hagglund, as executor of the will, stated that all of Christine Morton's children, including John, were living in Washington. No towns were specified.

John's younger sister Clara may have seen him in the Bellingham area as late as September or October 1913. She alluded to this in an October 31, 1913 letter to her 10-year-old niece, Edith Freberg, in Cedarhome. Clara was living in Bellingham.

"Dear little Edith," she began. After reporting that her infant son, Corwin, had won first prize at a "baby show," and then telling Edith about a wisdom tooth "on a rampage" that limited her diet to milk and broth, Clara ended with this postscript:

"Do you know where Uncle John Morton is? I have not seen nor heard of him for about a month."

Various family members have recalled that he "disappeared" as a young man.[114] His oldest sister, Anna, is said to have searched in vain for him in Bellingham at some point.

I found several traces of his adult life path but not its end. In 1918, he was living in the small South Dakota town of Salem, the seat of McCook County. Salem is about 130 miles due north of Madison, Nebraska, on what at the time was called the Meridian Highway (now U.S. Route 81), the main road from Canada to Mexico, built early in the 20th century parallel to the land division marker known as the 6th Meridian.

John listed Salem as his home address when he registered for the military draft on September 12, 1918. He put his age as 32 and his birth date as December 14, 1885. (He actually was born one year earlier, December 14, 1886. His mother had given birth to Blanche in May 1885, so basic human biology tells us he couldn't have been born in December of the same year.) John reported his occupation in Salem as thresherman and his employer as John Hinz. He listed his father, "L.G. Morton" of Route 2, Stanwood, Washington, as his nearest relative, although I believe his brother Harry was living in Nebraska.

(In what I believe is nothing more than a coincidence – remarkable as it may seem – another World War 1 draft registrant named John Morton listed the same birth date — December 14, 1885 – and registered on the very same day as the John Morton in South Dakota — September 12, 1918. The other John Morton listed a Seattle address for his residence and said his wife was Ruth Lena Morton.)

For more than a decade after that, his trail vanished. John did not stay in Salem much beyond 1918; he was not there for the 1920 census. I don't know where he went. Some in the family have said John moved to Wyoming to farm and was never heard from again. I found no written record of him residing in Wyoming.

In court documents settling John Hagglund's will in late 1926, John Morton is listed as an heir to his grandparents' estate, along with the other Morton children. The 1926 court document cites him as a resident of San Francisco, with no further details. The only other clue in the Hagglund probate records is a document dated April 25, 1925 in which he signed a record of acceptance for his inheritance of $81; It includes his signature – "J.A. Morton" – above a note saying he was residing in San Francisco at 76 Third Street. That address is near Mission Street, just north of the old Southern Pacific railyard, not far from the entrance to what would become the Bay Bridge.[115]

He later lived at least 12 years in Missouri.

He appears in the 1930 census in Kansas City as John A. Morton, age 43, born in Nebraska to parents born in Sweden. His address appeared to be a hotel, since he is among a large number of people listed as lodgers and guests at 803 Oak Street. He is listed as divorced. Something was written in the census box for "Age at First Marriage," but it was crossed out and is illegible. I found no marriage or divorce record for him. He listed his occupation in 1930 as painter and his industry as printing.

He also is listed in a 1930 Kansas City business and residential directory as J.A. Morton residing at 803 Oak. The only other information provided in this entry is his occupation: interior decorator. I could not find a listing for him in the 1929 Kansas City directory, but the 1935 directory has a J.A. Morton, painter, at 818 East 12th. That is the same address listed for him in the 1940 federal census, which says John A. Morton, age 54, born in Nebraska, was at East 12th Street, with no house number given; it says he had been at the same address since at least April 1, 1935. He is designated as a "lodger" – one of many dozens – at what apparently was a residential hotel. His occupation: painter and contractor.

The Kansas City connection is further confirmed by a World War 2 draft registration card for a John Albert Morton born in Madison, Nebraska. On that 1942 document he again put his birth date as December 14, 1885 instead of 1886, but this certainly is the same man. He listed his home address as 818 East 12th Street in Kansas City — the same place he had been living since the 1930s — and his occupation as self-employed "paint contractor." Curiously, on the line asking for "the person who will always know your address," he wrote Paul Streeter of 3120 Main Street, Kansas City, Missouri. I could find no record of such a person.

I found no record of John's death, so the mystery lives on.

John's younger brother, Harry, also took a different path from Nebraska, although he eventually wound up in Washington and remained there. Harry was 4 years old when his mother died. Like

Clara, he was raised by his big sister, Anna; the siblings lived with Anna and Carl in Boyer, Iowa, after they married in 1900, and while Clara likely moved west with them in 1903, Harry, at age 15, appears to have stayed behind.

The 1910 census lists Harry as a "hired man" in the household of Herbert and Ida Perdy, a young couple operating a farm in the Stanton County, Nebraska township of Dimick. His uncle Oscar Hagglund's family was living in Ramshorn township, adjacent and to the east of Dimick, which is a rural farming area on the Madison County border. The following year, on June 7, 1911, Harry married 21-year-old Matilda K. Wieland (daughter of German immigrants whose surname originally was spelled Wyland) in Madison, Nebraska. "Tillie," as she was sometimes called, was born and raised in Madison. She gave birth to their first child, Hyacinth, in Madison that same year.

Harry's World War 1 draft registration card shows he was still living in Madison in 1917, a father of four children, employed as a mailman. By 1920, Harry and Tillie and the children were living in Norfolk, about 15 miles north of Madison; he was a railroad brakeman.

By the mid-1920s he and Tillie had moved to Everett, Washington, and Harry was working in a lumber mill. They remained there at least into the mid-1930s. By 1942 he was living in Hoquiam, Grays Harbor County, Washington, where he worked in a shingle mill and had the scars to prove it. Asked on his World War II draft registration card whether he had any distinguishing physical marks, he reported that one finger on his left hand and two on his right had been "sawed thru joint."

Harry died in Hoquiam in August 1957 at age 68. Tillie died in Everett in December 1964.

26

Iowa Again

By June 1900 most of the Mortons had migrated to Iowa.

Blanche had just turned 15. She was still in Sac County but had shifted from the Brown farm to the home of William and Hannah Paul a short distance away in Wheeler township, where she was a domestic servant. It's unclear what, if any, connection Lars had to this English immigrant family.

Mabel Morton, who had been living with the Selanders in 1895, is listed in the census five years later as a domestic servant in the home of another Swedish immigrant couple, August and Tilda Linman. She was now 16. August Linman came to Crawford County with his parents in 1869, one year after the Hagglunds, and grew up not far from the Hagglund family farm. The Linman farm was about four miles east of Kiron and just below the Sac County line. This meant Mabel in 1900 was several miles from Blanche and probably within a mile or so of the Boyer farm where her siblings Harry and Clara were living with Carl and Anna.

Lars Morton, meanwhile, had moved to the Kiron area with all or most of the farm equipment and livestock he had acquired during his years on his Nebraska homestead. This would suggest he intended to continue farming, but that ambition did not last long. On February 27, 1900 – the day before Anna and Carl's wedding – he auctioned off the equipment as well as livestock and household items: a table, a bureau with mirror, a coal stove, two bedsteads "and a lot of other articles," according to a notice published a week earlier in the *Odebolt Chronicle*.

"Having quit farming," his ad began, he was employing the services of an auctioneer to dispose of his property, using August Linman's place as the venue. Among the animals for sale: four horses, including a 12-year-old gray mare; six head of cattle, and eight "brood sows" (female pigs). He also sold off a lumber wagon, a 16-inch walking plow, two corn plows, a disc harrow and a corn planter. Several pieces of farm equipment were listed as "nearly new": a two-seat buggy, a McCormick binder, a Deere mower, and a "sulky plow," which was a type of horse-drawn riding plow – a forerunner to the mounted tractor plow.

The fact that he staged the auction at the Linman place suggests the possibility that Lars was living there at the start of 1900, perhaps with Mabel. By the time of the census in June, however, he was in Kiron. The census lists him as a "laborer" living in the home of one of the town's best-known businessmen, George A. Norelius, whose father, Andrew Norelius, was pastor of the Swedish Baptist Church in the early years of the Hagglunds' time there. George's son, Everett A. Norelius, would later buy the 40-acre Otter Creek farm once owned by the Hagglunds, and most of that acreage remained in a Norelius family trust well into the 21st century.

I could not determine whether Lars had close ties to the Norelius family, but the fact that he lived in George's home at the turn of the century suggests the possibility that the arrangement reflected the Hagglunds' long association with the family, based on their shared Baptist faith, their links to Vasa, Minnesota, and their arrival in the

Kiron area at nearly the same time in 1868. George was the same age as Martha Hagglund; as children they may have attended school together.

During some portion of 1900 — likely while living in the Norelius home — Lars worked as a railroad section hand, meaning he laid or maintained track. He was probably making $1.25 a day, judging from news accounts from that period. The pay was not high, but the physical toll was. A local newspaper item in November reported, "Our friend and section man, L.G. Morton, is confined to his bed with a complicated back and limb trouble this week." He had just turned 53 years old.

At this point, in the summer of 1900, Anna and Carl Freberg were renting a farm near the Crawford County village of Boyer, along the Boyer River, several miles east of Kiron. I could not find their exact location, but it was remarkably close to where John and Anna Hagglund had been tenant farmers in the late 1870s. Living with Anna and Carl were her younger brother Harry, age 11, and the baby of the Morton family, 8-year-old Clara. To Anna's credit, both kids were attending school.

Anna's diligence in these trying times set an example that earned the respect of many. Generations of descendants marveled at how she managed the responsibility of looking after her siblings while she herself was only a teenager.

Two decades after Anna's death, her niece Philip Smith told the 1983 Everett family reunion that she deserved enormous credit.

"Aunt Anna, she was the head of the family," he said. "She helped raise those (five) kids."

Initially I thought this comment, which captured Anna's heroic effort and strong will, had understated the burden her father bore as a grieving widower. But later I came to realize that Anna's challenge was even greater than I had imagined. It turns out that in late March

1901, Lars moved to Princeton, Illinois, the Bureau County town where several of his siblings had been living since the 1860s. He appears to have gone alone, again separating from his children.

"We are sorry to lose friend Morton from our locality," the *Denison Review* wrote, "and trust it will be but for a short time." [116] The article said Lars had "secured a good position" in Princeton and intended to stay "through the balance of the year."

Anna was now 19 and had just become a first-time mother. Her youngest sibling, Clara, was only 9. Without judging Lars, it is striking that he would feel compelled to move so far away to find work, even if he intended to return by year's end.

Lars kept a low public profile throughout his life — so much so that I found it difficult to track him, even in public records like the census. He was no publicity hound. In 1902, however, he made quite a splash on the front page of the Princeton newspaper. The story detailed Lars' recollection of a run-in he'd had years earlier in Iowa with Leslie M. Shaw, a banker and lawyer who later served two terms as the state's governor and vaulted to national prominence in January 1902 when President Theodore Roosevelt chose him to be treasury secretary.

It's entirely unclear what prompted the *Bureau County Tribune* to publish this account, but I wouldn't rule out a political ploy — not by Lars but by the newspaper's editor. Otherwise, you would have to conclude that Lars had just wandered into the newspaper's offices one day and offered up an unsolicited recollection of Shaw, who was four days away from taking up his new duties as treasury secretary. I can't rule out that Lars did initiate this news story, but it seems unlikely. In an era of openly and explicitly partisan newspapers, the *Tribune* favored Democrats, and thus it may have been inclined to welcome any dirt on Shaw, who was about to assume a top Cabinet post in a Republican administration.

"L.G. Morton, of this city," the story began, "has a vivid recollection of an interview he once had" with Shaw. After digressing to recount Shaw's rise to political prominence and take a swipe at his character – "a money loaner and financial sharp, keen as a razor and hard as steel, absolutely devoid of compassion or mercy for the man in a hole" – the story got around to Lars' recollection of Shaw, with whom Lars was acquainted from his years in Crawford County, Iowa. Shaw was a lawyer in Denison, and Lars was a farm hand in the area.

"One day while residing there, Mr. Morton bought a horse of a young man who warranted the animal to be sound and true," the story said. Unfortunately for Lars, the horse turned out to be a loser. "Mr. Morton found he was as tricky as the average politician" and so weak or unwilling that he "would not pull a tired man to his feet."

Lars marched the horse back to its original owner, whom he found on a Denison street. He demanded his money back, but the owner refused and ducked into Shaw's law office. Lars followed and spotted the two men conferring out of earshot and glancing in his direction. It appeared the Swedish immigrant commoner was about to lock horns with a titan of late-19th century Iowa politics.

In Lars' recollection of the moment, Shaw suddenly was "advancing on Morton in a menacing manner [and] exclaimed in a loud and threatening voice: 'You want to create a disturbance, do you? I'll give you all the law you want and make you plenty of trouble if you don't quiet down.'"

Shaw's courtroom reputation for crafting iron-clad arguments was such that an admirer in Iowa once asserted it was "well-nigh impossible to answer him."[117] Lars, however, was not easily impressed. Nor, in the case of Shaw's verbal threats, was he amused. As the Princeton newspaper story put it, Shaw's words "had the reverse effect of what Mr. Shaw intended, for it so angered Mr. Morton that he seized Shaw by the shoulder, gave him a twirl, and while scarcely able to resist the impulse to knock him down, informed him there would be plenty of trouble right then and there unless the deal was squared and he received his money."

The reader is left with the impression that Lars won the day, but the story did not say exactly how the confrontation concluded. The story ended with a verbal jab at Shaw.

"Mr. Morton says Mr. Shaw was very unpopular in his home county and never could carry it in local elections on account of his crafty, selfish and money-grabbing nature." (If true, this is a side of Shaw that was not reflected in the generally positive press coverage he received in Denison during his political career.)

I could not determine how long Lars stayed in Princeton, what sort of work he did there or where he went next, although I presume it was to Cedarhome.

Lars never remarried, but he seemed to hold a special place in his mother-in-law's heart. In an addendum to her final will and testament, Anna Hagglund made a point of leaving to him "my new Bible."

* * *

Three Annas and an Emma

Anna Freberg not only played the role of surrogate mother to her sisters and brothers, she also made lifelong friends during the short period she lived in Iowa. I managed to learn a little about three of them and was surprised to find yet another link to the Brown family.

One friend was Anna Mathilda Anderson. The two Annas – Freberg and Anderson – were nearly the same age. Anna Anderson was born in Odebolt, Sac County, Iowa, in October 1881. By the turn of the century she was a near neighbor of the newlywed Frebergs in Boyer; she was living with her Swedish immigrant parents, Gust and Emma Anderson. The two Annas apparently became acquainted during this period.

In February 1911, Anna Anderson married Henry Brown, the younger brother of Adolph Brown. The ceremony was held in Boyer. By that time, Anna and Carl Freberg were living in Cedarhome, but the two Annas apparently stayed in touch for many years. Evidence of this is an "Anna Brown" entry in Anna Freberg's personal address book, which appears to date to the late 1940s or early 1950s and was preserved by her youngest daughter, Annabelle. The handwritten entry says, "Anna M. Brown, Route 1, Albert City, Iowa, c/o Waldo H. Brown." I have no doubt this was the former Anna Mathilda Anderson. Waldo Henry Brown was Anna's eldest son; she apparently lived with him after her husband died in the early 1940s – thus the "in care of" designation.[118]

A second Iowa friend of Anna Freberg's is listed in her address book as "Mrs. Doc J.D. Cornish, Odebolt, Iowa."

Determining the identity of Mrs. Cornish proved especially difficult. J.D. Cornish – Julius Dawson Cornish – was married three times in a span of 32 years; He was nicknamed "Doc" even though he was a farmer and had only a grade-school education. His first wife was Clara Alice Shives, whose younger sister, Maud, married Harry Brown – the same Harry Brown whose housemate in 1895 was Blanche Morton and who appeared in a wedding photo with Anna and Carl Freberg in 1900. "Doc" married Clara Shives in 1902 in Boyer. Since Carl and Anna were living in that area at the time, they likely were acquaintances if not neighbors.

Clara and Doc had five children together. Clara died in 1915. The following year Julius married Agda E. Westerlund, a native of Minnesota born to Swedish immigrant parents. He and Agra had four children before she died in 1928. I have no indication that Anna Freberg knew Agda.

Six years after wife No. 2 died, Doc remarried a final time. The bride was Emma Anderson, a cousin of Anna Mathilda Anderson (their fathers were brothers). I believe Emma was the "Mrs. Doc J.D. Cornish" in Anna Freberg's address book.[119] I'm quite sure it was neither of his first two wives. Wife No. 1, Clara, died in 1915 and Anna's address book seems to be of more recent vintage. The second wife, Agda, is ruled out for the same reason, having died in 1928.

This brings me to the last of the three Iowa women who remained in touch with Anna Freberg, and this is where the blood relations among them get especially entangled.

It turns out that Emma Anderson, the third wife of Doc Cornish, had an older sister named Anna Mathilda. Yes, Emma had a sister AND a cousin of the exact same name – Anna Mathilda Anderson. Perhaps to distinguish her from her cousin, the Anna Mathilda who was Emma's sister was known in the family as "Thilda."

Anna Freberg knew both Anna Mathilda Andersons – and Emma, to boot.

The Anna Mathilda known as Thilda married a man named Olof Larson in Seattle in March 1918. I deduced that Anna Freberg knew her from the fact that Anna Freberg's address book has an entry for "Thilda Larson" of Seattle.[120] Olof Larson (not to be confused with the Olof Larson who was Anna Hagglund's brother) died in Mt. Vernon, Washington, in November 1951 and is buried there. Thilda died in Chehalis, Washington, in November 1972.

(Fun footnote: Thilda and Olof gave their second-born son, William, the middle name Odebolt, apparently after the Iowa town that played a central role in Thilda's family history.)

(Small-world footnote: The other Anna Mathilda Anderson, the one who married Henry Brown, had a younger brother named Elwood

Gustaf Anderson, whose family burial plot in Kiron Cemetery in Iowa includes the grave of John and Anna Hagglund's son, Oliver.)

I might never have unraveled the knot of Anna Freberg's Anderson connections if I had not found Kathryn Peper, a granddaughter of Emma Anderson Cornish by Emma's first husband, Edlef Henricksen. When I contacted Kathryn in California in 2015, she was understandably skeptical of a stranger rooting around in her family history.

"Honestly, I can't decide whether to be impressed or appalled at what you were able to find out," she wrote back. Later, perhaps still wary, she said she was a "dead end" for me, but in fact she graciously steered me to important facts and helpful clues.

* * *

The Close-out years in Iowa

Carl and Anna started a family soon after marrying. Floyd was born February 2, 1901, followed almost exactly two years later by Edith on February 8, 1903. Various official records cite their birthplace as Kiron; that may be because Carl and Anna lived in town for a period, although the chronology is unclear after June 1900, at which point they were renting the Boyer farm.

In 1901 Carl tried his hand at what might loosely be called the hospitality business. Local newspaper reports said that in mid-October 1901 he and Anna moved into a newly built Kiron residence owned by John Jacobson, which they rented and used as a boarding house.

"We royally extend to them all the success possible in their new undertaking," the *Denison Review*'s Kiron correspondent wrote. Anna's sisters, Mabel and Blanche, moved in with her and Carl, but that arrangement and their business seems not to have lasted more than a couple of months. In mid-January Carl and Anna vacated the residence.

It's unclear how all of this unfolded.[121] The same newspaper item in January 1902 that said Carl and Anna had vacated what was called the Jacobson house also reported that Carl had been running a Kiron hotel but gave it up for a lack of patrons. My hunch is that the "hotel" and the "boarding house" were one and the same.

"The hotel not securing all the patronage, partly on account of lack of rooms, Mr. F could not find it paying," the report said, using only an "F" for the surname. "We are sorry to see him go out of business and more so the removing of this couple from our town."

The newspaper said Carl and Anna moved from Kiron to what it called the "John F. Engberg place" northeast of Kiron in Stockholm township.[122] Engberg was the eldest son of C.E. Engberg, a Swedish immigrant who was among Kiron's early settlers.

The Frebergs moved to Washington some months after Edith's birth in 1903, possibly in October.[123]

Once the young Freberg family had arrived in the Puget Sound area, they did not immediately settle in Cedarhome. They started in the Whatcom County city of Bellingham, where Carl found work in the timber industry, which was booming. A 1902 business directory listed 91 shingle mills in Whatcom County. Some of them employed as few as five men; none employed more than 34.

From at least 1904 to 1907, Carl worked at the Whatcom Falls Mill Co., originally built on Whatcom Creek.[124] The mill specialized in Western red cedar and manufactured a variety of products including bevel siding, sash and doors, porch columns and lumber. A new plant, built in 1903 at the bottom of Bellingham's "G" Street, eventually produced only cedar lumber and shingles.

While in Bellingham, Carl and Anna had their third child, Francis, born September 2, 1905. As recorded in his Petition for Naturalization filed in Snohomish County in September 1936, Carl moved his family from Bellingham to Cedarhome in January 1908. His sworn witnesses for naturalization were Anna's uncle John J. Hagglund and Harry Tackstrom, son of Anna's aunt Martha Tackstrom. (The witnesses were required to state when they first met Carl. Both were specific: October 26, 1903. That might have been the date Carl and Anna arrived in Washington, although John J. Hagglund certainly had known Carl before that because he attended Carl and Anna's wedding in Iowa in 1900.)

Just months after the move to Cedarhome in 1908, Anna gave birth to daughter number two, Erma, born on her father's birthday, May 13.

Not long after they resettled, Carl and Anna bought a 10-acre parcel less than half a mile from her grandparents' place. 1910 plat map of Snohomish County shows Carl's place on Cedarhome Road – designated as a "wagon road." Next door was a 17.5-acre parcel owned by Anna's father, Lars Morton.[125]

Even after settling in Cedarhome, Carl seems to have spent at least a short period working elsewhere. His 1917 military draft registration says he was working for the Hazel Mill Co. in Blanchard, about 25 miles north of Cedarhome. He may have lived in mill workers' housing there; he listed Anna as a Stanwood resident. Their eldest daughter, Edith, recalled many years later that the family lived on Bow Hill, near Blanchard, for a time, although she did not mention the specific year. Edith recalled being there during the summer – perhaps in 1916 only – while her father and older brother Floyd did mill work.[126]

Mabel and Blanche remained close amid the family upheaval after their mother's death. They were living in or near Kiron, Iowa in late 1901, after their father had moved to Illinois. Mabel was 17 and Blanche was 16. (Kiron is the town just north of the original Hagglund homestead in the Otter Creek area of Crawford County.) A newspaper item suggests they either worked at or lived in a local hotel, which might have been the boarding house their brother-in-law Carl had just opened.

"The Misses Mabel and Blanche Morton have severed their connection with the City Hotel and on Wednesday left for Ida Grove to remain," the *Denison Review*'s Kiron correspondent wrote in the newspaper's November 8, 1901 editions. "It was with the greatest of regrets that Kiron saw these two ladies going away."

Ida Grove is the seat of Ida County. The town sits about 12 miles northwest of Kiron and about 11 miles due west of Odebolt, the main town in adjacent Sac County.

The following spring, the Morton sisters made their way to Washington state, presumably by train.

"The Misses Mabel and Blanche Morton arrived from Ida Grove last week to visit friends over Sunday. On Monday they started for New Whatcom, Wash., where they expect to remain," the Denison paper reported in April 1902. (New Whatcom was the name initially given to the merged Whatcom County towns of Whatcom and Sehome. In 1903 the "New" was dropped, and Whatcom merged with Fairhaven to create today's city of Bellingham.) Mabel was 18. Blanche was one month shy of her 17th birthday.

It didn't take Mabel long to get her bearings in her new surroundings. On August 27, just four months after arriving from Iowa, she married a Bellingham mill worker, Peter Peronteau, in Stanwood. At the wedding, Blanche was her official witness.

Mabel and Peter lived for a number of years in Blanchard, a now-defunct town on Samish Bay in Skagit County. For a period in the 1920s, the town's residents included the Roscoe and Ethel Murrow family, whose youngest son was Egbert, who would become famous as Edward R. Murrow, the CBS radio and television journalist whose trademark words, "This – is London," crackled over the airwaves during the German bombardment of Britain in 1940-41 and catapulted him to international fame. Born Egbert Roscoe Murrow in North Carolina, he moved to Blanchard with his family in 1913 at age six.)

Mabel and Peter had no children of their own, but they raised Althea Viola, whose biological parents were Ella and Earl Nims. After Ella (niece of Anna Hagglund and younger sister of Lewis Hagglund's wife, Martha) died in April 1906, 11-month-old Althea was taken in by Mabel and Peter. Similarly, Ella and Earl's first child, Vernon, born in December 1903, was raised by Lewis and Martha Hagglund.

Peter and Mabel and daughter Althea moved from Blanchard to Everett at some point in the 1920s and then to Bellingham in about 1928. Peter died the following year. Mabel did not remarry. She died in Bellingham in 1977 at age 93 and is buried in Cedarhome Cemetery beside Peter.

Blanche remained single only slightly longer than Mabel. She married Eudell "Dell" Revere Smith on July 26, 1905 in Bellingham.[127] He was nine years older than Blanche and a native of Sutton, Nebraska. His family had moved to Bellingham from Nebraska in 1900.

Blanche and Dell's marriage certificate lists his occupation as "candy and cigars." For a number of years he ran "The Club," a combination cigar store and pool hall in Blanchard. It folded in about 1924, and he and Blanche moved to Everett, where they initially suffered hard times as a result of his bankruptcy in Blanchard. They had five sons and a daughter.

Dell and Blanche both died in Everett, he in 1951 and she, at the age of 95, in 1980. Blanche is buried in Cedarhome Cemetery beside Mabel and their father.

Clara Morton, who was 8 years old when Anna and Carl got

married, was 11 when they moved to Washington, presumably with her in tow. By 1910, Clara was working as a telephone operator in Bellingham and living as a boarder in the home of Arthur H. and Winifred E. Pence at 1409 Central Avenue.

A year later, on August 8, 1911, she married Grant E. Stanley in a Baptist church in Seattle. He was a native of Wisconsin and 13 years older than Clara. She was his second wife.

Grant and Clara had a son, Edward Corwin Stanley, born in February 1913 in Bellingham, and a daughter, Betty, born in Idaho in 1920. Clara and Grant moved back to Bellingham at some point before 1930; he died in Bellingham in February 1953, and a short time later she moved to Laramie, Wyoming, where, as I described earlier, she married Charles Eckdahl, a tailor whose mother, Anna (Morton) Eckdahl, was Lars Morton's older sister. Thus, Charles and Clara were cousins. They moved to Bellingham in the late 1950s, perhaps in 1958; Clara died there on May 15, 1969 at age 77 and he in March 1970. He is buried in Laramie, beside his first wife, Jennie, joined later by their son, Clifford.

Clara's remains were cremated in Ferndale, Washington, at Green Acres Memorial Park.[128]

27

Some to Cedarhome, Some to Bellingham

Once August and Martha Tackstrom had committed to moving to Washington in 1899 in answer to Andrew Tackstrom's call for help, the Hagglunds followed from Nebraska in fairly short order.

Lewis and his family moved to the Bellingham area in March 1900 and stayed for the remainder of their lives. Lewis's younger brothers Oscar and John moved at about the same time – Oscar to Bellingham and John to Cedarhome; both would backtrack to Nebraska for personal reasons soon after arriving in Washington, but they eventually rejoined the others on Puget Sound.

Andrew Hagglund was last in his family to make the move, in 1902. He chose Cedarhome.

The exact timing of John and Anna's move to Cedarhome is in some doubt. One of their grandsons, Oliver "Bob" Hagglund, recalled that John and Anna moved to Washington "late in 1900" and lived on a two-acre tract of cleared land in a two-bedroom log house. He remembered it was "well built" with a large unfinished attic. (A home fitting that general description still stood, and was occupied, at approximately the same location on Cedarhome Road more than a century later.)

Bob was a little off on the timing. John and Anna's first appearance in official records as Cedarhome residents is in the 1900 census, taken in June, but it's clear they had arrived several months earlier.

The following lines from the 1983 Everett account suggest John and Anna moved in 1899:

"Anna persuaded John to follow the Tackstroms to the west coast. They stayed with August and Martha for a short time then, in 1900, John bought a tract of timber land near Cedar Home, a Swedish Settlement."

County land records show that John bought property in Cedarhome in February 1900. Given the time required to find and arrange the purchase, it's logical to conclude that he and Anna had been in the area some months before February.

John bought several parcels of land February 20 in two separate deals. Both sellers were in Boston. John paid $560 to Charles E. Dyer and his wife, Olive M. Dyer, for three parcels totaling 80 acres near and along what would become Cedarhome Road. Separately, a Boston widow, Ruth A. Bradford, sold John three other parcels totaling 70 acres in the same area of Township 32 North, for $490.[129]

The warranty deeds in which these transactions are described also note that the Hagglunds leased these same properties in 1899 – another indication that they likely were living in the area prior to 1900.

John concluded a third purchase on July 11, 1902. He paid $500 to a Seattle-based merchandising and land development company, Schwabacher Bros. & Co., for a 40-acre parcel — the southwest quarter of the southeast quarter of Section 5, also in Township 32 North. Schwabacher was a well-known and highly successful company, perhaps best remembered as the main outfitter of prospectors seeking their fortunes in Alaska during the gold rush years. The stampede north to the Yukon started when a steamship laden with gold from Bonanza Creek arrived in San Francisco and another arrived two days later at Schwabacher's dock on Seattle's Elliott Bay on July 17, 1897 with what newspapers reported was a "ton of gold." The Schwabacher brothers built a merchandising empire based mainly in Seattle and Walla Walla.

Their purchase of 40 acres from Schwabacher meant John and Anna had control of the 80-acre south half of the southeast quarter of Section 5 – having bought the adjacent 40 acres in February 1900. Their son, Andrew, later would inherit those 80 acres and operate a sawmill there with his brother John. Another Andrew – Andrew Tackstrom – owned the 80-acre north half of the same quarter section, according to the 1910 plat map, which includes a note that School No. 38 was situated in the northeast corner of Andrew Tackstrom's parcel.

In sum, John and Anna paid $1,550 for 190 acres just north of what came to be called Munson's Corner and just east of Lake Ketchum. At some point prior to 1906 they added 10 acres in the northeast quarter of the northwest quarter of Section 8. The properties' value rose quickly. By January 1907, the combined 200 acres was appraised at $4,620 – about triple the sum John paid for it several years earlier.

At nearly the same time they were buying property in Cedarhome, John and Anna were selling their homestead in Nebraska. They were in Stanwood when they signed the sales contract on February 10, 1900. On that date, in their presence, their signatures were notarized by Whitfield C. Brokaw, who a few years later would be among the founders of the Bank of Stanwood. Terms of the contract suggest John and Anna were in a hurry to make a deal; it committed the buyer, George H. Walker, to paying only $1,100 of the $6,000 sale price in the first three years of a seven-year deferred payment plan.[130]

Once settled in Cedarhome, John and Anna were quick to plug back into the Swedish Baptist community. They became founding members of what initially was called the Swedish Baptist Congregation of Cedarhome. They joined on March 25, 1900, putting them at the bottom of a chronological list of what the church calls its 30 charter members, starting in 1890. This distinction means their lives in America were bookended by pioneering moments in Swedish Baptist church history — first as founding members of the church in Kiron, Iowa, in the summer of 1868, and then in the same role in Cedarhome 32 years later.

The Cedarhome congregation was slow in formalizing. It was started in February 1890 by seven people, with meetings held in homes until a church was built in 1900 in an area then known as upper Cedarhome. Records from the early years are extremely limited, with no membership list beyond the 30 charter members, although other documentation shows John J. Hagglund joined the church shortly after his parents, and his brother Oscar served as superintendent of the Sunday school in 1927. In 1922 a new church was built in what was known as lower Cedarhome, west of today's Interstate 5, and the name became Cedarhome Baptist Church, dropping the word "Swedish."[131]

John and Anna never moved again. They had no reason to. They'd finally found home. They were getting up in age, and in Cedarhome they were among family, including not only three of their grown children but also their eldest granddaughter, Anna Freberg, and her still-growing family.

Anna Freberg (my grandmother) was the only one of Lars and Christine Morton's children to live in Cedarhome. She was there from 1908 until her death in 1967, which happened to mark 100 years since her mother left Sweden as Kerstin Johansdotter and arrived in America as Christine Hagglund, along with her parents and three siblings.

Anna and Carl built a home on their 10 acres fronting Cedarhome Road. They raised chickens, grew raspberries and other fruits, and had a small number of dairy cows on pastureland behind the house. The land and house were sold after Anna and Carl died, but the house stood until 2016 when the owner tore it down to make room for a new, modern residence. Replacing the old with the new is a familiar theme in the cycle of life, and yet when that old thing has stood squarely in your mind's eye since childhood, its physical disappearance can be jolting. I'll always regret not having taken a final look sometime during my adult years.

Carl worked in lumber mills, including the Wisconsin Timber Co. (later Clough Mill Co.), in Stanwood, until about 1930. By 1940, at the age of 67, he was working as a watchman at a vegetable cannery in Stanwood. According to family legend, he walked to and from work, a distance of about three and a half miles each way. He was 90 when he died of a heart attack at Northern State Hospital in Sedro-Woolley in March 1963. Sadly, he was unhappy with his hospital confinement. I can recall my father telling me that he dreaded visiting Carl there because it meant facing his heartbreaking pleadings to be taken back home.

Anna remained in their home until her death in February 1967 at age 84. She and Carl are buried in Cedarhome Cemetery; their plots are a short distance from her father's grave.

After the birth of Erma in 1908, Anna and Carl may have thought they were done enlarging their family, but nearly two decades later, on May 15, 1926, another baby girl came along. She was Annabelle Carlene, known by many in the family as "Toots." She was my mother. On May 8, 1948, she married Robert Walter Burns, an auto mechanic. They made their home in East Stanwood, down the hill from Cedarhome, and had four children: Barbara Ann, born in August 1950, Deborah Kay in August 1953, Robert Wayne in January 1955, and Roger Warren in July 1961.

Annabelle died in a Seattle hospital on February 21, 2011 after a fall at home, and Robert died of lung cancer at home in Stanwood on September 29, 2014. Their graves rest side by side in Cedarhome Cemetery, within whispering distance of her parents, her grandfather and many other relatives.

Annabelle was not yet two when her Grandpa Morton died on December 10, 1927. The Freberg family photo collection includes one of Lars posing with baby Annabelle. He is in bib overalls, a flat cap shading his eyes. Sporting a white goatee and mustache, he is reclining on his side on the Frebergs' front lawn, propped up on his left elbow as he leans toward Annabelle, who looks to be about one year old. She is sitting upright on the grass in a white dress, looking toward the camera with a mix of puzzlement and bemusement. The photo has no date, but my guess is summer 1927.

Lars died of a cerebral embolism, or stroke. He was 80. He is buried in Cedarhome Cemetery, near three daughters but far from the unmarked Nebraska grave of his long-departed Christine.

* * *

Stanwood and Cedarhome

The spot on the Stillaguamish River delta that became the town of Stanwood was first populated in the mid-1860s by pioneers whose sense of adventure must have been as strong as the area's native cedar trees. Some were East Coast transplants, including Daniel O. Pearson. He came to the Puget Sound in 1866 from Lowell, Massachusetts, with his mother and a sister as members of what came to be called the second Mercer Expedition — a creative scheme by Asa S. Mercer[132] to "import" from Massachusetts dozens of single women and Civil War widows to remedy an acute shortage of marriage prospects for Seattle's men.

Pearson was joined two years later by his future wife, Clara Jane Stanwood, also of Lowell. Initially settling on Whidbey Island, they moved to a tiny trading post at the mouth of the Stillaguamish in 1877, where he built a wharf, opened a store and became postmaster. When requested by the Postmaster General to change the name from Centerville to something less common, he chose Stanwood in honor of his wife's family.

Stanwood is a name with a history of its own.

Clara, the daughter of William Edward Stanwood and Rachel Page, was descended from a centuries-long line of Stanwoods, starting with Philip Stanwood (he spelled it Stainwood), who came from England in 1652 to settle in the Colony of Massachusetts Bay, at the town of Gloucester, northeast of Boston. (Some 600 years before Philip Stainwood emigrated, the name in its ancient Saxon form – Staneude – was known in England. It was a hamlet, owned by the king, in the County of Hampshire.) Even today the Stanwood name is visible in Gloucester. In recognition of the many Stanwoods who lived there, the city includes a Stanwood Avenue as well as Stanwood Point, which is a cape, or headland, in Gloucester's inner harbor.

In 1903, the year Stanwood was incorporated, Daniel Pearson was elected its first mayor. The little town was proudly Scandinavian – the kind of place where the local druggist sold what he advertised as "Scandinavian medicines."

In those days, Cedarhome was hardly a bend in the road; in fact, there were not many roads at all. Situated just northeast of Stanwood, the settlement had a two-story schoolhouse, three churches, a saw mill called the Cedarhome Cedar Lumber Co., and a small mercantile store owned and operated by Gustaf Nickalson. A later version of that store stood in nearly the same spot when I was growing up nearby in the 1950s and 60s. We called it simply "the Cedarhome store," as it was the community's only store.

No one seems to know for sure who chose the name "Cedarhome," or why. Some have said it was in keeping with the abundance of cedar trees, some more than 200 feet tall, that populated the hillsides above the Stillaguamish. In the early years, the name was commonly spelled as two words: Cedar Home.

Whatever its origin, Cedarhome was an apt name for a wooded and welcoming settlement on the doorstep of the Cascade Mountains. It was a homey, modest and unassuming place that embraced simplicity — a perfect match for the Hagglunds.

The area's pastoral, even tranquil, setting was one of its selling points. In a "farm for sale" advertisement in the September 9, 1902 edition of the Swedish-language *Svenska Amerikanska Posten* in Minneapolis, a Cedarhome farmer named John Holm pitched his 25 acres as a place where "storms, hurricanes and malnutrition are unknown."

Author Thomas Ostenson Stine wrote in a somewhat syrupy ode to Cedarhome in 1900, "If it had been whittled out to order for a quiet, sober and intelligent people, nothing more consistent could have been expected." In Stine's telling, the "father" of Cedarhome was a Swedish immigrant named John Anderson, who traveled extensively before settling on 160 acres at Cedarhome in 1876, then known unofficially as "The Burn." That odd name refers to the aftermath of fires that scorched the timberland in the 1870s, leaving what many dismissed as scarred wasteland unfit for human habitation. Hopeful settlers came anyway. Greenery returned and lives flourished.

In her account of Cedarhome history, Stanwood native Grace Ryan Cornwell said there were two such devastating blazes.[133]

"The Stanwood 'men folk' had many a hearty laugh at the 'rubes' who came West from the Dakotas or Minnesota to buy this rough land up on the 'Burns,'" she wrote, adding that the street now called Cedarhome Road was then called "Burn Way." The fires scorched Cedarhome as well as the nearby settlements of Victoria, Freeborn, Village and Bryant.

Stanwood and Cedarhome are among villages, towns and cities across Washington state that acquired a distinctly Scandinavian profile in the late 19th and early 20th centuries. Danes flocked to Enumclaw east of Tacoma, Icelanders to Blaine on the Canadian border and Swedes to Poulsbo on the Kitsap Peninsula on the western shores of Puget Sound. Stanwood and Cedarhome drew Norwegians and Swedes. Among the first to reach the Stillaguamish River valley at what later became Stanwood was a Norwegian immigrant named Oliver B. Iverson. He arrived in 1876 from South Dakota in search of unspoiled land and a climate more to his wife's liking.

In South Dakota the weather wore poorly, Iverson wrote in the first of a series of retrospective articles published in the Stanwood News in October 1920. "There was too much climate, 110 degrees-plus in summer and 40 degrees-minus in the winter." Although he valued the fertile Dakota prairie, his wife did not.

"I had come to the conclusion that if I wanted to keep her I would have to find a different climate," he wrote.

The Puget Sound weather may have been a less compelling consideration for the Hagglunds, Mortons and Frebergs, but it probably suited them. At least they were freed from worry about tornadoes, prairie fires and drought that had threatened them all too often in Iowa and Nebraska. Nor did they face blizzards of the kind that had made an ordeal of Lewis Hagglund's move to Nebraska in 1880-81.

28

Lewis and Two Marthas

L ewis, arguably the most adventurous Hagglund in his youth, settled down once he and Martha and their three daughters arrived in Bellingham. They added a fourth child, Esther, in January 1901. Five years later they took in and raised Martha's nephew, Vernon, who was two when his mother, Ella Nims, died.

Although he ended up in Bellingham, Lewis's initial destination from Nebraska was Stanwood. Parts of that cross-country journey — as with his snow-slowed trek in the winter of 1880 from Crawford County, Iowa to Madison County, Nebraska — can be reconstructed more than a century later, thanks to the extensive paper trail he left in the public record.

Lewis wrote a fascinating account of the March 1900 train trip that took him and his family from Stromsburg to their new life on Puget Sound. Under a miniature headline — "Hagglund's Journey to The Promised Land" — it was written in Stanwood on April 20 and published in the Stromsburg Weekly News in two parts, on May 10 and May 17. The travelogue offered commentary on the landmarks and cities the family saw during their six days on the rails. True to form, Lewis also managed to comment on the heathen habits he observed along the way — "the presence of saloons everywhere" in the vicinity of rail stations, for example.

"Even places that had hardly anything else would have a saloon or two. That is to say the least, a horrible condition of affairs," he wrote.

Lewis said he and Martha and their children were joined aboard the Union Pacific's Express No. 3, which began its run on Monday evening, March 12, at Valley, Nebraska, by "my brother with his family from Madison." He didn't say which brother; I'm not sure whether it was John or Oscar.

After struggling to stay awake to see the Platte River town of Gothenburg, near the Swedish Crosses Cemetery, the Hagglunds slept through the rest of Nebraska and awoke in Wyoming. They missed the train's brief dip into the northeastern tip of Colorado at Julesburg, an old Pony Express stop, but were able to stretch their legs during a 25-minute stop at Cheyenne.

Among the great landmarks the Hagglunds marveled at through their train car windows — in addition to a huge sign Lewis quoted as reading, "Divide of the Continent" — was the legendary Deer Creek trestle bridge in Albany County, Wyoming, about 20 miles southeast of Laramie. At 128 feet high and spanning some 700 feet, it was reputed to scare the living daylights out of passengers as the train, seemingly floating in the air, slowed to make its crossing above an imposing rock canyon, the ribbon of rail sometimes swaying in the wind.

"In looking down from the train as it passed over the bridge we could see dwelling houses which seemed to us about the size of pigeon houses on the banks of the stream below," Lewis wrote in a matter-of-fact tone. If he or others had been frightened, he hid it well.

As a devout Baptist, Lewis seemed even less impressed with Salt Lake City, which he and his family made a side-trip to visit during a layover in Ogden.

"We had not gone far in the city before we were unmistakably convinced that we were at the very seat of Mormonism, for there in the center of the public street ... stands the statue of Brigham Young about 30 feet high with his arms stretched out seemingly assuming an attitude of authority over the city. To us 'gentiles,' as these saints call those not belonging to their church, it seemed very humiliating" for the trains to have to maneuver in order to get by the statue.

He worked a little humor into his commentary, noting that although eastern Wyoming seemed barren — "nothing but red gravel and limestone, sagebrush and buffalo grass" — the state's capital city had redeeming qualities.

"At Cheyenne we got all the coffee we wanted at 10 cents a cup. What do you think of that?"

On the morning of their fourth day they stopped at Meacham in what today is known as the Umatilla National Forest in northeastern Oregon. (The town is about 20 miles northwest of La Grande, where I spent a night in December 1977 after my car broke down in a heavy snowstorm while making my way from Seattle to Jefferson City, Missouri, to begin my Associated Press career.) Lewis was less than pleased with Meacham, despite what he described as pleasing scenery.

"The first station we saw after daylight was Meacham, which is only a small place but will certainly become famous for raising the price of bread — the price was raised more than the bread," he wrote. Told the loaves cost 10 cents each, "and small loaves at that," he left empty handed. "Here would be a good opening for some of Stromsburg's restaurant men, especially if the saloon forces them out."

The Hagglunds' route took them along the Oregon side of the Columbia River as they headed toward Portland.

"Streams of water rushing down the mountain sides makes a very handsome picture," he wrote. "Wish we could send some pine and sycamore trees to our Stromsburg friends, for here are thousands of them along the railroad and they are very beautiful.

"A little further on we caught our first glimpse of Oregon flowers, the ground being covered with them in places, and cattle on green grass, and plum trees in bloom (on March 15)."

He added: "In these mountainous regions you can see mountain peaks only a few rods in circumference but upright as a steeple hundreds of feet high with green trees growing on the very top of them — a curious sight to behold. At one place we noticed a planing mill which was run by water that came from the top of a high mountain, the water being led by means of a great spout."

From Portland, which Lewis described as "very fine" despite a city ordinance that banned spitting on sidewalks "or upon the floor of any building within the city limits," they crossed the Columbia aboard a ferryboat he said was large enough to carry two engines and about 20 passenger cars. That almost certainly was a train ferry called the *Tacoma* (previously called the *Kalama*), which transported Northern Pacific traffic — passenger cars and all — across the Columbia to a landing at Kalama, Washington, where the train would proceed to Tacoma and Seattle. The ferry became unnecessary in 1908 when a train bridge was completed over the Columbia, connecting Portland and Vancouver, Washington.

The Hagglunds made it to Seattle on Friday morning — Day 5 of the journey — only to find that their train connection to Stanwood had just left. Since there also was no boat service that day, they stayed overnight in Seattle. Lewis marveled at a cityscape with buildings "four, five and six stories high." He described climbing "the big bluff on which King County court house is located just east and several hundred feet above the city, where we had a grand view of the whole city, the wharf, the great Puget Sound, the great snow-covered mountains west of the sound, West Seattle on the other side of the sound, the great Mt. Good [*Hood*]."

For all of its fine features, one thing about Seattle baffled Lewis. He was mystified by "that most odd-looking heathen idol of which we heard mention while in Stromsburg." It stood on the street, 50 feet tall and "bears the image of all the ugliest-looking creatures under the sun, being covered with such ghastly looking carvings all the way from bottom to top."

A totem pole? He didn't say.

Lewis and his fellow passengers finally arrived in Stanwood at 10:30 a.m. on Saturday, March 17.

He ended his story with one of his favorite subjects — the weather, which he said was not as bad as commonly believed elsewhere in the country.

"I like the climate here, it being real balmy and the weather has been most beautiful every since we came," he wrote. "We have had a few gentle rains since we came, but only of short duration, it has not been a continuous rain like we were made to believe in Nebraska, neither have the rains been accompanied by thunder and high winds," as they often are in the Midwest.

Lewis, like younger brother Oscar and other transplanted members of the family, initially found work in the timber industry. After a brief stay in Stanwood, he and Martha settled in the town of Geneva on Lake Whatcom, just east of today's Bellingham. He toiled at the Bellingham Bay Improvement Co., a lumber mill and later at the Bellingham Bay Lumber Co. and the E.K. Wood Lumber Co.[134]

Later, for at least several years, Lewis worked at the Bloedel-Donovan mills, a fast-growing forest products company that traced its roots to a mill started on Lake Whatcom in 1898. Bloedel-Donovan also logged and milled on the Olympic Peninsula and eventually was bought out by Weyerhauser, the forest products giant. (Bloedel Hall on the University of Washington campus is named for one of the company's founding partners, Julius Bloedel.)

For many years after leaving Nebraska, Lewis kept up his correspondence with Stromsburg newspapers. Some of his letters touched lightly on his new life in the Pacific Northwest. A few months after resettling he told the Weekly News he was working in a Whatcom County shingle mill for $2 a day. "He says he is very much pleased with the climate of that country," the paper reported. Six years later he ended a letter by saying his family was "fairly well" and "doing nicely out here generally."

By 1930, Lewis had retired, and he and Martha were living in the home of daughter Esther and her husband, Samuel R. Kagey, a mill worker, and their 2-year-old daughter, Marcelline. They were in Custer, an unincorporated area north of Ferndale.

Lewis's knack for appearing in newspapers followed him to the grave. When he died in September 1938 in Whatcom County, Esther sent word to an Ida County, Iowa, farmer named Verne Howard Meleen, whose parents, Ola and Minnie Meleen, apparently were friends of the Hagglunds during their years in the Otter Creek area. Verne Meleen relayed the news to the Odebolt (Iowa) Chronicle, which published a short obituary calling Lewis "a former pioneer resident of Kiron ... who is well remembered here."

"Mr. Hagglund has written on several occasions for the Kiron News," the obituary said.[135]

The Chronicle obituary mentioned that the Rev. Gordon Carlson of the Bellingham Baptist Church officiated at Lewis' funeral service. Carlson had been pastor at the First Baptist Church in Kiron, starting in 1928. That was long after Lewis and the other Hagglunds had left Kiron, but the link may have been important to Lewis. Or maybe the Kiron connection was just a coincidence.

Lewis succumbed to heart failure caused by chronic myocarditis.[136] He passed away on the morning of September 7, 1938 after four days in a Bellingham hospital. He was 79. Martha died 15 years later, on March 29, 1953 in Bellingham after what her obituary in the Bellingham Herald called "a short illness." She was 87.

Lewis and Martha were buried next to each other in Enterprise Cemetery a few miles north of Ferndale. (Lewis is in grave 1, lot 4, block 9-H, and Martha is in grave 4, lot 4, block 9-H.)

The other Martha Hagglund – the one who became Martha Tackstrom — had two more children after she and August moved to Cedarhome. Ruby was born in June 1904 and Hazel in September 1906. Her Nebraska-born sons, Lawrence and Harry, made what was probably their first appearance in the local newspaper shortly before Christmas 1904. The "little tots," as the Stanwood Tidings called the boys, wrote "Dear Santa Claus" letters, perhaps with a parental assist. Both boys asked Saint Nick to remember a gift for their baby sister, Ruby.

"I would like a picture book and a little train," 7-year-old Harry wrote. "I have a little baby sister and I wish you would please bring her a rubber ring."

Declaring himself old enough to hunt, Lawrence, 10, asked for a story book, a BB gun "and some shots." For his sister: "I wish you would bring her a rubber doll." He ended with a final wish that Santa's reindeer not "freeze their ears."

Having been raised a Baptist, Martha apparently kept it in the family. Notes preserved by the Cedarhome Baptist Church include a church member's recollection that Harry was confirmed as a Baptist sometime between 1914 and 1916, which were his late teen years. There was nothing fancy about this. Harry and two others were baptized in the shingle bolt pond of the Sjolander Shingle Mill on Fisher Creek. Shingle bolts, which are blocks of wood from which roof shingles are cut, were often stored in a pond created by damming a portion of a creek. The pond water sometimes became turbid, even filthy.

"They pushed 3 or 4 shingle bolts back until (the pastor) could baptize one of them and then they would go upstairs by one of the shingle saws and change into dry clothes," the note said.

Martha lived a full life but died younger than either of her parents or any of her grown siblings, other than Christine. Martha was 75 when she died on February 22, 1944 at Northern State Hospital, where she spent the final 16 months of her life. The recorded cause of death was arteriosclerotic heart disease – hardening of the coronary arteries.

August died in April 1939 at age 78.

Martha and August are buried in the Tackstrom family plot at Cedarhome Cemetery along with a daughter they outlived, Anna V. Allison, who died at age 30, and their son Lawrence and his wife, Margaret.[137] The 12-grave plot was purchased in 1898 by August's brother Andrew to bury his wife Hannah and their daughters Nellie and Mabel.

* * *

Whiskers

Andrew Hagglund, who had been his father's right-hand man for years in Nebraska, stayed there for two years after his parents moved west, possibly because he was involved in multiple business and real estate ventures in Madison at the turn of the century. When he tidied up his affairs and left for Cedarhome in April 1902, he closed the book on a two-decade Hagglund era in Madison County.

The 1900 census lists Andrew as a 43-year-old boarder in the home of John C. Botts, 51, a farmhand who two years later bought two town lots in Madison from John and Anna Hagglund. The census taker's handwriting in the column listing Andrew's occupation is almost indecipherable but the entry appears to be "wells & pumps," which had been one of his business interests since the early 1890s.

Andrew left little record of his personal life, but the scraps I did find portray an energetic man who was part engineer, part farmer, part woodsman and a bit of a scholar. Of the original Hagglunds, he was the only one who never married.

Like his father, Andrew was committed to the temperance cause; during his years in Nebraska he belonged to the Madison Lodge of the Independent Order of Good Templars, which advocated for the prohibition of alcohol. In 1892 he attended a Good Templars district convention in nearby Wilson, Nebraska.

Descendants remember Andrew was called "Whiskers" for his bushy, red-tinted beard. Through the eyes of a child he could seem a raggedy Andy. Gloria Mathews, who grew up down the road from Andrew in the 1930s, recalled her great uncle many years later as an unkempt visitor next door at her Grandma (Anna) Freberg's house.

"There would be this old man in her kitchen, and she would be fixing something" for him to eat, Gloria recalled in 2019. "His clothes were very shabby. He always wore a hat and had a big beard. We called him Whiskers."

In his declining years, Andrew may not have looked like much. But as a younger man he was the standout entrepreneur in the family. In addition to farming and his failed investment in the "hydrocarbon burner" in 1887, Andrew dealt in windmills as well as tubular wells in the 1890s, and he was partners with his brother John in a small sawmill after he moved to Cedarhome.

He started a plumbing business in 1891 or 1892. In the summer of 1892, he began promoting it with display ads in the Madison Independent Reporter (later the Madison County Reporter) that gave a detailed rundown of his qualifications, specialties and most attractive sales items.

If his business had a name, he didn't use it in advertising. He simply put his name atop his Reporter ads, which said he was a dealer in "windmills, pumps, plumbers' supplies, steam fittings, water tanks, etc., etc." He sold well-known windmill brand names: Adams, Dempster Vaneless (made by the Dempster Mill Manufacturing Company in Beatrice, Nebraska with an innovative design that maneuvered the mill into the wind without need for a tail vane, or rudder) and the all-steel Queen City, also by Dempster. He seemed particularly keen on selling the "Excelsior Windmill Attachment and Feed Grinder," which his ad called "just the thing" for farmers looking for a simple but versatile tool.

"For the grinding of feed, shelling corn, sawing wood, turn your fanning mill, grind stones, churns, etc., and do it at the least expense and with the least labor" the ad said.

Andrew also advertised himself as a "licensed city plumber," which likely was a good business in Madison during in the 1890s as businesses and some homes began getting hooked up to a city water system. A blurb in the Reporter in January 1892 referred to him as "the city plumber" who was "superintending" the installation of a city water line into the Beuttner & Zessin men's clothing store.

"I carry the only complete line of Plumbers' supplies in the county and am prepared to do first-class work in that line," his Reporter ads said in the summer of 1892. "As I handle only first-class goods I am prepared to meet all competition and can give you the very lowest prices. Tubular wells a specialty."

Andrew began buying this advertising space in July 1892. To help promote that first ad, the Reporter ran a short story on the same page.

"Andrew Hagglund calls the attention of our readers to his business by an advertisement to be found in the columns of this issue," it said. After highlighting some of his services, it added, "By calling on him at his shop near the depot you can obtain full particulars of everything in his line, and you will find that he can sell you goods as cheap as anyone in the same business."

He stopped advertising in the Reporter after his sister Christine's death, perhaps reflecting the family's anger at the newspaper and its editor, J.H. Mackay, who was involved in the surgical operation the night she died.

Starting in June 1896, Andrew advertised his well-drilling services every week in a rival newspaper, the Madison Star. He seemed to have dropped out of the windmill business. His small, text-only ad was the same every week, arranged simply with the words "Tubular Wells," followed by, "I am now prepared to put down tubular wells at a reasonable figure." At the bottom: "Andrew Hagglund, Madison, Nebraska." He stopped advertising in July 1901.

Andrew's name popped up from time to time in local newspapers during the Nebraska years, sometimes in the briefest way. The Norfolk Daily News, for example, reported on April 29, 1891: "A.J. Hagglund [was a] visitor in the city from Madison last evening." Tidbits of that kind were a staple of local news in those days.

A later news item was much more revealing. It appeared in the Madison Star on August 2, 1901. In addition to describing a sudden financial setback for Andrew, it suggested that he had made enemies — or at least he believed he had.

"A.J. Hagglund's steam threshing machine was destroyed by fire last Friday night, inflicting a damage of about $800," the story began. Apparently, Andrew had a threshing outfit in addition to his tubular wells business. He hired out his crew of threshermen to harvest wheat or oats using a steam-powered machine that threshed the crop to separate the edible part from the stalks. This was an advance from the older systems of beating the stalks with a hand-held flail or walking horses or other livestock over the straw so that the impact of their hooves knocked loose the grain.

The Star story hinted at intrigue.

"It is a puzzle to Mr. Hagglund how the fire originated, for when he quit the outfit at night, extra precaution was exercised in examining the firebox of the steamer to see that the coals were all dead," it said. "The door to the firebox fastened securely when the workmen left for the night, and even if a live coal had remained there was no danger of it doing any harm."

Andrew seemed determined not to let the disaster kill his business.

"Mr. Hagglund will have a new outfit here this week and all engagements will be filled," the story said. "The accident is a considerable loss to the owner and will retard his work just at this busy time."

But was it an accident? The story ended with a startling accusation.

"There is but little doubt that the fire was of incendiary origin, perpetrated through jealousy by some of his contemporaries," it said. In other words, it was an act of sabotage. It's not clear whether this was what Andrew believed or was the writer's conclusion based on his conversation with Andrew.

I found no follow-up newspaper references to the incident.

This was an especially busy time for Andrew, and probably a difficult one, too, with his parents and siblings all gone. In addition to tending to his business interests, he was engaged in what today we would call distance learning. He was taking classes by correspondence to earn high school credits, and he apparently was doing well by the time he was ready to move to Washington.

"A.J. Hagglund, machinist, well and windmill man of this city, who has been a student for some time in the American School of Correspondence, Boston, has just been awarded two certificates for free scholarships in that school," the Madison Star reported on April 4, 1902, just days before he left for Cedarhome.

"He will be glad to turn these over to two of our readers who are anxious to study steam, electrical or mechanical engineering," it added. "Write or call on him at once."

The American School of Correspondence was founded in Boston in 1897 by R.T. Miller and a group of graduates and faculty members from the Massachusetts Institute of Technology and Harvard University. It provided a path to a high school diploma for those unable or unwilling to attend a school, and the idea was a winner. The company was still in business as of 2019 and claims an eclectic group of "alums," including former tennis star Andre Agassi, the Everly Brothers singers and members of the Flying Wallenda circus family. I contacted the school in 2017 to request copies of any record of Andrew's work and was told by a spokesman that a search of company archives turned up no documentation.[138]

I don't know for sure how many years of school Andrew attended as a child; the 1940 census says it was five. The 1870 census, taken while the Hagglunds were newly arrived in Crawford County, Iowa, lists 13-year-old Andrew as "at school." Ten years later the census counted him as a teacher at age 23.

After his parents left Madison, Andrew made a few more local real estate deals. In March 1902 – just one month before leaving Nebraska – he bought Lots 1, 2 and 3 in Block 53 of the Railroad Addition for $375, apparently as an investment. He was in Cedarhome when he sold the properties in April 1906 for $400 to a Madison man, Isaac B. Potter, a former neighbor who had been a competitor in the wells and pumps business.

In June 1906, Andrew took a loss on Lot 14 in Madison by selling it to his brother John for $150 – $75 less than he had paid for it 12 years earlier. Two months after John bought it, he resold it at a further loss to a Madison businessman, Peter F. Oberg, for $100. Oberg was yet another competitor of Andrew's in the plumbing and windmills business; he also had gained local notoriety with his assault on J.H.

Mackay, the Madison Reporters editor and publisher.

Perhaps learning lessons from his business dealings in Nebraska, Andrew started a saw mill in Cedarhome. This seems to have been the venture mentioned in the May 1902 Madison Star newspaper item, which said Andrew intended to go into the timber business with brother John. I don't know what year it was established, but I found a newspaper reference to the Hagglund Mill Co., in December 1915, and the last mention I could find was in a 1919-1920 Polk's business directory. It was on Cedarhome-Highland Road, four miles northeast of East Stanwood.

"Manufacturers of all kinds of rough and dressed lumber and shingles," a directory entry says.

Oliver "Bob" Hagglund, a son of Oscar and Millie Hagglund, made a reference to Andrew and John's shingle mill when he wrote years later of his recollections of seeing Cedarhome for the first time.

Bob mentioned that two eight-man bunkhouses stood on John and Anna's property in 1924. The structures were built, he said, "when a shingle mill had been operating on ... Andrew's property across the road." Bob wrote that the 20 acres of Cedarhome property that Oscar had inherited when his father died in 1906 – and which Oscar remembered as a valuable stand of old-growth cedar and fir – had by the mid-1920s been reduced to "an almost worthless 'stump ranch.'"

Stumps were not worthless, of course – particularly cedar stumps. They were cut and split into "bolts," or wedges, from which shingles were made at mills like Andrew's.

Like his parents, Andrew lived out his remaining years in Cedarhome, except for a period, possibly starting in 1935, when he lived in the Josephine old folks home in Stanwood, now called the Josephine Sunset Home. He had just passed his 87th birthday when he died March 11, 1944 at Northern State Hospital in Sedro-Woolley, where he had been a patient for nearly two months. The recorded cause of death was cerebral arteriosclerosis –hardening of the arteries in the brain.

About 10 days after Andrew entered the hospital, his niece, Clara (Morton) Stanley mentioned him sympathetically in a letter to her 17-year-old niece in Cedarhome, Annabelle Freberg. Clara seemed to wish for a merciful end to his suffering.

"Too bad about Uncle Andrew!" she wrote from her home in Bellingham. "It would be a blessing if he could 'go on.' What keeps people here when they are so helpless?"

Andrew rests in an unmarked grave beside his father in Cedarhome Cemetery.[139]

29

Death and New Paths

In the first decade of the 20th century, more Hagglunds died young. The first was Oscar's wife Bertha in 1902, at age 25, followed two years later by John's wife Hattie, at 28. Also, Anna Hagglund's niece, Ellen Larson, who had moved from Stromsburg, Nebraska, to Washington state and married Earl D. Nims in January 1903, died in Bellingham three years later as a 24-year-old mother of two.

The deaths of Bertha and Hattie set their husbands, Oscar and John, on new paths.

John and Hattie had been in Cedarhome only about a year when she gave birth to their second child, Edna Christina in May 1901. (The first, Anna May, was born in Nebraska in May 1898.) They seemed settled, having joined the Swedish Baptist Church shortly after arriving. John appeared many years later in a newspaper photo of the church's "pioneer members." He might have joined as early as 1900, the same year as his parents. An article in the November 15, 1900 edition of the *Seattle Post-Intelligencer* cites "Mr. and Mrs. Hagglund" as among Cedarhome delegates to a conference in Bellingham of the Swedish Baptists of Western Washington. That could have been John and Anna Hagglund, or, just as likely, John and Hattie; the other delegate from Cedarhome was Erick N. Sjolander, the church's first pastor.

This apparent stability for John and Hattie collapsed quickly. Around 1902, they and their two girls moved back to Nebraska, settling in Stanton County, one county east of Madison County. The reason and exact timing are unclear.[140]

Perhaps the move was related to Hattie's health problems. A couple of years after they resettled, Hattie died. A Stanton Register obituary published three days after her death said she succumbed on August 16, 1904 to "a compilation of diseases." No details were offered.

"The deceased leaves a devoted husband and two little girls to mourn her untimely death," the obituary said, adding that she was buried at Newman Grove, the little town in Madison County where she and John were married in 1896.

Paul Cederlind, a Newman Grove mortician, told me that Hattie was buried in Hope Cemetery. Cederlind said she was buried as "Mrs. J. J. Hagglund," with no date recorded and no grave marker. "The records are poor," he wrote in a June 2016 letter. Cederlind said a "Gust Granlund and wife" also are buried there; that would be Hattie's older brother Gust and his wife, Hannah.

Hattie's obituary in the Stanton Register ended with this:

"We extend our sympathy to the bereaved husband and daughters. May they so live that they may meet her in Heaven when they too are called away."

Below the obituary is a "Card of Thanks" to neighbors and friends "who so kindly assisted us during the sickness and death of our beloved wife and mother." It was signed, "J.J. Hugglund [sic] and Daughters."

The obituary said the family was living in Butterfly township, named for the creek that runs through it, on "the Scripture land," which would appear to refer to Herbert E. Scripture, a local cattle rancher who perhaps employed John and rented to him. The article says the Hagglund family "moved there about a year and a half ago," which would be early 1903.

After Hattie's death, John and the girls moved back to Cedarhome sometime between 1907 and 1910, when the census shows them living in Cedarhome, and their household included his mother Anna. Ten years later, John and the girls were living in the same place in Cedarhome with a lodger, Christian Peterson, a Norwegian immigrant.

On September 7, 1927, John remarried. His bride was a Swedish immigrant, Frida Elisabeth Persson, who had Americanized her surname to Pearson.

Frida was born May 14, 1881 in Jämtland, the same area in Sweden from which the Hagglunds had emigrated. Frida's family name was Vågström; she married Karl Johan Axel Persson in the village of Gevåg, along the Indalsälven River, on February 2, 1902. He moved to the U.S. later that year, and she and their two children – Martha, age 3, and Olof, a newborn – followed in May 1903, traveling aboard a steamship called the SS *Ivernia*. (Reflecting a trend toward resentment of immigrants who arrived penniless and often were seen as a public burden, all passengers aboard the *Ivernia* were asked: "Whether in possession of money, and if so, whether upwards of thirty dollars, and how much if thirty dollars or less." Frida's answer: $15.)

By 1910, Frida and her family were living on 70 acres in Cedarhome, a short distance southeast of the Hagglunds and Frebergs. Axel Pearson, as he was known, died in 1913. Five years later Frida married Mathew Welch, a blacksmith of Irish descent, and in the 1920 census they are listed as residents of Silvana, a village a few miles upriver from Stanwood. The marriage was short lived.

John and Frida were married in Seattle and made their home in

Cedarhome; the 1930 census shows them living on the Bryant Road, with five children from Frida's two previous marriages – four boys whose father was Axel Pearson and a girl, Hazel, born in 1919, whose father was Mathew Welch, according to census data. (One of Frida's sons, Carl Anton, married a great niece of John's – Erma Christina Freberg, a daughter of Anna and Carl Freberg, in January 1927.)

John died on November 17, 1966 at age 93. Thus, the last-born of John and Anna Hagglund's ten children lived the longest – three years longer than Oscar. John's death certificate says he died at Zenith Sanitarium, which apparently was situated in or near the south Seattle suburb of Des Moines. His "usual residence" was listed as 119 Mirror Lake Park, Federal Way. The recorded cause of death was C.V.A., or stroke, after "many years" of "generalized arteriosclerosis." He was buried two days later in Washington Memorial Park cemetery near Seattle-Tacoma International Airport.

Frida died in Everett on August 9, 1970 and was buried in Anderson Cemetery in Stanwood beside her first husband, Axel Pearson.

* * *

South Dakota and a bungled birth record

Oscar Hagglund lost Bertha in 1902. Although he and the children had barely settled into their new lives in Washington before the death, Oscar quickly moved the family back to eastern Nebraska. There he remarried and remained for the better part of two decades before becoming the last of the original Hagglunds to resettle permanently in Washington.

Oscar and Bertha first moved to the Bellingham area sometime in the second half of 1899 or in early 1900. He is listed in an 1899

Madison, Nebraska business directory as O.F. Hagglund, "thresher and laborer."

By the time of the 1900 census, recorded on June 18, Oscar and Bertha and their two sons, Clarence, 4, and Leonard, 1, were living in the Bellingham area. They did not stay long. A third son, George, was born in Bellingham on August 29, 1900. He was followed by Theodore on July 2, 1902. Five days later, Bertha died. Her death certificate cites child birth as the cause.

Shortly after losing Bertha, Oscar and his four sons headed back to northeastern Nebraska, where he married a farmer's daughter, 17-year-old Mildred "Millie" A. Carleton, on June 6, 1905 in Stanton County. Millie was 18 years younger than Oscar; he may have known her family in the 1890s, since the Carletons were living in the Warnerville area of Madison County for at least a portion of that decade.

Oscar and Millie farmed on rented land in Ramshorn township, an unincorporated area of Stanton County about ten miles east of Madison. A widowed John J. Hagglund and his two daughters were living in the township just to the north, Butterfly.

In 1906, Oscar's two older boys, Clarence and Leonard, made a train trip West, apparently to visit their grandparents and other relatives in Cedarhome. This was just a few months before their grandfather, John Hagglund, died. The Stanton Register reported on June 22 that Millie had departed for Norfolk to catch the Union Pacific to Portland, Oregon, "to visit and bring home her two boys, who have been out there with relatives." The U.P., as it was known, ran its Overland Limited service to Portland, which it advertised as "many hours quicker" to the West Coast than its competitors – 58 hours to Portland. From Portland, Millie would have gone by rail on a Great Northern line to Stanwood.

By 1909, Oscar and Millie had produced three children – Pearl,

Oliver and Dora – bringing the family total to seven.

At that point Lady Luck intervened, and Oscar and Millie rather suddenly became homesteaders. This was thanks to the federal government's decision to "settle" large portions of two Indian reservations – the Cheyenne River reservation in South Dakota and the Standing Rock reservation that stretches from the northern reaches of South Dakota across the border into North Dakota. In 1909 the government held a lottery to determine who would be allowed to enter homestead claims on the land. In an account of the decision to open the reservation to white settlers, the *Bismarck Daily Tribune* called it "the next opportunity for the land-hungry people."

Whatever his appetite, Oscar tossed his name in the lottery pool and came up a winner. His was among 6,100 names picked in October 1909 from a pool of 80,142 entrants. Oscar was pick No. 4,850, meaning the choicest land would be taken by the time it was his turn to select 160 acres, although it turned out that more than half of the winners never filed claims.[141] No doubt many shied away from a Dakota badlands challenge that only the toughest settler could embrace.

Oscar apparently saw this as a challenge worth facing – and worth uprooting the family, though not immediately. Millie was pregnant with Irwin, who was born in February 1910.

A full year after his stroke of lottery luck, Oscar auctioned off his livestock at their rented farm in Ramshorn. He bought a display ad in the October 14, 1910 edition of the local weekly newspaper, announcing that on October 18 he would offer for public sale five horses, 68 head of cattle and 48 shoats, or young pigs. For purchases of $10 or less he required cash payment. Those spending more than $10 could pay over ten months on "good bankable notes at 8 percent interest."

To whet the public appetite, he tossed in this tidbit: "Free lunch at

11 a.m., sale immediately after."

Sometime after that, he traveled to South Dakota and filed his claim for 160 acres in the northwest corner of the Standing Rock reservation, whose boundaries included all of Corson County.

Corson County is on the North Dakota state line and is bordered on the east by the Missouri River. The Grand River flows east across the county and spills into the Missouri just beyond the town of Little Eagle. The old Black Hills Trail, which some called the Bismarck Trail, ran just north of Oscar and Millie's claim and turned southwest into the Black Hills, which became the destination for thousands of speculators during the gold rush of the mid-1870s.

This flood of white people to territory that had been granted to the Sioux by the 1868 Treaty of Fort Laramie created conflicts that historians say led to the Great Sioux War of 1876, ending with Custer's Last Stand. Peace had been restored by 1890. None of that history likely mattered to Oscar or Millie, who may or may not have known they and other homesteaders were staking claims on traditional Sioux hunting grounds.

I don't know exactly when the Hagglunds filed their claim but it likely was in the fall of 1910. His land patent, number 296346, signed by President William H. Taft, was dated October 12, 1912. The 160-acre homestead was the northeast quarter of Section 18, Township 22 North, Range 19 East of the Black Hills Meridian. It was in Custer township, Corson County, just south of the tiny South Dakota town of Keldron, which today is an unincorporated area not tracked by the Census Bureau.

In describing the area many years later, a fellow homesteader named Torval Idso said it was covered with buffalo grass so famous for fattening livestock that ranchers in Texas would ship their longhorn steers to the Dakotas to graze. Torval's family moved there in June 1910 as lottery winners, just like Oscar and Millie.[142] The Idso family almost certainly knew the Hagglunds; the 160-acre Idso homestead, in the southwest corner of Section 17, was catty corner from the Hagglunds' place in the northwest corner of adjoining Section 18. Oscar eventually sold his land to Torval's father, Adolph T. Idso, a Norwegian immigrant.

Adolph Idso had been working as a butcher in Alden, Iowa, a small town about 60 miles north of Des Moines, when, at age 54, he decided to try his hand at homesteading. His son Torval, 12 years old when they left Iowa, said the family doctor had advised his father to move to a drier climate.

"The prairies of South Dakota seemed to be the answer," Torval wrote in a booklet about the family's homesteading years. He likened the experience to conquering a wilderness. The times, he wrote, were both trying and rewarding. But they were not for everyone.

"Quite a number of homesteaders got discouraged in the fall of 1911 as they had not had a crop for two years and were completely without funds," he wrote.

Some families, he said, lived almost entirely on jack rabbits. One fellow who gave up and left had this verse painted on the side of his covered wagon:

"10 miles from water,

20 miles from school.

Hot as hell in summer,

Cold as the devil in winter.

I'm leaving this God forsaken country forever."

Torval stayed longer than many, but he, too, eventually gave up.

"The cattle market went down to almost nothing and the following years till 1928 were just one hard streak of luck after another until I decided the good Lord wanted me to leave Dakota, and that's exactly what I did," he wrote. "In fact, the last few years brought such bad luck that I couldn't bring myself to write about it."

During their short time in Corson County, Oscar and Millie had a daughter, Anna Elsie, on November 30, 1911 and a son, Myron, on January 1, 1913. (They would eventually have 12 children together, giving Oscar a total of 16, including the four with Bertha.) Oddly, Anna Elsie's birth record was riddled with errors, and I don't mean minor mistakes like typos. Her birth name was recorded as Marie and her mother, Millie, was recorded as Mary. Millie's age was wrong by seven years and her maiden name was incorrectly recorded as Johnson. The mistakes were enough to make you think the babies had gotten mixed up. About the only thing they got right was Oscar's name, and even his surname was misspelled as Haggland. In August 1943, seven years after Millie died, Oscar filed paperwork in Snohomish County, Washington to correct the original record, changing the daughter's name to Anna Elsie. He also corrected the mother's name from Mary Johnson to Mildred Ada Carleton.

The birth record also incorrectly said the baby's parents were born in Minnesota, and it misstated Oscar's age by five years. Those errors were not fixed.

I found very few details about Oscar and Millie's life in South Dakota, including what sort of start they made on farming the 160 acres, but the land venture gave them a significant financial boost, as Oscar apparently had expected it would.

Settling on Indian lands was an attractive proposition for lottery winners like Oscar, even though they did have to pay several dollars an acre for their claim, plus fees. Non-reservation homestead claims, like those by the other Hagglunds and Lars Morton in Nebraska, were free except for small administrative fees. The big attraction for Oscar and Millie in South Dakota was the projected resale value of the land – as much as $20,000 for the choicest claims and an average of $2,500, according to a newspaper account at the time.

Oscar "commuted," or bought out, his claim, on June 26, 1912 through the federal Land Office at Lemmon, South Dakota. He and Millie paid $3.25 an acre, or a total of $520, according to his official claim number 022306. He also paid $4 in commissions and fees, plus $1.50 in "testimony fees."

They then sold the 160 acres to Adolph Idso, their neighbor, for $1,800 in November 1913.[143]

Earlier in 1913, Millie and the children had moved to Creighton, Nebraska, a small town in Knox County about 20 miles south of the Missouri River where it forms the border with South Dakota. (By coincidence, this is the town in which Andrew and Johanna Tackstrom lived in the mid- and late-1880s.) Oscar stayed behind in South Dakota to complete the property sale. Millie signed the deal through a notary public in Knox County, and he signed in Corson County, South Dakota.

After the deal was done, Oscar joined the family in Creighton. There they remained until they picked up and moved to Cedarhome, once again making the transition in stages, starting in August 1924.

* * *

Retracing the Oregon Trail

The first stage of that move to Cedarhome was a humdinger. Years afterward, Bob Hagglund, a son of Oscar and Millie, recounted the five-week journey in an artfully written and delightfully detailed account he titled "Overland Westward: Nebraska to Washington with the Hagglunds."[144]

Their path literally retraced parts of the old Oregon Trail — and shadowed long stretches of the Union Pacific rail route Lewis and Martha Hagglund had taken from Nebraska a quarter century earlier.

Bob began by puzzling over why his parents chose to leave Nebraska. "I do know that neither Dad nor Mother had been very well, and that Dad had a serious back problem," he wrote. As part of Oscar's dray, or goods-hauling, business he moved mail from the rail depot to the Creighton post office. This work, Bob wrote, added to his dad's back problem and "may even have caused it."

Bob mentioned that his grandmother Anna Hagglund had died a year earlier, leaving Oscar the home in Cedarhome that she and John had lived in since moving to Washington. This may have been at least part of the reason Oscar decided to move. The house, Bob said, was situated on two acres of cleared land. It had two bedrooms, a living room, kitchen and pantry. "It was a well-build log house with a large attic, unfinished but usable if floored," he added. (The house stood in the southwest corner of the northwest quarter of the northwest quarter of Section 8 in Township 32 North, Range 4 East. With the execution of his father's will in 1926, Oscar inherited the 2-acre parcel, plus the 20 acres formed by the north half of the northeast quarter of the northwest quarter of Section 8.)

Oscar and Millie knew the house would be awaiting them on arrival from Nebraska. Less certain was how they would get there. Oscar decided to stay behind temporarily to sell his Creighton dray business, so he loaded Millie and eleven of their kids into an imaginatively modified vehicle and pointed them west.

Millie and the kids – including 2-year-old twins – crossed the country in a 1916 Model 86, a touring car built by the Overland Company. With help from a blacksmith in their Creighton neighborhood, Oscar cut off the body just behind the front seat and installed a 6-by-8-foot flatbed.

"I don't know if it was a throwback to the covered wagon or a forerunner of the camper. One or the other," Bob wrote.

Their supplies were minimal: an 8-by-10-foot tent, a two-burner kerosene stove and a Coleman gas lantern.

Without a map or other instruction on how to get from Creighton to Cedarhome, they relied on what Bob called "word of mouth information" along the way. They set out on August 21, 1924, which happened to be Bob's 17th birthday. (They originally planned to leave in July, but neighbors complained about the wisdom of entrusting a 16-year-old driver with the lives of 11 other people, so they waited another month.)

"Much later I wondered why Dad didn't work out a route for us to follow," he wrote. "I suppose it implied confidence in my ability to get us there."

That confidence was well-placed. Despite what he called "troubles and frustrations" along the way, Bob performed what looks in hindsight like a series of mechanical miracles. Their overworked vehicle developed a bedeviling habit of coming up lame. The most frequent problem was flat tires, and they had no spare.

Bob was not just good, he was lucky, too. One day, after yet another flat tire, he began walking toward the nearest town in search of a valve stem. Although they had often driven for hours without meeting a car, on this day one came along as soon as Bob started out. The driver happened to be a sales representative for Bowles Seal-Fast tire repair materials. He had a supply of value stems in his car and gave Bob several, along with tire-patching materials. The man refused payment, asking only that the Hagglunds keep his brand in mind in the future. Bob wrote that in the 60 years he subsequently worked in the car business he "never willingly purchased or used" any other brand of tire repair materials.

Some days earlier, along a stretch from Casper, Wyoming, to Billings, Montana, the engine quit.

Bob described the scene:

"A hundred miles away from the possibility of getting parts, the only solution was to disconnect the vacuum line, plug the inlet hole, drain gas into one of Mother's cooking pans, fill the pick-up supply tank through the hole provided for emergency filling, clear and re-install the spark plugs and start the engine."

This he did. It worked. But the day's challenges were not over.

"The pick-up tank held only a quart of gas, so when the initial quart was used the engine quit," Bob wrote. "We poured in another quart, drove until that was used up, poured in another quart and on and on for over a hundred miles." There was one bright spot, however. "We only had three flats on the way back (to Casper)."

That spirit of optimism seemed ingrained in the Hagglunds, or as Bob put it, "High hopes were a part of the family nature." It came in handy on the way to Cedarhome.

"In defiance of problems, rough rides on springless seats, heat and dust, Mother and the kids sang and joked their way nearly halfway across the U.S.," he wrote.

Bob recalled the moment they came upon the Columbia River, 40 miles north of Pendleton, Oregon.

"What a sight that was to a bunch of dried-out small-town hicks from the sand hills of northeastern Nebraska," he wrote. It was, he said, "the greatest body of water we had ever seen."

They arrived in Cedarhome, apparently no worse for wear, on September 25.

Back in Creighton, it took Oscar a few months to tidy up his affairs. The local paper reported on December 18, 1924 that he sold his dray business to Chris Blair, who had been "assisting Mr. Hagglund for a short time getting next to the ways of the business" –- in other words, getting acquainted with it before taking over.

"Mr. Hagglund will leave for East Stanwood, Washington, where he will join his family, as soon as he can get his business affairs cleaned up, which he thinks will be about the first of the year," the article said.

His trip presumably was less eventful than Millie's.

In a 1983 video-taped retelling of the "Overland" trip, Bob summed it up simply, in unadorned words that could apply as well to the decades-long Hagglund odyssey from Sweden to and across America.

"But anyway, we made it," Bob said. "We got there."

* * *

Oscar's Final Stop

During their first years back in Cedarhome, Oscar and Millie stayed in touch with folks in Creighton. Millie wrote a letter to the *Creighton News* in October 1930 to share news that their son Ervin had married Naomi F. Tate in Mt. Vernon that month and had moved onto a farm on Guemes Island, just north of Anacortes.

"We are all quite well and busy," she wrote. "Oscar still works in the Clough Lumber Mill, and the children are in school." She was referring to the Clough mill in Stanwood, site of the Hamilton smokestack that was a Stanwood landmark during my childhood and for many decades beyond.

In her letter, Millie alluded to the hard times felt from coast to coast in the early stages of the Great Depression. "There is quite a slump in both labor and wages out here making it very hard to make both ends meet," she wrote. She signed off as, "Your old friend, Mrs. Oscar Hagglund."

Millie died in April 1936 in Cedarhome and was buried in Cedarhome Cemetery. Two years later, Oscar married a widow, Lena Carlson, a Kentucky native whose husband of more than 40 years, Swedish immigrant Carl E. Carlson, died in 1936. Lena and Oscar were married in Seattle in March 1938, but the union did not last long. Oscar married for a fourth and final time a year later, in July 1939. Wife No. 4 was Opal G. Rumsey, a California native, 31 years his junior.

Oscar's death certificate says that when he died in 1961, he was living at an Everett address – 2007 Cleveland Avenue, on the city's east side. In his final years he suffered from a hardening of his arteries. This led to myocardial degeneration, or heart muscle disease. The immediate cause of death on January 24, 1961 was recorded as pulmonary edema, or excess fluid in the lungs. He was four months shy of 91.

On his 90th birthday in April 1960, Oscar posed for a photo with a copy of the *Everett Herald* in his lap. The newspaper published the picture on April 13 with a caption that said, "Oscar Hagglund, 2007 Cleveland, is 90 years old today and still going strong." It said he had moved to Everett from Seattle two months earlier.

"He has 16 children, 35 grandchildren and 33 great-grandchildren," it said.

Oscar, like his brother John, was buried in Washington Memorial Park Cemetery near Seattle-Tacoma International Airport. He was joined there seven years later by Opal.

30

The Home Stretch

John and Anna defied the odds by reaching what would be considered old age even in the 21st century, although John didn't last long once he and Anna arrived in Cedarhome. A Stanwood doctor began treating him for heart trouble in the summer of 1904, and he died of heart disease on October 27, 1906. He was 78.

In his final years, John remained a man of modest means. He and Anna had, however, risen above the grinding poverty of the peasants' life they left behind in the rocky soil of Jämtland County, Sweden.

No one was getting rich in Cedarhome. John and Anna's land holdings had expanded in size and value since their days farming on 40 acres in Iowa, but they were a long way from wealthy. In his will, written and signed at home in Cedarhome on June 19, 1905, John gave $5 each to his five surviving children — Andrew, Lewis, Martha, Oscar and John — and he left $1 for each of the six children that "my deceased daughter Christine Morton left behind her."

His legacy was love, not money.

To "my beloved wife Anna Hagglund" he left the rest of his personal property and empowered her to sell their land holdings or use them as she saw fit. Whatever she retained at the time of her death would go to the five Hagglund children in equal shares, and to Lars Morton, "the surviving husband of our said deceased daughter Christine Morton." (By the time Anna died 18 years after this will was written, the $1 sums John had bequeathed to each of the Morton children had grown to $81.)

The Hagglund property in Cedarhome, as inventoried and assessed for the court in January 1907, a few months after John died, totaled 200 acres and was valued at $4,620. His animals, valued at a combined $172, consisted of two milk cows, four "young cattle," two calves and one horse.

The gap between life as we know it in the early 21st century and the experiences of the Hagglunds and other immigrants of their day must be measured in more than time and money. The rhythms and patterns of life were different then, even if basic aspirations – to be productive citizens, reliable friends and loving parents – were similar. Thus, it is not possible to see perfectly through their eyes or into their hearts to know what satisfaction their long journey brought.

This much is clear: It was not a fortune they sought in America; it was a future. And, along the way, they demonstrated the same faith and dedication that sustained and rewarded an entire generation of immigrants and enriched a nation not always welcoming of newcomers.

John's passing touched people far and wide, including in Nebraska. An obituary published in the *Stanton Register* on November 9 offered a touching tribute that may have been written by his namesake son John, who was living in Stanton County at the time.

"He was a kind father, a strong Christian and temperance man," it said.

A brief death notice appeared in a Swedish-language newspaper, the *Svenska Amerikanaren* (the Swedish American), published in Chicago. It noted his name and date of death, misstated his age as 79 and his residence as Bellingham, and added without further comment: "Leaves behind a spouse and five children."

John was buried in Cedarhome Cemetery, a simple, secluded graveyard barely a mile from his and Anna's home, on the highlands above Stanwood. He lies in grave No. 4, Lot 48, in what was known at the time as the A.O.U.W. – Ancient Order of United Workmen – Cemetery, later expanded to form today's Cedarhome Cemetery. His grave is marked by an upright stone monument scarred by weather and adorned with a two-dimensional carving of a lamb in repose, a traditional symbol of the gentleness and purity of the deceased. On the monument's face is an engraving of a scene framed by what look like stage curtains pulled back just enough to reveal what may be a church setting – perhaps intended to depict sanctuaries of Old Jerusalem. Like his and Anna's long immigrant path, many details in the engraving have worn away with time.

Anna, who lived longer than any of the original seven Hagglund immigrants, went next. She died on a Sunday evening, December 2, 1923. She was 93. Her death certificate cites "acute pleurisy," which is inflammation of the lung lining, sometimes caused by a viral infection.

She was buried three days later. That week's *Stanwood News* reported that her funeral was held at the Cedarhome Baptist Church – presumably the new one built just a year earlier. The following week the paper published a more conventional obituary, noting she was survived by four sons and a daughter and that she left 33 grandchildren and 21 great-grandchildren. She also left a less obvious legacy: All five of her married children – Lewis, Christine, Martha, Oscar and John – named a daughter after her. All but Oscar did so with their first-born daughter.

For unknown reasons, there is no grave marker for Anna in Cedarhome Cemetery, and the incomplete records held by the

Stanwood funeral home that manages it include no reference to her.[145] Her death certificate, however, says she was buried Decemer 5 at "Cederhome," and that the undertaker was Aaron Light of Mount Vernon. There is a second cemetery in Cedarhome; it is called the Pleasant Hill Cemetery and is associated with the original location of the Cedarhome Baptist Church. The limited records of Pleasant Hill show no mention of Anna, however, and I see no reason to doubt that Anna lies beside her husband in the other Cedarhome cemetery, where other Hagglunds and their descendants rest. I believe she is in grave No. 5, Lot 48, in the cemetery's original A.O.U.W. section.

The uncertainty about where Anna was buried is a shame, since the location obviously was known to her immediate family. It also is a metaphor for this book project. Many of Anna's descendants, including me, had long assumed she lay in Cedarhome Cemetery, but none looked close enough to notice the absence of a headstone or other marker; or, if some did notice, they did not look for an explanation until it was too late to find one. In the same way, I had long overlooked virtually every aspect of Hagglund history, including their journey to and across America. By the time I grew interested, the people who knew the story, in pieces or in whole, were no longer alive, and it was too late to learn with certainty the answers to many basic questions, including why John and Anna decided to leave their homeland. And yet, it is possible a century and a half later to weigh the meaning of John and Anna's odyssey.

In the end, the Hagglund story is about beginnings. It's about starting a second family after the first was taken in flames; about making a fresh start as near-penniless immigrants; about starting a Swedish Baptist church on the Iowa prairie, and about starting over as homesteaders in Nebraska. Finally, at the dawn of a new century, it was about making one last new beginning in Washington, where they ended a journey that began 56 years earlier on a trail of hope.

It's hard to know what ultimate goals Anna and John had in mind when they said farewell to Sweden in June 1867 and climbed aboard the *Tyne Queen* at Trondheim a month later, but it's clear they achieved at least one: a more promising future for their children and for the generations that followed.

The challenges they faced along the way – the backlash for being Baptists in Sweden, the anxious voyage across the Atlantic, the recurring personal tragedies, and the struggle for survival through periods of economic depression -- may not have been unusual for their time but are hard to fully comprehend so many years later.

Still, knowing at least the outlines of their story allows an appreciation for the spirit and wisdom of Johan Andersson and Anna Larsdotter — ordinary farmers who seized a chance to live their dream and now rest in peace.

It was a long way home.

Acknowledgements

This book is about family in more ways than the obvious one. It bears the imprint of love and support from my wife Liz and our two adult children, Bobby and Libby, who patiently waited for my obsession with the Hagglund story to run its course. Liz read a draft of the manuscript, tolerated my research trips and offered helpful suggestions; Libby lent her creative touch to the book's artwork, and Bobby's curiosity about his ancestors gave me hope that the book's value will endure.

My siblings played key roles from start to finish. Barbara gave advice and insights on medical matters and more, Debbie was my guide to resources of the Stanwood Historical Society, and Roger kept a lookout for research clues that helped my cause. All three share my interest in our heritage.

I missed a lifetime of chances to quiz my mother, Annabelle, about the Hagglunds and Mortons before she died in 2011. My father, Robert, had limited knowledge about the Hagglunds, but in his final years he gladly dug through dresser drawers and storage shelves in search of ancestral nuggets.

Among relatives in Sweden, I relied often on the gracious indulgence of Marie Bergstrom, a second cousin whose grandfather Set was a younger brother of my maternal grandfather, Carl Emil Freberg. Marie answered many questions about our common lineage, discovered important Swedish records for me and patiently translated – sometimes single words, sometimes whole documents. Likewise, I am grateful for the generous help of Josefin Ekman, who is descended from Carl Freberg's older sister Ida Kristina. Josefin and her mother Annika tutored me in family history, provided family photos and thrilled me by sharing copies of letters I had written and sent across the Atlantic many years earlier to Berta Svensson, a niece of Carl Freberg.

Matts Svensson, a grandson of Berta, also provided helpful information about family connections. He and his wife, Helena, hosted us when my wife and I and my parents and younger brother Roger visited them in 1985.

I also benefited greatly from the help of several archivists at the national archives of Sweden and Norway.

In the four states in which the Hagglund family lived – Minnesota, Iowa, Nebraska and Washington – I met and learned a great deal from genealogists, church officers, county government officials, librarians, archivists, and others who indulged my many questions. I am especially grateful for the assistance of five people in Iowa who helped start me down my research trail in 2014-15: Norm Prince, an amateur genealogist; Denise Meeves, the Crawford County Recorder of Deeds; John Larson, who led me to the unmarked grave of Olof Hagglund and shared his cemetery records; Violet Finstrom, who gave me a personal tour of Kiron on my first visit, and Pastor Bruce Kaihoi of the Kiron Baptist Church, who trusted me – not once, but twice — with irreplaceable records stored in the church basement.

I regret that Bernard Anderson, a gentle soul who patiently shared with me his recollections of the history of his beloved Vasa, Minnesota, did not live to see this book published.

Finally, I offer a special thanks to Eileen Nelson King, to whom I am distantly related through the Hagglunds. Eileen's family lived near mine in Stanwood when I was a kid. I barely knew of her, but at a stage in my research when I was stuck in a rut, she performed

Ancestry.com magic to direct me to valuable new clues in Swedish church records. Like the story of the Hagglunds, her intervention is a reminder of the enduring importance of family roots.

Bibliography

Sweden

Barton, H. Arnold, *Letters from the Promised Land; Swedes in America, 1840-1914.* 1975. University of Minnesota Press, Minneapolis.

Barton, H. Arnold, *The Search for Ancestors: A Swedish-American Family Saga.* 1979. Southern Illinois University Press, Carbondale, Illinois.

Herring, the Rev. Armine Styleman. *Letters from Abroad with Hints to Emigrants Proceeding to the New Dominion of Canada.* 1871. Publisher unknown.

Howard, Mark. "Robert Steele and Company: Shipbuilders of Greenock." The Northern Mariner, Vol. 3, No. 3, July 1992, pp. 17-29.

Johansson, Hilding, *Saleby, Trässberg, Härjevad: A History of Three Västergötlands Parishes, 1969.* Publisher unknown.

Johnson, Emery. *Eric Norelius, Pioneer Midwest Pastor and Churchman.* 1954. Augustana Book Concern, Rock Island, Illinois.

Johnson, Emery. *Early Life of Eric Norelius, 1833-1862, a Lutheran Pioneer.* 1934. Augustana Book Concern, Rock Island, Illinois.

Lewenhaupt, Carl. "Report of Count Carl Lewenhaupt on Swedish-Norwegian Immigration in 1870." Translation published in Swedish-American Historical Quarterly, January 1979, Vol. 30, No. 1.

Lovell, Odd S. *Across the Deep Blue Sea; The Saga of Early Norwegian Immigrants.* 2015. Minnesota Historical Society Press. St. Paul, Minnesota.

Ljungmark, Lars. *Swedish Exodus.* 1979. Translated by Kermit B. Westerberg from original published in 1965 under the title *Den Stora Utvandringen.* Southern Illinois University Press. Carbondale, Illinois.

Moberg, Vilhelm. *Unto a Good Land.* 1954. Albert Bonniers Förlag AB, Stockholm. 1952. Translation by Gustaf Lannestock.

Nelson, Olof Nickolaus. *History of the Scandinavians and Successful Scandinavians in the United States.* Vol. 1. 1893. Tribune Job Printing Co., Minneapolis.

Norelius, Eric, and Marion Siegfried Norelius. *Vasa Illustrata.* 1905. Swedish Evangelical Lutheran Church, Vasa, Minnesota. English version printed 2004 by Graphic Design Inc., Hastings, Minnesota.

Ostergren, Robert C., *A Community Transplanted.* 1988. University of Wisconsin Press, Madison, Wisconsin.

Pacific Marine Review, Vol. 9, No. 2, Feb. 22, 1912. Seattle.

Persenius, Ragnar. "Baptism and Membership in the Church of Sweden," p. 183 of *Baptism and the Unity of the Church,"* Michael Root and Risto Saarinen; 1998. William B. Eerdmans Publishing Co., Grand Rapids, Michigan/Cambridge, England.

Schroeder, Gustavo's W., *History of the Swedish Baptists in Sweden and America.* 1898. Published by author, "greater New York." Digitized version, Princeton Theological Seminary Library.

Stephenson, George Malcolm. *The Religious Aspects of Swedish Immigration: A Study of Immigrant Churches.* Arno Press, New York. 1969. Reprint of 1932 edition.

Sundbärg, Gustav, *Sweden, it's People and its Industry.* Swedish government handbook. 1904.

Sveriges Officiela Statistik (Swedish Official Statistics), 1866-1870.

From a series, 1863-1912. Jämtland County.

General

Baxter, Maurice G., "Encouragement of Immigration to the Middle West During the Era of the Civil War." 1950. Indiana Magazine of History, Volume 46, Issue No. 1.

Blake, Kellee, "First in the Path of the Firemen," Prologue Magazine, Spring 1996, Vol. 28, No. 1. The National Archives and Records Administration.

Bogue, Allan G., "Farming in the Prairie Peninsula, 1830-1890," *The Journal of Economic History.* 1963. Cambridge University Press.

Bogue, Allan G., *Money at Interest; the Farm Mortgage on the Middle Border.* 1955. Cornell University Press, Ithaca, New York.

Bradsher, Greg, "How the West was Settled," Prologue magazine, Winter 2012 issue, National Archives and Records Administration.

Castle Rock Writers, *Chronicles of Douglas County, Colorado.* 2014. The History Press, Charleston, South Carolina.

Hall, Basil, Captain, Royal Navy, *Travels in North America in the Years 1827 and 1828.* 1829. Cadell and Co., Edinburgh and Simpkin and Marshall, London.

Hansen, Marcus Lee, *The Immigrant in American History.* 1940. Harper & Row, New York, Evanston and London.

Holbrook, Stewart H., *The Story of American Railroads.* 1947. Bonanza Books. New York.

McConnell, Richard George, "Preliminary Report on the Klondike Gold Fields." 1900. Geological Survey of Canada.

Olson, Ernest W., *History of the Swedes of Illinois.* 1908. Engberg-Holberg Publishing Co., Chicago. Digitized by Google.

Taber, Clarence W., and Edward J. Boecher. *Breaking Sod on the Prairies: A Story of Early Days in Dakota.* 1927. World Book Company, New York.

The Englishman's Illustrated Guidebook to the United States and Canada. 1875. Chiswick Press, London.

The Pacific Tourist. Williams' Illustrated Trans-Continental Guide of Travel from the Atlantic to the Pacific Ocean. 1876. Henry T. Williams, editor. New York.

The Gold Mining Industry in Alaska, Alaska Review of Business and Economic Conditions, University of Alaska Institute of Business, Economic and Government Research. March 1965.

Turner, T.G. and C.E., *Turners' Guide from the Lakes to the Rocky Mountains.* 1868. Spalding & LaMontes, Chicago.

Weinstein, Allen, *Prelude to Populism: Origins of the Silver Issue, 1867-1878.* 1970. Yale University Press. New Haven and London.

White, Richard, *Railroaded: The Transcontinentals and the Making of Modern America.* 2011. W.W. Norton & Company, New York.

Wyte, William E., *"O'er the Atlantic,"* 1870. The American News Company. New York.

Yesterday and Today: A History of the Chicago and North Western Railway System. 1910. Chicago and North Western Railroad Company. Chicago.

Minnesota

Anderson, Philip J. and Dag Blanck, *Swedes in the Twin Cities.* 2001. Minnesota Historical Society Press, St. Paul, Minnesota.

Bodien, the Rev. Olof, "The Swedish Baptists of Minnesota," an essay starting on page 251 of *A History of the Swedish-Americans in Minnesota*. Edited by Algot E. Strand. 1910. The Lewis Publishing Company, Chicago.

Mitchell, W.H., *Geographical and Statistical Sketch of the Past and Present of Goodhue County*. 1869. O.S. King's Book and Job Printing House. Minneapolis.

Wood, Alley & Co., *History of Goodhue County*. 1878. Red Wing, Minnesota, Harvard University Library digital collection.

Iowa

Ahlström, Louis J., *Eighty Years of Swedish Baptist Work in Iowa – 1853-1933*. 1933. Swedish Baptist Conference of Iowa, Des Moines. Text digitized by Google; original held by the University of Wisconsin.

Davenport family papers, 1800-1941. Collection #539. Division of Rare and Manuscript Collections, Cornell University Library. Ithaca, New York.

Grant, H. Roger, editor, *Iowa Railroads: The Essays of Frank P. Donovan, Jr.* 2000. University of Iowa Press, Iowa City, Iowa.

Hart, William H., *History of Sac County*. 1914. B.F. Bowen & Co., Inc., Indianapolis, Indiana.

History of Western Iowa, it's Settlement and Growth. 1882. (No author cited) Western Publishing Company. Sioux City, Iowa. Digitized by Google.

Houlette, William, D., *Iowa, the Pioneer Heritage.* 1970. Wallace-Homestead Book Co., Des Moines, Iowa.

Meyers, Frederick W., *History of Crawford County, Iowa*. 1911. S.J. Clarke Publishing Co. Chicago.

Mitchell, the Rev. S.H., *Historical Sketches of Iowa Baptists*. 1886. Burdette Co., Burlington, Iowa.

Richards, Charles B., *Annals of Iowa, a Historical Quarterly*. Vol. XI, No. 1. 1913. Iowa Historical Department. Des Moines.

Schwieder, Dorothy. *Iowa, the Middle Land*. 1996. University of Iowa Press, Iowa City, Iowa.

Thompson, William H. "Transportation in Iowa, a Historical Summary." Iowa Department of Transportation. 1989. Ames, Iowa.

W.W. Walker, "First Report of the President and Directors of the Cedar Rapids and Missouri River Rail Road," June 1860. Beach and Barnard Printers, Chicago.

Winters, Donald L., "Tenant Farming in Iowa, 1860-1900: A Study of the Terms of Rental Leases," Agricultural History Society, Agricultural History, Vol. 48, No. 1, *Farming in the Midwest, 1840-1900: A Symposium.* January 1974, pp. 130-150.

Yesterday and Today: A History of the Chicago and North Western Railway System. 1910. Third edition. Published by Chicago and North Western Railway Company. Chicago. Digitized by Google.

Nebraska

Birge, Julius C., *The Awakening of the Desert*. 1912. The Gorman Press. Boston.

Bly, Nellie. "Nellie Bly with Starving Nebraskans," dateline Valentine, Nebraska, January 19, 1895, and "The Wish to Own a Home," dateline Butte, Nebraska, January 25, 1895. Originally published in the New York World newspaper. Reprinted in Nebraska History magazine, Vol. 67, 1986, the Nebraska State Historical Society, original text via University of Minnesota Library.

Cather, Willa. *My Antonia.* 1918. The Houghton Mifflin Co., Boston.

Compendium of History, Reminiscence and Biography of Nebraska. Alden Publishing Co. Chicago. 1912. (No author cited; apparently a state government publication.)

Danbom, David B., *Sod Busting. How Families Made Farms on the 19th Century Plains.* 2014. Johns Hopkins University Press, Baltimore.

DeMilt, A.P., *Story of an Old Town.* 1902. Douglas Printing Co., Omaha.

Fitzpatrick, Lilian L., *Nebraska Place-Names.* 1960. University of Nebraska Press, Lincoln.

Fremont, John C., *Report of the Exploring Expedition to the Rocky Mountains in the Year 1842 and to Oregon and North California in the Year 1843-44.* Washington, D.C., Gales and Seaton, 1845. Republished in 2012 by University of Nebraska Press, Lincoln and London, as *Fremont's First Impressions, the Original Report of His Exploring Expeditions of 1842-1844.*

History of Stromsburg, 1872-1997, by Stromsburg Woman's Civic Improvement Club. 1997. Service Press, Henderson, Nebraska.

Long, Francis A. *A Prairie Doctor of the Eighties.* 1937. Huse Publishing Co., Norfolk, Nebraska.

Meyer, Jane Sleeper. *One Wideawake Sleeper. 1990.* Realy Rapid Printing, Prescott, Arizona.

Morrill, Charles H. *The Morrills and Reminiscences.* 1918. University Publishing Co., Chicago and Lincoln, Nebraska.

Munson, Myron Andrews. *The Munson Record: A Genealogical and Biographical Account of Captain Thomas Munson and His Descendants.* 1896. The Tuttle, Morehouse & Taylor Press. New Haven, Connecticut.

"Northern Nebraska." The American Agriculturist, 1883. Vol. 42,

p. 389.

Story of a Live Town, a Photographic Review of Madison, Madison County, Nebraska. May 1910. The account was sponsored by Madison Commercial Club.

"The Official State Atlas of Nebraska." 1885. Cornell University Library.

Van Hoff, Joseph John. "A History of the Czechs in Knox County, Nebraska," July 1938. Thesis paper, Department of History, University of Nebraska, Lincoln.

South Dakota

Idso, Torval. *Survival on the Prairie, or Homesteading on the Standing Rock.* 1971. Unknown publisher.

Washington

An Illustrated History of Skagit and Snohomish Counties; Their People, Their Commerce and Their Resources. 1906. The Interstate Publishing Co., Chicago. Digitized by the Internet Archive.

Bagley, Clarence B. "The Mercer Immigration: Two Cargoes of Maidens for the Sound Country." The Quarterly of the Oregon Historical Society, Vol. 5, No. 1, March 1904. Pp. 1-24.

Baker, the Rev. J.C., *Baptist History of The North Pacific Coast.* 1912. Publisher unknown.

Bolton, Ethel Stanwood. *A History of the Stanwood Family in America.* 1899. Rockwell and Churchill Press, Boston.

Coates, Ken and Bill Morrison. *The Sinking of the Princess Sophia.* 1991. University of Alaska Press, Fairbanks, Alaska.

Conant, Roger. *Mercer's Belles: The Journal of a Reporter.* 1960. Edited by Lenna A. Deutsch. Seattle. University of Washington Press.

Dahlie, Jorgen. "Old World Paths in the New: Scandinavians Find Familiar Home in Washington." Pacific Northwest Quarterly. Vol. 2, No. 2. April 1970.

Engle, Flora A. "The Story of the Mercer Expeditions." The Washington Historical Quarterly, Vol. 6, No. 4, October 1915. Pp. 225-237. University of Washington.

Hines, the Rev. H.K., *An Illustrated History of the State of Washington.* 1894. The Lewis Publishing Co., Chicago.

Hunt, Herbert and Floyd C. Kaylor. *Washington, West of the Cascades.* 1917. S.J. Clarke Publishing Co. Chicago, Seattle and Tacoma.

Iverson, O.B. "From the Prairie to Puget Sound." Series of articles in the Stanwood News, 1920-21, Stanwood, Washington. Republished in "Norwegian-American Studies," Vol. 16, 1950, by Norwegian-American Historical Association.

McGoffin, Mary J., *Under the Red Roof, One Hundred Years at Northern State Hospital.* 2011. Self-published. Sedro-Woolley, Washington.

Rasmussen, Janet E. *New Land, New Lives, Scandinavian Immigrants to the Pacific Northwest.* 1993. University of Washington Press. Seattle.

Stine, Thomas Ostenson, *Scandinavians on the Pacific, Puget Sound,* 1909. Publisher unknown. Seattle.

Appendix with Photos

Nebraska Homesteads

Here are key details of the Homestead Act claims by John Hagglund, Lewis Hagglund and Lars Morton in Madison County. Sources: National Archives, Bureau of Land Management.

John Hagglund

160 acres. South half of southwest quarter (80 acres) of Section 1, and north half of northwest quarter (80 acres) of Section 12, in Township 22 North, Range 1 West of the 6th Principal Meridian. He entered his claim at the General Land Office in Norfolk on September 7, 1881. Homestead application number 7779. Final certificate number 5106. Land patent issued March 27, 1889.

John and Anna sold the homestead in February 1900 to George H. Walker for $6,000.

Lewis Hagglund

160 acres. South half of southeast quarter (80 acres); northwest quarter of southeast quarter (40 acres); northeast quarter of southwest quarter of Section 30 in Township 23 North, Range 1 West of the 6th Principal Meridian. He entered his claim at the General Land Office in Norfolk on May 13, 1880. Application number 7376. Final

certificate number 4925. Land patent issued May 21, 1889.

Lewis sold the homestead in February 1894 to Jacob D. Horner for $1,700.

Lars Morton

160 acres. Southwest quarter of Section 28 in Township 23 North, Range 1 West of the 6th Principal Meridian. He entered his claim at the General Land Office at Neligh on October 8, 1884. Application number 9577. Final certificate number 5796. Land patent issued February 18, 1891. He originally filed a Timber claim (formally a claim under the Timber Culture Act of 1873) for this parcel on December 7, 1880, then converted it to a Homestead Act claim in October 1884.

Lars and Christine sold the homestead in February 1892 to Thomas Malone for $2,400.

The land patent for John and Anna Hagglund's Nebraska homestead is dated March 27, 1889.

In November 1880, after moving from Crawford County, Iowa, John A. Hagglund paid a $2 fee to file a Declaratory Statement at the General Land Office in Norfolk, Nebraska, registering his intent to claim 160 acres of land in Township 22 North, Range 1 West of the 6th Principal Meridian in Madison County. This would be the Hagglund homestead for the next 20 years.

John A. Hagglund received his Certificate of Citizenship on September 11, 1885 in Madison County, Nebraska, five years after he formally declared his intention to become an American citizen. This automatically made his wife, Anna, a citizen also.

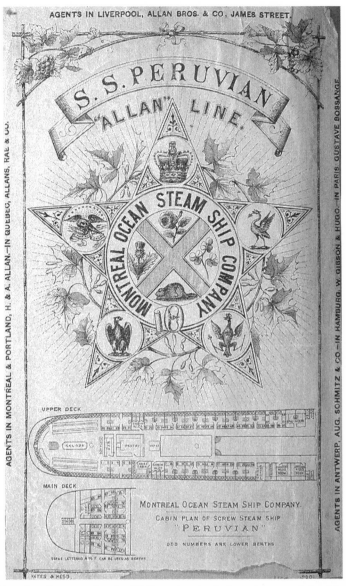

This advertisement for the SS Peruvian includes a layout of the ship on which the Hagglund family spent 14 days at sea, from Liverpool, England to Quebec, Canada. Photo used with permission of the McCord Museum, Montreal. Yates & Hess, engravers and printers, Liverpool, circa 1870.

Left, Andrew J. Hagglund, circa mid-1890s in Madison, Nebraska. Right, John J. Hagglund (standing, left) and his brother Oscar, circa 1880s in Norfolk, Nebraska.

John Hagglund and his son Andrew sued the inventor of this "hydrocarbon burner" after he accepted their $150 promissory note but failed to provide them with a prototype. Image source: U.S. Patent and Trademark Office.

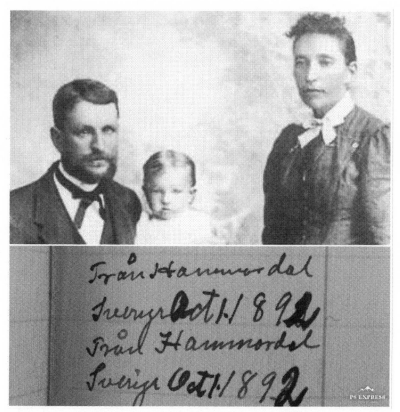

Top, Lewis and Martha Hagglund with daughter Anna, circa 1894. Photo courtesy of Pam Brown Persson. Bottom, records of the Swedish Baptist Church of Stromsburg, Nebraska include a note about Martha's parents, Olof and Christina Larson. "From Hammerdal, Sweden, Oct. 1, 1892."

Left, Oscar Hagglund and his first wife, Bertha, married in Stanton, Nebraska in 1894. Right, John J. Hagglund and his first wife, Hattie, married in Newman Grove, Nebraska in 1896.

Christine and Lars Morton with three of their children, circa 1890-92.
Photo courtesy of Suzanne Hawley.

Andrew Tackstrom, left, in undated photo courtesy of Eileen Scott-Zinck.
Right, Andrew's younger brother August with wife Martha, circa 1890s.
Photo courtesy of Greg Dodson.

Carl and Anna Freberg wedding photo, February 1900, Denison, Iowa.

353

*Clockwise from top left, Christine (Hagglund) Morton, her eldest son John
A. Morton, her eldest daughter Anna (Morton) Freberg, and Anna's
youngest daughter, Annabelle (Freberg) Burns.*

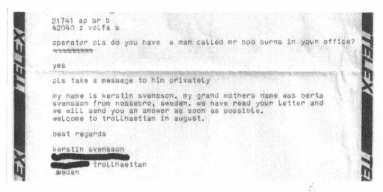

```
21741 ap br b
42040 z volfa s

operator pls do you have  a man called mr bob burns in your office?


yes

pls take a message to him privately

my name is kerstin svensson. my grand mothers name was berta
svensson from nossebro, sweden. we have read your letter and
we will send you an answer as soon as possible.
welcome to trollhaettan in august.

best regards

kerstin svensson

                trollhaettan
sweden
```

*This telex opened the door to the trip of a lifetime for my mother — a visit
to the ancestral home of her father, Carl Emil Freberg. I received the telex
in my Associated Press office in Brussels, Belgium in the spring of 1985.
We made our visit to Sweden in June. (Kerstin Svensson home address
edited to protect her privacy.)*

Notes

1   My account of the circumstances and timing of Johan and Anna's emigration
    is derived mainly from Swedish church records as well as emigration records
    held by the National Archives of Norway. Data on emigration from Jämtland in
    1867-69 is from Sveriges Officiela Statistik (Swedish Official Statistics) for the
    years 1866-70.

2   Weather details for central Sweden in 1867 are from "250 Years of Weather Obser-
    vations at the Stockholm Observatory," January 2006, the Swedish Meteorological
    and Hydrological Institute (SMHI), Norrköping, Sweden. Also, web postings by
    SMHI, including "The Exceptionally Cold May Month of 1867," published May
    15, 2017. A 1977 documentary, "Ett Satan's år," about the extreme weather of
    1867 in Norrland, which includes Jämtland, was later developed into a book of
    the same title by Olle Häger and Hans Villius.

ANNA MEETS JOHAN

3   Personal and family history for Anna and Johan is from church records, and
    in Johan's case I also obtained information via email from a researcher at the
    Swedish National Archives. I relied on a brief account of Hagglund family history
    ("the Everett account") that was prepared for and distributed at a 1983 family
    reunion in Everett, Washington; portions were collected by Conley Smith of
    Mount Vernon, Washington, whose grandmother, Mary Blanche (Morton) Smith,
    was a granddaughter of John and Anna Hagglund. I tried unsuccessfully to obtain
    the complete collection of his underlying research materials. Portions of the
    Smith collection were graciously shared by his niece, Suzanne Hawley of Seattle.

4   "long lifers" is from descendant Phil Smith speaking at the 1983 family reunion.

SHARING SPACE WITH RATS AND DISEASE

5   Information about Johan and Anna's travel aboard the *Tyne Queen* is from records
    held in the Norwegian National Archives and obtained via their digital data
    service. In December 2018 I obtained a scanned copy of the emigration registry
    that listed Johan and Anna and their five children, identified by name, age and

gender. This record is in "Trondheim politikammer, 1/32 Emigrant protocols, No. 1: Emigrant protocol No. 1, 1867-70." It also listed the passengers' place of origin and destination. It indicates that Johan and Anna paid 203 kronor for the family's passage. The emigration protocol serial numbers for the seven family members are 1249 through 1255.

6   I could not determine exactly where the *Tyne Queen* arrived in eastern England. It was either at Hull or, more likely, Newcastle on the River Tyne.

7   For information about the history of the *Peruvian* I relied on Mark Howard's article, "Robert Steele and Company: Shipbuilders of Greenock," *The Northern Mariner*, July 1992.

8   The passenger manifest for Johan and Anna's voyage aboard the *Peruvian* is available from the Library and Archives of Canada: "Passenger lists of the Peruvian arriving in Quebec, Que., on 1867-08-14." Microfilm reel number C-4522, List number 81, Record Group 76, Item number 317.

9   "a regular old salt, blunt, uncourteous and undignified in his manner": William E. Whyte, *O'er the Atlantic* (New York: The American News Company, 1870).

10   "I did not like the look of my sleeping space ...," is from "Letters from Abroad with Hints to Emigrants Proceeding to the New Dominion of Canada," Herring, May 1871.

11   "Like pigs vomiting in all directions": Canadian Institute for Historical Microreproductions Collection, No. 41405.

12   The fact that the U.S. government did not begin tracking immigrants entering from Canada until 1895 is from U.S. National Archives and Records Administration, Prologue Magazine, "By Way of Canada," Fall 2000.

NO GOING BACK

13   Johan's younger brother Olof also was officially labeled a Baptist by local authorities in the 1860s while living in Gävleborg county. Anna's brother Olof Larsson and his wife Kerstin Månsdotter got the same treatment in Hammerdal parish in the early 1870s. Parish authorities wrote a special note on the 1884 birth record of Olof and Kerstin's son Elias: "Parents refuse to allow baptism of the child." (In Swedish: "Foräldrarn vägrat låta döpa barnet.")

MINNESOTA FOR A MINUTE

14   "They considered it a great privilege to be free," is from an essay, "The Swedish Baptists of Minnesota," by the Rev. Olof Bodien, in Algot E. Strand, *A History of the Swedish-Americans in Minnesota*.

15 I found out in late 2018 that Bernard Anderson, the gentleman who shared memories of his pioneer Vasa family during my 2017 visit, had died in the summer of 2018. Bernard was one of the closest (non-relative) connections to the Hagglunds that I encountered in my research; His great-grandfather Bengt Anderson was living in Vasa township when the Hagglunds arrived in 1867.

16 In addition to his biological children, Johan's younger brother Olof also had two stepchildren; his wife Christina had a son and a daughter by her first marriage: Daniel Pehrsson, born in July 1858, and Margreta Pehrsdotter, in July 1861. The father, Pehr Pehrsson, died one year after Margreta was born. Although Olof and Christina emigrated in 1882, church records also list them (incorrectly) as having left for America from Bergsjö in May 1869. For some reason they did not leave in 1869. Records show that in November 1870 they moved to Hassela, the birthplace of Olof's wife, and they remained there until they left for America in June 1882.

17 "I know that when I left my home": Eric Norelius, *Early Life of Eric Norelius.* Eric Norelius wrote his memoir in Vasa, Minnesota in 1916. After appearing in the Swedish church periodical, *Augustana*, it was translated into English by a colleague, the Rev. Emeroy Johnson, and serialized in a Lutheran publication, *The Lutheran Companion.* In 1934 the same translated work was published in book form, titled *Early Life of Eric Norelius (1833-1862); a Lutheran Pioneer,* by the Augustana Book Concern of Rock Island, Illinois.

I also found useful insights in *Eric Norelius, Pioneer Midwest Pastor and Churchman,* Rev. Emeroy Johnson; Augustana Book Concern, 1954.

A coincidence of note: In his memoirs, Eric Norelius mentioned that on his voyage to America in 1850 he met a fellow passenger named Olof Stolt, and that Stolt later moved from Illinois to a Swedish enclave in western Iowa. I came across the Stolt name while reviewing records of the Swedish Baptist Church in Kiron, which included a letter written in 1961 by an Ester (Stolt) Lame of Tacoma, Washington, responding to a request for recollections of the church. It turns out that Ester was a granddaughter of Olof Stolt, and her mother, Mary Josephine (Norelius) Stolt, was a daughter of Andrew Norelius.

SWEDEN IN AMERICA

18 Mattson's 1856 account is from *Vasa Illustrata,* p. 190.

19 "There is perhaps ..." is from "Vasa, the Characteristic," p. 259 of *Vasa Illustrata,* a small book originally written in Swedish in 1905 by the Rev. Erik Norelius. The English version was produced by the Vasa Museum and collaborators to coincide with the 150th anniversary of the founding of the Vasa Lutheran Church.

20   Information about Andrew Norelius's years in Isanti County, Minnesota is from records of the Isanti County Historical Society at Cambridge, including "Life Sketch of Andrew Norelius," courtesy of Lynne Dablow, director.

21   Eric Norelius preached mainly in Indiana and Minnesota, but he also wandered far and wide to spread the word. In 1885-86 he traveled up and down the West Coast, and in October 1885 he met in Astoria, Oregon, with a local minister as well as the Rev. L.O. Lindh, described in Emeroy Johnson's account as a Lutheran pastor from La Conner, Washington. The following April, Lindh took Norelius to La Conner, where they "spent a few days."

22   George Norelius's recollections of the family's move from Swede Bend to Kiron were published in the Odebolt Chronicle in 1938: "Swedish People Founded Kiron," by G.A. Norelius, as told to V.W. Crain.

ON OTTER CREEK

23   "As fertile and desirable as any in America": W. W. Walker, vice president of the Iowa Rail Road Land Company, Cedar Rapids, Iowa, 1871 advertisement. Source: Library of Congress.

24   The Rev. William M. Haigh's writings about Swedish immigrants are in the November 1897 issue of *The Home Mission Monthly*, published by the American Baptist Home Mission Society of New York.

25   "much sought after here": Jesse W. Denison in a letter to his land company, July 22, 1867, re-published in the centennial edition of the Denison Bulletin newspaper, August 24, 1956. The comment about Swedes coming in "successive waves from Minnesota" is from *Crawford County History*, by the Writers Program of the Works Project Administration, 1941, available in the University Library Digital Collections of Iowa State University in Ames.

26   "I could usually discern through cracks": Louis J. Almstrom, *Eighty Years of Swedish Baptist Work in Iowa*, p. 396.

27   Hall's observations about the Iowa prairie are from *Travels in North America in the Years 1827 and 1828*, Vol. 3, p. 385.

28   Waldemar's recollections of prairie fires as well as the Easter tornado of 1878 and other local events are from his account, "Pioneer Memories of Waldemars and the First Settlers," original publication date uncertain, probably in 1930s or 1940s, possibly in the Kiron News. Portions are reprinted on a website called Kiron Kountry, maintained by Glenn W. Gustafson of Thousand Oaks, California. Some of Waldemar's writings are incorporated into Ahlstrom's *Eighty Years*.

29   The 1876 travel guide is *The Pacific Tourist: Williams' Illustrated Trans-Continental*

Guide of Travel from the Atlantic to the Pacific Ocean.

30   Information about Jesse Denison and his land dealings is from several sources, including letters he wrote to his land company in the 1850s, reprinted in the Denison Review newspaper in 1952 and 1956. Also, General Land Office records held by the Bureau of Land Management, and Frederick W. Meyers' *History of Crawford County, Iowa.*

31   Sources of information about Abraham Lincoln's land claim in Iowa include, "Lincoln's Iowa Lands," E.R. Harlan, State Historical Society of Iowa, Spring 1927; "Lincoln Land in Iowa," Abraham Lincoln Online; Denison Review, April 15, 1874; Denison Bulletin, February 17, 1909, and my own examination of property tax records at the Crawford County courthouse, Denison.

32   "A Moses in those days" is from a December 31, 1875, story in the Chicago paper reproduced by the IAGenWeb Project, a web-based genealogy site.

33   The reference to Kiron having a Swedish-language newspaper in 1903 is from the Denison Review, November 11, 1903, p. 6. Regrettably, no copies of the paper seem to have survived.

THE BAPTISTS

34   It is worth noting that in a few accounts of Otter Creek history, faulty memories have substituted John Hoaglund and his wife Annika for John and Anna Hagglund. The Hoaglunds were Swedish immigrants who settled on Otter Creek in 1869, a year after the Hagglunds. The Hoaglunds stayed much longer than the Hagglunds, which might explain the mixup in later years.

35   Frodig's notes from the June 13, 1876 meeting were translated for me in May 2015 by Marie Bergström of Stockholm, Sweden. She is a granddaughter of Set Friberg, younger brother of my maternal grandfather Carl Emil (Friberg) Freberg.

36   "Led to his exclusion" is from "A Centenary History, as Related to the Baptist General Conference of America," by Adolf Olson. Circa 1952. Isanti County Historical Society.

LANDOWNERS AT LAST

37   W.W. Walker's report of June 1860, "First Report of the President and Directors of the Cedar Rapids and Missouri River Rail Road." Beach and Barnard Printers, Chicago.

38   The warranty deed for the Hagglunds' 40-acre parcel is on file at the Crawford County Recorder's office in Denison, Warranty Deed No. 132, Book "H", pp. 480-481.

39   Olof Wick settling later in Wyoming is from an obituary published December 31, 1909 in the Pine Bluffs Post, Laramie County, Wyoming.

40   The Hagglunds' initial mortgage of 1872 is on file at the Crawford County Recorder's office, Mortgage Book "B," pp. 458-459. The March 13, 1875 mortgage is in Mortgage Book "C," pp. 467-468.

COMPETING FOR SETTLERS

41   To further explain the concept of a township: Each township is designated by a combination of letters and numbers corresponding to its position on the map grid. The township that became Otter Creek is T85N R39W5PM. The "T," or township, number indicates its position north or south of a designated base line; the "R," or range number, indicates its position east or west of a principal meridian. Thus, Otter Creek is in the 85th tier of townships north of the Clarendon Base Line, which runs west across Arkansas from the mouth of the St. Francis River, and is 39 townships west of the 5th Principal Meridian, which runs perpendicular to the Clarendon line.

42   "made a new life in the farming community around Kiron": C.J. Johnson in *History of the First Swedish Pioneers Who Settled Otter Creek Valley, Situated in Otter Creek and Stockholm Townships from 1867 to present time, 1915."*

43   John I. Blair as "a human dynamo" is from "Railroad Construction and Influence in Iowa," p. 27, Chapter Two of *Transportation in Iowa, a Historical Summary.*

44   Peter Star's snake story is from Ahlstrom's *Eighty Years.*

A GROWING BROOD

45   Information on the individual farm production and values is from the 1870 federal census and its associated agriculture schedule.

46   Impact of the 1873 financial crisis is from "Crisis Chronicles: The Long Depression and the Panic of 1873," Federal Reserve Bank of New York. February 5, 2016.

   The Chicago Times story, "Pandemonium in New York," was reprinted in the Denison Review of October 8, 1873.

47   "Offers for sale," is from the Denison Review, August 20, 1873.

'A TERRIBLE SCOURGE'

48   The cemetery records were held by John Larson of Kiron. I reviewed them in his insurance office on Main Street in 2015.

KIRON, THEN AND NOW

49   Carl Waldemar's surname was his father's first name: The switching of surnames is an example of Swedish creativity and loose allegiance to family names; Carl's father apparently was given the name Waldemar in honor of Denmark's 12th century King Valdemar I, and when the family came to America that became the children's surname. Thus, Carl Waldemar was the son of Waldemar Peterson.

    The "Swedesburg" and Manchuria references and other Kiron history is from several sources, including an Odebolt Chronicle article by George Norelius, "Swedish People Founded Kiron," published August 25, 1938.

50   "At present, and in fact since its removal" is from the Denison Review, September. 2, 1902.

51   John and Anna's tax payment of $6.64 in December 1878 was one of their smaller property tax bills in the 1870s; for the 1875 tax year it was $11.74, including $2.71 in interest for paying late. They also were a year late paying these taxes in 1874 and 1875.

52   In the 1860s, Ira Davenport developed an innovative system for tapping into the western farm mortgage market. At the time, too little bank credit was flowing to recently settled areas like Iowa and Nebraska, where the risk of default was deemed greater and thus mortgage rates were higher. The money Davenport loaned was from his own family's $1 million fortune, which was built by his father and uncle in the mercantile, land and mining businesses in New York state. The key Ira Davenport innovation was to hire loan agents who lived near the properties in which Davenport invested; these agents – often a local lawyer or bank officer – selected prospective borrowers, set terms and serviced the loans. For this work the agent generally received a commission paid by the borrower.

    According to Davenport family records on file at Cornell University, Ira and his brother John owned or held part interest in 80,000 acres of land in several states, including Iowa and Nebraska, in the last three decades of the 19th century. This is from the Davenport Collection, 1800-1929, Division of Rare and Manuscript Collections, Cornell University, Ithaca, New York. Also, Bogue, *Money at Interest*.

53   The record of the Hagglunds' final payoff of their farm mortgage is in Mortgage Book "S," page 576. Final "satisfaction" paperwork filed with the Recorder's Office on August 18, 1880.

54   The Donald Winters work is "Tenant Farming in Iowa, 1860-1900: A Study of the Terms of Rental Leases," Agriculture History, Vol. 48, No. 1, January 1974. Also, *Farmers Without Farms: Agricultural Tenancy in Nineteenth-Century Iowa.* 1978. Greenwood Press.

STARTING OVER

55 My account of Lewis Hagglund's quest to file his homestead claim and other aspects of his resettlement near Munson was developed from Homestead Act records on file with the National Archives and databases of the Bureau of Land Management.

Lewis' claim was in the south part of Section 30, Township 23 North, Range 1 West of the 6th Principal Meridian.

56 The doctoral dissertation about the winter of 1880-81 is by Barbara E. Boustead, University of Nebraska, 2014.

"Black Winter" is from Chapter 7 of *History of Custer County, Nebraska: A Narrative of the Past,* by William Levi Gaston and A.R. Humphrey, Lincoln, Nebraska, 1919.

57 Details of the homestead claims of John Hagglund and Lars Morton are from records held by the National Archives and the Bureau of Land Management. Scanned images of their homestead paperwork were accessed through the Fold3 website.

The two 80-acre parcels that John claimed were in Township 22 North, Range 1 West of the 6th Principal Meridian. One was the south half of the southwest quarter of Section 1; the other was the north half of the northwest quarter of Section 12.

58 Dates on which John Hagglund and his sons Andrew and Lewis filed their initial naturalization paperwork in Denison were obtained for me from the Crawford County Courthouse by an amateur genealogist, Norm Prince, of nearby East Boyer Township.

LARS MORTON'S 'ORDINARY PRAIRIE'

59 Lars' claim under the Homestead Act was for 160 acres: the southwest quarter of Section 28 in Township 23 North, Range 1 West of the 6th Principal Meridian.

60 The book about life in Warnerville is Jane Sleeper Meyer's *One Wideawake Sleeper.* I was made aware of the book by Peg Timmer and reviewed a copy held by Earl Reed.

61 Oskarshamn is about 125 miles from the Falköping area of Skaraborg county, so it seems illogical for Lars to have begun his sea voyage there rather than at the southern Swedish port of Gothenburg, which is only about 65 miles from his home. Lar's siblings, Peter and Anna Christina, made the trans-Atlantic voyage two years earlier from Hamburg, via Gothenburg.

62 Information about Lars Morton's siblings in Princeton, Illinois, is from various sources, including census records. Also, archival records of the First Lutheran

Church in Princeton were copied for me and provided by Lynne Swanson and June Ohlson of Princeton.

'NEARLY WORTHLESS'

63   Francis A. Long's book is *Prairie Doctor of the Eighties* (Norfolk, Nebraska: Huse Publishing Co., 1937).

64   "Just a plain country doctor," is from a letter Dr. Long wrote to the editor of the Madison County Reporter, February 12, 1892.

65   Survey information and the surveyor field notes by Wiltse are from original General Land Office records, images of which are available online through the Office of the Nebraska State Surveyor. Nebraska land surveys were begun in the mid-1850s and were completed in the mid-1880s.

66   "Some wheeled portable cabins from claim to claim" is from "How the West was Settled," by historian and government archivist Greg Bradsher in the Winter 2012 edition of "Prologue," the magazine of the National Archives and Records Administration.

67   "An unproductive wasteland" is from Asa S. Mercer's *The Banditti of the Plains,* an 1894 account of what has been called the Johnson County War, in which dozens of cattlemen and their hired guns invaded the county in April 1892, allegedly to shoot or hang 70 men accused of being cattle rustlers. I have a copy of a reprinted edition published by the University of Oklahoma Press in 1954.

68   "Nearly everyone who comes" is from *Compendium of History, Reminiscence and Biography of Nebraska* 1912.

69   "No, we have a real home," the Madison News, June 16, 1932.

SUBDUING THE SOIL

70   The Pettitt sketch of Warnerville was created by Mabel Pettitt-Huggins in the early 1930s based on recollections by her mother, Maud R. Pettitt. A copy was provided by Earl Reed.

71   Andrew's 40 acres, purchased from the government for $50 in 1886, was the southeast quarter of the northwest quarter of Section 12.

72   The Elkhorn Valley News article about Lewis Hagglund's wedding is a reprint from the Denison Review of March 13, 1885. A separate account was published in the Nebraska State Journal at Lincoln on February 21, 1885.

73   Lars reported his yearly crop yields in paperwork filed in 1889 to "prove up" his homestead claim. For unknown reasons, such statistics were not included in the available homestead paperwork for Lewis or John.

In what looks to me like a quirk of the Homestead Act paperwork required to "prove up" a claim, the claimant was asked how many acres he had in crops each year and their yield in bushels – but not their dollar value. However, a similar questionnaire required from witnesses in support of the claimant *did* ask about crop values per year. Thus, Lars Morton reported that he had 10 acres in corn in 1882, yielding 50 bushels. But he was not asked to put a dollar figure on the harvest. A neighbor who provided witness testimony, Charles Rice, reported that Lars earned $12 from those 50 bushels. I assume Rice got the figures from Lars.

In total, Rice reported Lars' yearly activity as follows: 1882, 10 acres of corn, 50 bushels, worth $12; 1883, 15 acres of corn and oats worth $120; 1884, 20 acres of corn worth $110; 1885, 28 acres corn and wheat worth $180; 1886, 36 acres corn and wheat worth $190; 1887, 34 acres corn and oats worth $290; 1888, 20 acres corn worth $85, oats destroyed by hail; 1889, "crops consisting of 35 acres not harvested."

The agriculture supplement to the 1885 Nebraska state census provides a more detailed breakdown on the Mortons' farm yield from 20 acres for 1884, as follows: Corn, 12 acres, yielding 300 bushels; oats, two acres, 60 bushels; rye, four acres, 75 bushels; wheat, two acres, 60 bushels. They also had one acre in potatoes, yielding 40 bushels. In addition to the 20 acres planted in grains, 100 acres was grasslands, of which 30 acres was harvested for a total of 40 tons of hay.

1890S: DRY DECADE, HARD TIMES

74   The Morrill memoir is Charles H. Morrill, *The Morrills and Reminiscences* (Chicago and Lincoln, Nebraska: University Publishing Company, 1918).

75   "I saw nothing but misery and desolation," Nellie Bly article for the New York World newspaper, "Nellie Bly with Starving Nebraskans," datelined Valentine, Nebraska, January 19, 1895.

    "It is a horrible and ghastly delusion," Nellie Bly article for the New York World newspaper, "The Wish to Own a Home," datelined Butte, Nebraska, January 25, 1895. Both Bly articles reprinted in Nebraska History magazine, Vol. 67, 1986, Nebraska State Historical Society, original text via University of Minnesota Library.

76   My description of the fire that consumed the 1890 census records is based in part on Kellee Blake's article, "First in the Path of the Firemen," in Prologue Magazine, Spring 1996, Vol. 28, No. 1, the National Archives and Records Administration.

77   The March 1888 lawsuit by Lewis and John Hagglund was against William Harvey and A.L. Harvey. The appearance docket, which was the only reference available when I reviewed district court records in April 2016, does not explain the dispute

or further identify the disputants. The docket calls the suit an "appeal from Justice Court," referring to a court convened by a justice of the peace, of which there was one in each township in the county. These justices usually were not lawyers and rarely had legal training. Under Nebraska law, these courts have jurisdiction mostly over non-criminal cases and civil actions such as contract disputes. On the appearance docket, the Hagglund/Harvey case has a date stamp of March 20, 1888. Beside the date is a series of notations, including "bill of particulars," "summons," "subpoena," and "verdict," indicating it proceeded through April 1889, but it says nothing about how the case ended.

78 Record of Andrew's mechanic's lien is in Madison County District Court, Mechanic's Lien Record, No. 2, page 348, January 30, 1891.

REAL ESTATE SHUFFLE

79 Information on property transactions and mortgages by the Hagglunds and Mortons is from warranty deed books, mortgage books, and other records on file with the Madison County Register of Deeds in Madison. I also obtained copies of a portion of Madison County tax rolls for this period, with thanks to History Nebraska, formerly known as the Nebraska State Historical Society, in Lincoln.

Among many puzzles presented by the tax records, I found that for the 1890 tax year, Lars and Christine Morton were listed separately on the tax rolls as owners of their property, making separate payments of $3.99 ("C. Morton, Mrs. L.G.) and $3.00 (L.G. Morton). Both payments were made on October 31, 1891 with separate receipts. In earlier years the property and the payments were listed only in Lars' name.

80 Three weeks before Cramer sold the properties to Anna, the local newspaper said he was "seriously ill with la grippe," a common 19th century term for influenza. Eleven months later, in December, he died. Cramer was a Civil War veteran who served at the rank of private in the 128th Infantry Regiment from New York from August 1862 to September 1863, according to the Veterans Schedules of the 1890 federal census, one of the few parts of the census that survived the 1921 records fire in Washington, D.C.

81 Information about businesses on Pearl Street in 1892 is from a Sanborn insurance map published that year; available from the Library of Congress.

82 County assessor records show this single parcel — #590003895 — in 2016 was comprised of what had been designated in the 1890s as Lots 15, 16 and 17, plus portions of Lots 13 and 14. Andrew once owned three of those: numbers 14, 16 and 17. In the early 1890s he ran his windmill and plumbing shop from one of those lots, probably No. 16; a newspaper item in July 1892 mentioned that his

shop was "near the depot," referring to the Union Pacific depot that stood about 100 yards west of Lot 16. Lot 14 was a bit closer to the depot, but Andrew did not purchase it until 1894. Andrew's rate of return on his properties was meager. Fifteen years after he bought Lots 16 and 17 for $160, he sold them to Frank Kaderavik of Madison for $150, "plus $12.50 in back taxes." At the time of the sale in 1907, Andrew was living in Cedarhome.

83 The story of the naming of Enola is from *Nebraska Place Names*, by Lilian L. Fitzpatrick, originally published in 1925 by the University of Nebraska at Lincoln. In 1960 it was reprinted as part of a collection by the University of Nebraska Press.

84 In 1902, the year he notarized the documents for the Hagglunds, Whitfield Brokaw advertised himself in the Snohomish County business directory as a "dealer in hay, grain, farm implements, real estate and insurance."

85 John and Anna's 1894 mortgage and loan: They took out a five-year, $1,500 mortgage on April 2, 1894, four months after paying off the previous $1,500 mortgage. For collateral, they used the same 200 acres they had used in the 1888 loan. They paid it off on time, on April 3, 1899, including 7 percent interest. At the same time, in April 1894, they took out a one-year loan for $119.25 at 10 percent interest, using the same 200 acres as collateral. This also was paid off in April 1899. The lender was the Abstract and Loan Office of R.A. Maloney of Madison. Using the remaining 80 acres of their holdings as collateral, they took out a separate $195 loan in July 1895. In September 1898, they borrowed $391.25 from S.O. Campbell, a local lawyer, using 200 acres as collateral. That loan was repayable in six months.

A 'MEDICAL IGNORAMOUS'

86 I obtained information about Christine Morton's death and the doctors who were present at the time, as well as the public dispute that followed, largely from contemporary local newspaper accounts. I was able to locate Christine's unmarked grave through the assistance of Karen Tiedgen Reed of Battle Creek, Nebraska (who accompanied me to the cemetery and put her dowsing rod to work), and, later, Eugene Trine of Madison, who was the keeper of cemetery records and was able to confirm the grave's location.

87 The unsigned item in the December 29, 1893 edition of the Reporter suggested that others besides Hutchinson were fed up with public criticism and were planning to light off some legal fireworks. "From present indications there is likely to be a shaking up of the town generally before long in the courts," it said. "Charges will be met with counter charges and the people implicated will surprise

the public. Libel, slander, adultery, criminal acts are among the charges to be investigated."

88   Mackay delivered his speech to the Missouri Valley Medical Association in Kansas City, Missouri; it was published in the "Medical Arena," Vol. 4, December 1895.

89   Norfolk Daily News, April 25, 1896, p.1.

90   Madison Independent Reporter, March 24, 1892.

KEEPING ON

91   Bertha Anderson likely was born in Cuming County, which lies two counties directly east of Madison County. The 1880 census shows her, at age 3, on her family's farm in Wisner township, Cuming County. Bertha's father, Gilbert, and her mother, Inga, (maiden name Knutson) were both natives of Norway.

At about the turn of the century, Bertha's mother died; the 1900 census lists Bertha's father as a widower living with Bertha's 24-year-old brother Ole Anderson and his wife and daughter in Elkhorn township, Stanton County. Many years later, Clarence and Leonard Hagglund would return to visit their Uncle Ole.

92   The military service history of Hagglund descendants is beyond the scope of this book, but I felt compelled to make limited exceptions in the case of Oscar Hagglund's eldest sons, Clarence and Leonard. Both fought in World War I – Clarence with the Army and Leonard with the Marines — and lived to tell about it.

Clarence enlisted in October 1917 at age 21. Leonard signed up two months later at 19. Both were in ground combat against German forces in France the following year.

Leonard told his former hometown newspaper, the Stanton (Nebraska) Register, shortly after he was discharged in August 1919 that he had fought in some of the American Expeditionary Forces' key battles, including the first U.S.-led offensive of the war, at Saint-Mihiel in northeastern France in mid-September 1918. He was a buck private with the 6th Marine Regiment, which was attached to the Army's 2nd Division. In the newspaper's telling, Leonard said he "sustained nothing but a slight shrapnel wound which did not even disqualify him for duty."

"He was but just recently discharged from the service and says that he would not take anything for his experience but would not go through it again for any amount of money," the story said, adding that Leonard was now "a picture of health and a splendid example of the American youth as all had to be to enlist in the Marines."

Leonard not only fought in the war but also served occupation duty in Germany after it ended. His discharge papers, which a granddaughter, Stacy Henry Saporito, permitted me to cite, say he was accepted for enlistment at Omaha and served with the American Expeditionary Forces in France from March 14, 1918 to December 13, 1918. He fought in the Saint-Mihiel offensive, as he told the Stanton Register, as well as the Meuse-Argonne offensive, in which Clarence also fought.

Leonard did post-war stints in two locations in Europe: first as a member of the Army of Occupation in Germany from December 13, 1918 to July 17, 1919, and then in France from July 17, 1919 to August 4, 1919 (including transit time to the U.S.). He sailed home from France aboard the SS Rijndam, departing Brest on July 25, 1919 and arriving at Brooklyn, N.Y., on August 4. Nine days later he was honorably discharged. His discharge papers say he was in excellent condition and was recommended for re-enlistment. (He chose not to re-enlist.) His military service number was 304839.

Clarence was not as lucky on the battlefield. Army Pvt. Clarence D. Hagglund shipped to France from Norfolk, Virginia, aboard a troop transport called the Pastores as "unassigned infantry," meaning he would be attached to a unit once he got to the war. His military service number was 2358089. He fought in the allies' climactic Meuse-Argonne offensive, near the Meuse River and in the dense Argonne forest. The offensive started in late September 1918 on the heels of the Saint-Mihiel battle and lasted until the war-ending armistice of November 11.

Clarence was shot in both legs during fighting in early October. In a letter to his father published November 7 in the newspaper in Creighton, Nebraska, where Oscar and Millie and much of the rest of his family were living at the time, Clarence said he was "getting along fine." For operational security reasons his location was not revealed; he wrote that he was "somewhere in France." The date was October 16. I determined that he was at American Expeditionary Forces Base Hospital No. 8, located in the city of Savenay in the western French department of Loire-Inferieure (now known as Loire-Atlantique), and he remained there for 47 days, from October 6 to November 22, according to records on file at the National Archives. The hospital was run by a U.S. Army medical group that set it up in a Savenay school in 1917; by August 1918, battlefield casualties had escalated to the point where surgeons and other doctors devoted all their time to the reception and preparation of cases for evacuation to the United States.

"Of course, I will be in the hospital for some time for it takes some time for a broken bone to heal," Clarence wrote. "I was shot in the right ankle and in the left leg and the ankle is broken but do not worry about me anymore, but I do not believe I will ever go to the front again for my ankle will never stand the strain and such a thing could be that I may go back to the states."

Clarence confided his hopes for peace and his concern for his brother.

"At times one would think the war would soon be over. They talked peace pretty strong for a while but without results. Still I don't think the war can last much longer. I have not heard from Leonard now for some time, so I wrote to him again today."

He signed off, "Your loving son, Clarence." The following April he was discharged, and in May he spent a few weeks visiting his deceased mother's brother, Ole Anderson, in Stanton County, Nebraska. The local newspaper, the Stanton Register, apparently interviewed him and reported some of his thoughts in a short story.

Clarence told the paper he had kept the machine gun bullet that doctors dug out of his left leg, "but the other passed right through the ankle." A description of his wounds is included in a military report from his time aboard a U.S. Navy hospital ship, the USS Comfort — a converted civilian passenger liner previously called the Havana. It said only, "Fracture, r. tibia, comp. gunshot." Clarence was aboard the Comfort from November 22 to December 10. The list of wounded was long; hundreds were put aboard the hospital ship the same day as Clarence or one day earlier – many with similar leg wounds but others with more serious damage that in many cases required amputation of a limb.

The Register story of May 8, 1919 said Clarence was looking forward to resuming civilian life.

"Mr. Hagglund limps considerably but says neither of the wounds are now painful, in fact, he thinks that in time he will be even better able to get around than at present," it said. "He states that he has been placed on a pension list, is entitled to an education to learn some line of work for which he will be able to qualify."

"I am sure that Uncle Sam will fix me out all right," he is quoted as saying.

93   In his naturalization petition in Everett, August misstated the year of his immigration as 1883.

94   Information about Ella and Lewis's divorce case is mostly from Butler County District Court records that I obtained by mail and email from court officials. Butler County District Court, appearance docket, Vol. 4, p. 236. Divorce decree, *Luella Hagglund v. Geo L. Hagglund,* Butler County District Court, journal, Vol. 5, p. 100, October 1890.

Information about Martha (Olsdotter) Hagglund's background in Sweden is from church records.

95   I reviewed handwritten 19th century records of the Stromsburg Baptist Church

courtesy of the church staff. Additional information and resources in Stromsburg were provided by Beth Sparrow, an amateur genealogist. I reviewed and collected property records and other information courtesy of Debra Girard, the Polk County Clerk/Register of Deeds, and her staff at the courthouse in Osceola.

96   It took me a long time to find Olof's death certificate. The Health Records Management Section of the Nebraska Department of Health and Human Services told me in 2015 that there was no official record of his death. However, on June 18, 2019 the state issued what it called "a true copy" of the original death records for him and Christina. It attributed his death to "senility" with no further explanation.

97   Further regarding the 1896 presidential election: McKinley, the "sound money" candidate, handily defeated the 36-year-old Bryan, who famously proclaimed at the Democrats' nominating convention in Chicago, "We will answer their demands for a gold standard by saying to them, you shall not press down upon the brow of labor this crown of thorns. You shall not crucify mankind upon a cross of gold." In 1900, the United States reaffirmed its commitment to the gold standard; the policy was ended in 1933 when the government ended convertibility of paper notes to gold.

MORE LIKE HOME

98   Nebraska Gazetteer listings for Andrew Tackstrom in the 1880s are courtesy of Andrea Faling of the Nebraska State Historical Society.

99   In "Washington, West of the Cascades," by Herbert Hunt and Floyd C. Kaylor, published in 1917, a brief recounting of Stanwood history notes that "Andrew Tackstrom opened a shoe shop and A. E. Klaeboe a drug store." No dates or details are mentioned, but Klaeboe's ad in the 1913 Polk directory (in which, incidentally, he said he sold "Scandinavian medicines") says his business was established in 1888.

My estimate of when Andrew arrived in Stanwood is based in part on the fact that 1889 appears to have been his last year in Creighton, and the 1889 Washington territorial census, the last before statehood was granted later that year, contains no mention of a Tackstrom in Snohomish County. If the 1890 federal census had not been lost to fire damage, it likely would have conclusively shown Andrew's whereabouts.

100 Andrew becoming Stanwood's postmaster in 1897 is from the Seattle Post-Intelligencer, October 24, 1897. His salary as postmaster is from *U.S. Register of Civil, Military and Naval Service, 1863-1959.*

Seattle's Diller is no longer a hotel, but the name lived on. In 2016 a bar called the Diller Room operated in what once was the hotel's lobby at 1st and University.

101 Stanwood men in Alaska is from "Stanwood Area Echoes," newsletter of the Stanwood Area Historical Society, Issue No. 21, Winter 2002. Reference to "Klondike" Anderson is from "Stanwood Area Echoes," Issue No. 16, Autumn 1999.

102 I wouldn't rule out that August and Martha Tackstrom traveled to Iowa to attend Anna and Carl Freberg's wedding in Denison in February 1900. One hint of this is a photographic portraiture, known as a cabinet card, or carte de visite, from the Freberg family collection. The unidentified man in the undated photo is dressed in formal wear and bears a striking resemblance to August Tackstrom. The only markings on the card are the photographer's imprint – A.H. Brown, who took the Frebergs' wedding pictures — and the studio location, Denison, the town where the wedding was held. If they were in Denison in February, they must have returned to Stanwood at least temporarily, since the 1900 federal census counted them in June as Stanwood residents.

The only other clue in the Denison newspaper blurb of October 14, 1903 is the heading under which it appeared: "Boyer Ripplings," a weekly column of news items from the village of Boyer, just east of Kiron. Carl and Anna were living in Boyer in 1903 and moved to Cedarhome late that year. It's possible that the Tackstroms were living there, too, and that both families moved west together in October.

Arguing against the Iowa scenario is the fact that a 1903 Snohomish County directory suggests that August was employed in Stanwood that year. The directory's Tackstrom entry requires some interpretation. It cites a "Tackstrom T, cutoff man, R.J. McLaughlin," in addition to a "Tackstrom Andrew, harness maker." I know of no Tackstrom in Stanwood at that time with the first initial "T." I believe this was simply a typo, and that it referred to August. My theory is strengthened by the following year's directory listings for Tackstroms, which are identical except the "cutoff man" is called "Tackstrom A." In both years' listing his employer was the same — Robert J. McLaughlin, a Stanwood shingle mill owner.

THE RUSH TO ALASKA

103 Regarding Oscar Tackstrom's life in the High North: Oscar became well-known in Fairbanks, where he was something of a transportation pioneer. His work was complicated by Alaska's long, harsh winters and treacherous terrain. He was quoted in the Fairbanks Daily Times on August 19, 1906, as boasting of plans to revolutionize a mail delivery service that until then had relied on pack animals and buckboards, which were four-wheel, horse-drawn carriages attached to a plank. Oscar was assistant manager of the Ed S. Orr Stage Co., which in 1906

introduced its more efficient system for delivering mail and passengers between Fairbanks and Valdez.

"With fresh horses every twenty miles, the best of ribbon-handlers, stock and equipment, we expect to make the distance between Fairbanks and Valdez in six days next winter," Oscar told the newspaper.

"The foregoing declaration, as welcome news as ever told to Fairbanks, is that of Oscar Tackstrom, who arrived from Dawson yesterday to complete preparations for winter mail service," the story said. "Tackstrom, who has been 'raised' in staging over sub-Arctic mud and ice, is the right-hand man of Ed Orr, who is the head of the big company organized to handle mail, passengers and express between here and Valdez next winter." Oscar, the story said, had been looking after Orr's business in Dawson, until it was decided to "move across the line," apparently meaning across the international boundary from Canada into Alaska Territory.

In 1911 Oscar moved to Ruby, a gold rush settlement on the Yukon River along what was known as the Iditarod trail to Nome. An item in the Alaska Citizen newspaper of Fairbanks on August 14, 1911 said, "Mr. and Mrs. Oscar Tackstrom and little son George, well known former Fairbanksans, are now in the Iditarod, arriving there a week or ten days ago." There, deep in Alaska's interior, Oscar was manager of the Independent Lumber Company. "He has a spacious frame residence under way in the most suitable portion of the residence section of the new camp," the Fairbanks Daily Times reported on April 15, 1912.

He was a prominent figure in what some called the Far Northwest. In their excellent book, *The Sinking of the Princess Sophia,* authors Ken Coates and Bill Morrison included Oscar among "the best and brightest" whose deaths in that long-forgotten disaster accelerated the economic decline of a vulnerable region.

104 "For a while there was some excitement but no panic," is from A.W. McQueen's letter as printed on page 1 of the *Alaska Daily Empire,* Juneau, October 30, 1918.

Details on the Princess Sophia disaster are from a combination of sources, including newspaper accounts, the Coates-Morrison book and records of the official inquiry: "Report of the wreck of Princess Sophia," Library and Archives Canada, Record Group 42, Marine Branch, Series B-1, Volume 290, File 47799.

105 Details on the deaths of Oscar and Christina Tackstrom and their two children aboard the ship are from Record of Deaths, Office of Territorial Registrar of Vital Statistics, Juneau; and California estate records, Alameda County Superior Court, Nos. 24885 and 24886.

On about November 9, two weeks after the tragedy, the bodies of Oscar, Christina and Margaret were among 156 recovered bodies – some still not identified — shipped south aboard the Princess Alice from Juneau. Little George's body was not recovered until December 30. The Alaska Daily Empire reported on January 4, 1919, that George's remains had been identified and would be shipped south aboard the City of Seattle.

106 Madison County Reporter, January 26, 1894. Among the Morton sisters at this time, Anna was two months shy of her 12th birthday, Mabel was nearly 10, Blanche was 8 and Clara was about to turn 2.

107 I visited the church in 2018 and reviewed a collection of church records, none of which included mention of the Freberg-Morton wedding.

Among surviving photos of Carl and Anna's wedding, one shows 16-year-old Mabel Morton standing beside the bride and groom. Seated in front of Mabel is Hattie Hagglund, and between Hattie and her husband John are 15-year-old Blanche and a little girl who appears to be Anna May, the first-born daughter of John and Hattie Hagglund. Anna May was 21 months old at the time. The photo was taken at the A.H. Brown studio in Denison, owned and operated by Albert H. Brown, no relation to the other Browns.

ODEBOLT OR BUST

108 Information on Carl Freberg's departure from Gothenburg is from the manifest of the SS Argo, where he is listed as Karl E. Gustafsson, age 20, of Trässberg, Skaraborg. His passenger ticket number was 1631. Emigrants were required to register with the local police — in this case, in Gothenburg. Source: Swedish National Archives.

109 List of passengers and date of departure of SS Berlin from Southampton, England on April 1, 1893, as reported by the Office of Customs at Southampton, via Ancestry.com, UK Outward Passenger Lists, 1890-1960.

110 My description of the historical context in which Anna Freberg filed a Petition for Naturalization, even though she had been born in the United States, is based largely on "Women and Naturalization, circa 1802-1940," in Prologue magazine, summer 1998, Vol. 30, No. 2, a publication of the National Archives and Records Administration. Her petition is on file with the National Archives, via Ancestry.com.

111 Information on the military history of Carl Freberg's father and other family members is from the Centrala Soldatregistret and from Swedish church records.

112 This interpretation of Friberg is courtesy of Marie Bergstrom, a granddaughter of Carl's brother Set.

113 Information about Gustaf Sixten Johansson is from parish records, the SS

Stockholm passenger manifest, and family records. By the time Sixten arrived in Illinois, Carl Moline probably was living in Harmon, a short distance from his officially recorded destination of Dixon, judging from the 1920 census.

THE MYSTERY OF JOHN MORTON

114 In a letter to my sister Barbara Christoferson in December 2015, a cousin, Gloria Mathews, recalled that as a child she heard family members discuss John's disappearance. Gloria, who was born in Cedarhome in 1929, wrote that Anna Freberg "went to Bellingham a couple of times looking for him."

115 Not surprisingly, there were quite a number of men named John Morton living in San Francisco in the 1920s. I found three that seem plausible matches. A 1924 city directory lists a John Morton, no middle initial, occupation "painter," residing at 3100 San Bruno Ave., as well as a John Morton, occupation painter and spouse named Viola, at 103 Dwight. A 1925 directory listed a John Morton, no occupation or middle initial listed, residing at 752 Lake, as well as the John Morton at 103 Dwight.

IOWA AGAIN

116 Denison Review, p. 8, March 29, 1901.

117 "Well-nigh impossible to answer him," is from "Leslie Mortier Shaw," an address broadcast over Station WSUI at Iowa City, Iowa, by William R. Boyd, former editor of the Cedar Rapids Republican. Manuscript filed in Iowa State Department of History and Archives, Des Moines. Published in the "Annals of Iowa," July 1958.

118 Henry and Anna Brown and their four children lived a number of years in Sac County, Iowa, and by 1930 had moved one county north to Buena Vista County. That year's census shows them in the Albert City area, and in 1940 they were a short distance farther north, near Marathon. Although I could not find official documentation of Henry Brown's death, some of his descendants say he died in 1941.

119 Emma Anderson Henricksen and Doc were married in April 1934. Both lived out their lives in Odebolt; he died there in 1958, and she in 1981. Henricksen was Emma's name by her first marriage. She and Edlef Henricksen married in 1913 and had two children; he died in 1927.

120 When Emma Anderson Cornish's mother, Augusta Wilhelmina, died in Odebolt in April 1927, a newspaper obituary noted that Emma's sister, Thilda, was unable to attend the funeral but sent a telegram from Seattle. "So sorry I cannot come, but goodbye, dear mother, will meet you in heaven. Thanks for all the you have

given me. Thilda."

121 Among the Denison Review newspaper reports on Carl Freberg's boarding house venture:

October 1, 1901: "Mr. Emil Freberg is thinking of renting it for a boarding house" – referring to a "new residence" that John Jacobson was finishing and making ready for occupancy "at once."

October 10, 1901: Jacobson was hurrying the completion of his house in the west part of Kiron "and we understand that he will rent it to Emil Freburg who intends to start a boarding house."

October 16, 1901: Emil and wife and Mable and Blanche "moved into the Jackson house last week and will commence their boarding house business this week." I assume "Jackson" was a mistaken reference to Jacobson.

122 Denison Review, January 17, 1902, page 8.

123 I could not determine the exact timing. If they were still living in or near Boyer in June 1903, they might have witnessed the June 2 visit to Denison by President Theodore Roosevelt, an event the local paper covered like the Second Coming. It was noted in the following week's paper that a number of Boyer residents had joined the throngs in Denison for the presidential visit, including Adolph and Harry Brown and their parents, as well as Harry's future wife, Maude Shives.

124 City directories provide a glimpse of Carl's whereabouts during his early years in Bellingham. In 1904 he and Peter C. Peronteau, the newlywed husband of Carl's sister-in-law, Mabel, shared a home at 1336 James Street, a residential area of Bellingham about a half-mile east of the city's center and near the intersection of James and today's Lakeway Drive. This spot is just east side of Interstate 5, which did not exist then. The following two years he was in the same neighborhood, at 1335 King. And in 1907 he was at 1316 James.

125 Carl and Anna Freberg's 10 acres in Cedarhome were in the northeast quarter of the southwest quarter of Section 8, Township 32 North, Range 4 East of the Willamette Meridian. This is where my mother, Annabelle, was born in May 1926.

Lars Morton is listed in the 1917 Polk directory as owner of the same parcel on Cedarhome Road that he had owned at least since 1910. Inexplicably, he does not appear in the 1910 federal census as a Stanwood or Cedarhome resident; indeed, I could not find him anywhere in that census.

126 Edith's recollection of living on Bow Hill is from the Frederick E. Smith papers, Center for Pacific Northwest Studies, Western Washington University, Bellingham.

127 Dell and Blanche had five sons and a daughter: The youngest son, Frederick, interviewed his mother in 1969 while researching a book about a socialist settlement called Equality Colony that was started in 1898 in the Blanchard area. In the interview, which he recorded on audio tape, Blanche expressed hard feelings about the colony socialists, whom she called "radical, crazy, uneducated people." The audio tape and other materials from Frederick's research collection are on file at Western Washington University in Bellingham.

128 Clara's remains were cremated on May 19, 1969 at Greenacres Memorial Park in Ferndale under the name Mae S. Eckdahl — Mae being her middle name and "S" perhaps standing for Stanley, her first husband's surname. According to Desiree Espericueta, who serves as a family service counselor at the Moles funeral service that operates Greenacres Memorial Park, Clara's cremated remains were returned to Jones Funeral Home in Bellingham, and there is no record of burial at Greenacres.

Clara was Grant Stanley's second wife: He and his first wife, Eva — maiden name Tuson and a native of Mount Pleasant, Michigan — were married in Port Angeles, Washington, in September 1899. The 1900 census shows them living on the Olympic Peninsula at Sequim, with a daughter, Verona, born in April 1900. Eva died sometime prior to 1910; in that year's census Grant and daughter Verona are listed as living with his parents in Seattle. Also in the household was Grant's 20-year-old brother Corwin. Both Grant and his father, Edward Stanley, were dentists.

SOME TO CEDARHOME, SOME TO BELLINGHAM

129 The three parcels totaling 80 acres that John and Anna bought from the Dyers in February 1900 were: SE quarter of the SE quarter of Section 5, plus the north half of the NE quarter of the NE quarter and the north half of the SW quarter of the NE quarter of Section 8 – all in Township 32 North, Range 4 East of the Willamette Meridian. Of the three parcels totaling 70 acres that they bought from Ruth Bradford, the most valuable was the NW quarter of the NE quarter of Section 8, totaling 40 acres; it was on this parcel that they cleared two acres to build their house. In this deal, they also received the south half of the NE quarter of the NE quarter, and the NE quarter of the NE quarter of the NW quarter of Section 8.

130 Brokaw as a founder of the Bank of Stanwood is from Stanwood Area Historical Society, "Echoes," Autumn 1999.

George H. Walker: Walker and his wife and children were on the property in June 1900, when the federal census was conducted in Madison County, but they didn't stay long. County land records show Walker sold the property two years later to Leopold Klug for $8,400.

131 Historical information about the Cedarhome Baptist Church is from the church's records collection, made available by Julie Pearce. These records include a copy of the original constitution of the church, handwritten in Swedish. The document includes no date, but Julie believes the constitution likely was written when the church was built in 1900.

132 Asa Shinn Mercer was an intriguing character, a promoter and schemer who succeeded modestly in some of his ventures but failed in many others. He was born (1839) and raised in Princeton, Illinois, which coincidentally is where Lars Morton's siblings settled after emigrating from Sweden. Mercer moved to Seattle in 1861, joining an older brother, and more or less fell into a job helping put up the first buildings on the grounds of the Territorial University of Washington. He became known as the first president of the university, although that title was bestowed on him mainly because he was nearly the only teacher on the payroll. Mercer was a man of many hats, including newspaper editor, educator, farmer, immigration commissioner and entrepreneur. He also authored a remarkable little book, *The Banditti of the Plains*, about the 1892 cattlemen-homestead war in Johnson County, Wyoming. My information about Mercer is from his book as well as a biography, *Asa Shinn Mercer, Western Promotor and Newspaperman*, written in 2003 by Lawrence M. Woods, and the papers of one of Mercer's granddaughters, Dorothy J. Weintz, on file at the University of Washington Libraries, Special Collections.

133 Grace Ryan Cornwell's account is from Stanwood Area Echoes, the Stanwood Area Historical Society, Issue No. 19, Spring 2001.

LEWIS AND TWO MARTHAS

134 Information about Lewis Hagglund's employment in Bellingham is from Polk directories as well as Bellingham city directories. For a time, Lewis lived very near Carl Freberg. From 1902 to 1907, for example, Lewis was at 1456 James Street, and Carl was at 1336 James in 1904 and at 1316 James in 1907.

135 "Mr. Hagglund has written on several occasions": I reviewed the very few surviving editions of the Kiron News, available on microfilm, but found nothing written by Lewis.

136 A Blaine doctor wrote on Lewis's death certificate that he died of chronic myocarditis and cerebral hemorrhage, and that hypertension was a contributing factor. Myocarditis is also known as inflammatory cardiomyopathy, or inflammation of the heart muscle known as the myocardium.

137 Also buried in the Tackstrom family plot at Cedarhome is Anna Allison's daughter, Lucille, who was born in August 1915 and died two months later. The grave marker says Lucille was buried in 1916.

138 The reply, from Jeff Cox, the school's chief marketing officer, said their records show no mention of Andrew. Cox said it is likely Andrew took only individual classes. "We have records of all of our graduates but we don't have records of those who may have taken individual courses with us," Cox wrote in an email, adding that it seems Andrew did not earn a diploma or degree from the school.

139 The grave is unmarked, but cemetery records say he was buried in grave No. 3, Lot No. 48, on cemetery's west side.

DEATH AND NEW PATHS

140 Regarding John and Hattie Hagglund's move back to Nebraska: A Denison (Iowa) Review newspaper article on January 17, 1902 said John was visiting relatives in Crawford County, Iowa; the one-sentence item referred to him as a resident of Madison, Nebraska, and said he was visiting friends and relatives "in these parts," which probably referred to his nieces, Anna Freberg and Mabel and Blanche Morton.

Another newspaper story of a year earlier is even more puzzling. The Newman Grove (Nebraska) Reporter newspaper said in January 1901 – five months before daughter Edna Christina's birth in Cedarhome – that Hattie was in town to see her brother, Gust Granlund. Newman Grove is about 20 miles west of Madison. "Mrs. Hagglund of Madison, sister of our townsman, Gust Granlund, was visiting at the latter's home the fore part of this week," the paper reported. I found this item reprinted in the January 5, 1901 edition of the Madison Star. The problem with this is that I don't believe she was "of Madison," unless the phrase was meant to indicate this was her former home. She and John were still Cedarhome residents.

141 Oscar as lottery pick number 4,850 is from the Omaha Daily Bee, October 29, 1909.

142 Information about the Idso family and their Corson County homestead is from a booklet, "Survival on the Prairie; Homesteading on the Standing Rock." Written by Torval Idso, unknown publisher, unknown publication date. The copy I obtained from an online seller has a note by the author on the inside cover, "To Don, with best wishes, Torv."

143 Information about Oscar and Millie's land patent is from the Bureau of Land Management archives. Information about buying out their claim is from records filed with the Corson County Register of Deeds on July 5, 1912. Information

about selling the land to Adolph Idso is from the warranty deed of sale, a copy of which I obtained from the Corson County Register of Deeds in McIntosh, South Dakota, in December 2015.

144 A copy of "Overland Westward: Nebraska to Washington with the Hagglunds," was provided by Maureen Gaffney Curtis, a descendant of Harry Morton.

THE HOME STRETCH

145 Information about burials at Cedarhome Cemetery is from personal visits and from records held by the Gilbertson Funeral Home in Stanwood, which operates and maintains the cemetery, courtesy of David Brandt.

Made in the
USA
Middletown, DE

74214836R00239